THE "Red Kelly" STORY

Leonard "Red" Kelly

with
L. Waxy Gregoire

and
David M. Dupuis

Published by ECW Press
665 Gerrard Street East
Toronto, Ontario, Canada, M4M 1Y2
416-694-3348 / info@ecwpress.com

Cover design: David A. Gee
Author photo: Bert Mason
Photos throughout are from the Kelly Family
Collection unless otherwise marked.

PRINTED AND BOUND IN CANADA
PRINTING: FRIESENS 5 4 3 2 1

Get the
eBook free!*
*proof of purchase
required

Purchase the print edition and receive the eBook free!
For details, go to ecwpress.com/eBook.

LIBRARY AND ARCHIVES CANADA
CATALOGUING IN PUBLICATION

Kelly, Red, 1927–, author
The Red Kelly story / Leonard "Red" Kelly ;
with L. Waxy Gregoire and David. M. Dupuis.

Issued in print and electronic formats.
ISBN 978-1-77041-315-3 (hardback)
ALSO ISSUED AS: 978-1-77090-932-8 (EPUB)
978-1-77090-933-5 (PDF)

1. Kelly, Red, 1927–. 2. Hockey players—Canada—
Biography. 3. Hockey coaches—Canada—Biography.
4. Canada. Parliament. House of Commons—Biography.
5. Legislators—Canada—Biography. 6. National Hockey
League—History.

1. Dupuis, David Michael, 1958–, author
II. Gregoire, L. Waxy, 1951–, author
III. Title.

GV848.5.K44A3 2016   796.962092   C2016-902380-X
C2016-902381-8

The publication of *The Red Kelly Story* has been generously supported by the Canada Council for the Arts, which last
year invested $153 million to bring the arts to Canadians throughout the country, and by the Government of Canada
through the Canada Book Fund. *Nous remercions le Conseil des arts du Canada de son soutien. L'an dernier, le Conseil a
investi 153 millions de dollars pour mettre de l'art dans la vie des Canadiennes et des Canadiens de tout le pays. Ce livre est
financé en partie par le gouvernement du Canada.* We also acknowledge the support of the Ontario Arts Council (OAC),
an agency of the Government of Ontario, which last year funded 1,737 individual artists and 1,095 organizations in 223
communities across Ontario for a total of $52.1 million, and the contribution of the Government of Ontario through
the Ontario Book Publishing Tax Credit and the Ontario Media Development Corporation.

Ontario
Ontario Media Development
Corporation

ONTARIO ARTS COUNCIL
CONSEIL DES ARTS DE L'ONTARIO
an Ontario government agency
un organisme du gouvernement de l'Ontario

MIX
Paper from
responsible sources
FSC® C016245

Canada Council
for the Arts

Conseil des Arts
du Canada

Canada

INTRODUCTION

It was a beautiful afternoon as little four-year-old Leonard Kelly accompanied his brother, Joe, and the others down to the swimming hole on the first bend of the Lynn River by the Kelly homestead. They had done this hundreds of times. It was what you did on a hot summer afternoon. It was fun and refreshing, a great place to play.

Leonard liked to be with the others. This time it was even more fun, as Stanton Berton and his younger brother Winston came along. Stanton was a friendly young college student. Every summer, when school finished in Michigan, he and his brother came to visit their grandparents at a neighbouring farm.

Leonard didn't know how to swim just yet, but that never stopped him from going. He waded in the shallow water to cool off. Sometimes he even went up to his neck, but he always stopped just before the ledge dropped off towards the middle of the river. There was a current there, and he had to be careful.

On this day, he stood in the water and watched the others jump into the deep water, laugh and play. He knew that when he got older, he would learn how to swim and join in on the fun.

When some of the older kids got out of the water, Leonard was still in it. With the screaming and yelling going on, it was noisy — hard to hear yourself think. Suddenly, Leonard found himself a bit too far from the shallows. Starting to panic, he was pulled in towards the centre by the current and had to stand on his tiptoes to keep his head above water. And then the slow current pulled him into the middle, where it was deeper, and he went underwater for the first time.

He thrashed his arms and managed to come up to the surface. He wanted to scream for help but was pulled back under before he could. When he was pulled back down for the third time, he figured it was the last. He was done.

On the riverbank, Stanton had just come out of the water and was drying himself off when he saw something out of the corner of his eye . . .

• • • • • •

It was Saturday night! Young Leonard came into the house excited. He took off his winter coat and boots and rushed into the living room. His mother was sitting on the couch, and his father had just turned on the radio and was about settle into his favourite chair. Leonard instantly slid to the floor in front of the big, old radio.

"Hello Canada and hockey fans in the United States and Newfoundland. This is Foster Hewitt speaking to you from Maple Leaf Gardens in Toronto . . . tonight the Toronto Maple Leafs and their captain Hap Day are hosting the Canadiens from Montreal and their captain Sylvio Mantha in what should be an exciting match."

Leonard shivered with excitement as he lay on the floor and put his ear right next to the radio. He didn't want to miss a moment of anything. The game began, and Hewitt's words sounded like a prayer as he described the back-and-forth action. Even through the sound of static, Leonard could hear the cheers of the crowd.

"Red Horner, the great Leaf defenceman, has the puck, he circles behind his net, crosses the blue line, dekes past a Canadien, and gets the puck up to Gentleman Joe Primeau, who is breaking at the Montreal blue line. Primeau cuts in and shoots . . . He scores!"

Leonard jumped up in the air.

"Primeau gets the goal, but all the work was the great rush and set-up by Red Horner," continued Hewitt. "Red Horner gets the well-deserved assist. Primeau and Horner are congratulating each other as the crowd goes wild."

Leonard listened carefully, eyes wide. He could picture Gentleman Joe Primeau breaking down the ice with the puck, and Red Horner, his favourite player, following up! Wow! To be like them . . .

● ● ● ● ● ●

It was the last minute of play in Game 6 of the 1967 Stanley Cup Final. The Stanley Cup was in the building. Toronto was leading the series 3–2 and the Leafs were ahead in this game 2–1, but the potent Montreal Canadiens offence was pressing for the equalizer and had managed to get a faceoff deep in the Toronto end, to the left of goalie Terry Sawchuk. The Canadiens pulled their goalie, Gump Worsley, and sent out the sixth attacker with fifty-five seconds left on the clock. This was it, the most important faceoff of the year.

Toronto coach Punch Imlach looked up and down his bench. "Kelly, Armstrong, Horton and Pulford. Stanley, you take the draw!" The sound of his own name made Leonard "Red" Kelly's adrenaline flow. He jumped onto the ice without hesitation. Punch had sent out his most seasoned veterans. Red knew what had to be done. They all did. This was it.

For Red, there wasn't much time to worry. But this could be

the last game of his 20-year NHL career. His last game! He had decided to announce his impending retirement after 1,316 regular season games. It was hard not to think of everything foregone — the farm, his parents, getting his nickname, Andra, the kids, Detroit, St. Michael's, Father Flanagan, the trade, teammates, foes, the game he loved — all of it. And Stanton Berton.

This was Red's 164th playoff game, the most of anybody who had ever played, even his buddy Gordie Howe. This could be his eighth Cup! *Imagine: Joe Primeau and Red Horner — me, eight Stanley Cups!*

The crowd was on its feet, the teams lining up. Sawchuk readied himself. The Canadiens were steely, determined to tie this game. Big Jean Béliveau was to take the draw opposite a serious Allan Stanley.

Just as they were about to drop the puck, Montreal forward John Ferguson came into the faceoff circle to whisper to Béliveau. Stanley turned his head slightly to listen. Béliveau nodded, and Ferguson left to position himself in front of the Toronto net. Stanley stepped out of the circle to talk to Red, who was situated just behind him in the corner. They exchanged a few words. Red nodded and moved over to Stanley's right, in front of the Toronto net, where most of the bodies were — particularly Ferguson — all set to dive into mayhem. Stanley moved into position. He put his head and stick down to face Béliveau. This was it. They set.

The puck dropped.

Stanley won the draw, pulled the puck back to near where Red had been, then blocked Béliveau's path to it. Red knew exactly what to do as he jumped into the void and snatched the loose puck.

A Canadien was racing towards him.

• • • • • •

Four-year-old Leonard disappeared under the water for the last time. Running hard off the bank, Stanton Berton dove in head first. He grabbed the drowning Leonard and pushed him up and out of the water. The little boy gasped for a breath, choking, coughing, scared, almost blue, but alive.

Stanton carried him over to the shore and put him down by the bank as Leonard continued to cough and sputter. The other kids rushed over and gathered around, shocked and scared — especially Joe. "You okay, Leonard?" he asked. Leonard nodded. Joe's little brother, Leonard, almost a goner! Wow! Everyone praised Stanton. *Atta go, Stanton!*

Leonard never forgot that traumatic moment or the heroics of the summer visitor. Stanton had saved his life.

· · · · · ·

Come the fall, life on the farm fell into the autumn routine. Leaves on the trees were starting to change colour, kids were back at school and the harvest was about to be brought in.

But then shocking news arrived from Michigan. Stanton Berton was dead, killed in a traffic accident.

Leonard cried. Stanton Berton, to whom he owed his life, was dead.

Why him? And just weeks after he had saved me! Why?

Leonard wondered. He would always wonder.

It would take him a lifetime to find that answer.

SEASON	TEAM	LEAGUE	REGULAR SEASON					PLAYOFFS					
			GP	G	A	PTS	PIM	GP	G	A	PTS	PIM	
1943–44	St. Michael's College Midgets	OMHA	8	10	5	15		—	—	—	—		Ontario Champions
1944–45	St. Michael's College Buzzers	OHA Jr. B	11	15	13	28	7	9	16	8	24	6	Ontario Champions
1945–46	St. Michael's College Majors	OHA Jr. A	26	13	11	24	18	12	2	8	10	0	Memorial Cup Finalists
1946–47	St. Michael's College Majors	OHA Jr. A	30	8	24	32	11	9	5	5	10	2	Memorial Cup Champions
1947–48	Detroit Red Wings	NHL	60	6	14	20	13	10	3	2	5	2	Finals, Calder 3
1948–49	Detroit Red Wings	NHL	59	5	11	16	10	11	1	1	2	6	Finals
1949–50	Detroit Red Wings	NHL	70	15	25	40	9	14	1	3	4	2	St. Cup, All-Star 2, Byng 2, Hart 10
1950–51	Detroit Red Wings	NHL	70	17	37	54	24	6	0	1	1	0	All-Star 1, Byng 1, Hart 3
1951–52	Detroit Red Wings	NHL	67	16	31	47	16	5	1	0	1	0	St. Cup, All- Star 1, Byng 2
1952–53	Detroit Red Wings	NHL	70	19	27	46	8	6	0	4	4	0	All-Star 1, Byng 1, Hart 3
1953–54	Detroit Red Wings	NHL	62	16	33	49	18	12	5	1	6	4	St. Cup, All-Star 1, Byng 1, Norris 1, Hart 2,
1954–55	Detroit Red Wings	NHL	70	15	30	45	28	11	2	4	6	17	St. Cup, All-Star 1, Byng 3, Norris 2
1955–56	Detroit Red Wings	NHL	70	16	34	50	39	10	2	4	6	2	Finals, All-Star 2, Hart 4, Norris 3
1956–57	Detroit Red Wings	NHL	70	10	25	35	18	5	1	0	1	0	All-Star 1, Norris 2
1957–58	Detroit Red Wings	NHL	61	13	18	31	26	4	0	1	1	2	
1958–59	Detroit Red Wings	NHL	67	8	13	21	34	—	—	—	—	—	
1959–60	Detroit Red Wings	NHL	50	6	12	18	10	—	—	—	—	—	
1959–60	Toronto Maple Leafs	NHL	18	6	5	11	8	10	3	8	11	2	Finals
1960–61	Toronto Maple Leafs	NHL	64	20	50	70	12	2	1	0	1	0	Byng 1
1961–62	Toronto Maple Leafs	NHL	58	22	27	49	6	12	4	6	10	0	St. Cup, Byng 4, Hart 8
1962–63	Toronto Maple Leafs	NHL	66	20	40	60	8	10	2	6	8	6	St. Cup, Byng 4
1963–64	Toronto Maple Leafs	NHL	70	11	34	45	16	14	4	9	13	4	St. Cup
1964–65	Toronto Maple Leafs	NHL	70	18	28	46	8	6	3	2	5	2	
1965–66	Toronto Maple Leafs	NHL	63	8	24	32	12	4	0	2	2	0	
1966–67	Toronto Maple Leafs	NHL	61	14	24	38	4	12	0	5	5	2	St. Cup, Hart 9
	NHL TOTALS		1316	281	542	823	327	164	33	59	92	51	

• • • • • •

CHAPTER ONE

GROWING
UP RED

"Ontario's South Coast" is the nickname for picturesque Norfolk County, an area along Lake Erie with a collection of charming towns and villages, their ports bustling and fields plentiful with fruits and vegetables. Its aqua-, agri- and culinary-tourism-based economy is flourishing, but it wasn't always so.

The development of communities such as Turkey Point, Port Rowan, Delhi, Port Dover, Long Point and Simcoe, where land meets water, was a credit to the pioneer determination to make the wild land home. The key to Norfolk's economic development has always been the allure and abundance of its shoreline waters, to go with some of the most fertile farmland in all of Canada. Case in point: its twin communities of Simcoe and Port Dover.

Port Dover, first known as Dover or Dover Mills, was the first of the two to be officially occupied when a man named Pete Walker planted roots in 1794. Settlers dammed the nearby river and established a grist mill in 1801, which encouraged the building of new homes nearby. The little settlement slowly grew, but international tensions bubbling between Upper Canada (or Canada West) and the Americans to the south would side-swipe it.

In the latter stages of the war of 1812, the Americans, emboldened by their success fighting on the shores Lake Erie, initiated their "Niagara Campaign." Sweeping through the southern region, they reached Dover on May 14, 1814, killing livestock and burning businesses and houses — only one was left standing. The British sacking of Washington and burning of the White House a few months later is believed to have been reprisal for the destruction of Dover. With peace declared shortly after Christmas, the inhabitants of Dover rebuilt anew but this time along the shore of the lake itself.

Fourteen kilometres inland, the town of Simcoe had a more auspicious beginning when it was personally chosen for a settlement in 1795 by the lieutenant-governor of Upper Canada himself, John Graves Simcoe. Originally comprising the hamlets of Birdville and Theresaville, it grew exponentially when businessman Aaron Culver established a saw and gristmill in the 1820s. The government of Canada West established a post office there in 1829, and Culver's suggestion that the two settlements become one and be renamed Simcoe was approved.

In the mid-1800s, Norfolk County, specifically the area around Port Dover and Simcoe, saw a large influx of Irish immigrants looking to start a new life in a new land. They were drawn by Norfolk's familiar rolling green hills of rich farmland. Among the newcomers from County Clare, in western Ireland, was a teenager named David O'Kelly, who arrived in 1853, and found work at one of the two tanneries in Port Dover. O'Kelly met and married Catherine Emmett O'Brien, who had emigrated from County Cork, Ireland, a year before he did. She was two years his senior.

When O'Kelly had saved enough money, he bought a strip of land along a road five miles outside of Simcoe, near Doan's Hollow. He and Catherine moved into a simple farmhouse he built on a hill overlooking his land and the nearby Lynn River, and took up the farming life. Children soon followed; among them was William Edward Kelly, born in 1866 — the *O'* seems to have fallen off the official spelling of the family name somewhere around this time.

William Kelly was raised on the farm and from a young age helped with the chores. When he was old enough, he attended school, walking the five miles every day with children from the nearby Forrest farm. It was clear from the beginning that William was scholarly. When his marks stayed high throughout his teens, and he showed no real interest in farming, his parents realized their son needed a higher education. They were devout Catholics but hardly rich, so it was likely a local priest who helped William get into St. Michael's College in Toronto, and from there into law school.

Soon after graduating, he met a local teacher, Annie O'Mahoney, whose family had a farm between Jarvis and Simcoe. They married at St. Mary's Catholic Church in Simcoe on May 30, 1894. He was 28, she was 25. That same year, William started his own law firm in Simcoe, called Kelly and Porter, with partner Jonathan Porter. Lawyering in farm country was not the most reliable work. Farmers didn't always have a lot of money, so it was not unusual for the Kelly front porch to be stocked with produce from the fall harvest or fresh-cut meat in exchange for his services.

William and Annie were blessed with seven children, but tragedy struck during a complicated and difficult final childbirth. The doctor and nurse attending her that day did all they could, but Annie and her unborn child died, leaving the distraught William Kelly a widower. The children learned to cook and fend for themselves, as their father was busy with his law practice. One of the boys, Lawrence, became adept in making chocolate pudding and fried eggs. Years later, William reacquainted himself with the nurse who had tried to save his wife years before, Lillian Hannick. Though she was 20 years his junior, a romance developed, and, at age 59, William married Lillian on August 3, 1925. In 1935, he was appointed Crown attorney for the region, and his work took him far and wide.

It was on his son Lawrence that the old farm cast its magical spell. From the moment he was old enough, Lawrence would head to his grandfather's to help with chores and harvesting. Into his teens, Lawrence's strength and brawn grew with him, a result of the daily physical grind on the farm. This came in handy in those days, because each of the local towns had its own teenage gang. Lawrence was the leader of the Simcoe gang, which included his brothers Leo, Bill and Dave. When a skirmish arose, Lawrence would hand his jacket to his brothers, pull up his sleeves and face the rival gang's leader "man to man." Many a score was settled successfully in this fashion, and so grew the county legend of Lawrence "Pete" Kelly.

If he was impressed with his son's bravado, William didn't much encourage it. Having eschewed the farming life himself, William felt strongly that education was a means to an end, and somewhere around 1915 he sent Pete to St. Michael's College. He wanted his son to get the good Catholic education that he had.

Pete Kelly entered St. Michael's eager to play hockey, something that had been forbidden by his father back home, for fear of injury. He and a pal ambled over to the Mutual Street Arena to try out for the St. Michael's team. Walking into the dressing room, he was met by a pudgy lad by the name of Jack Adams, who acted like he was an official with the team, but was merely trying out, like Kelly; Adams would later play a major role in hockey history. Pete Kelly made such an impression on the ice that the team manager told him that he would be signed and that he should go to a local sporting goods store, Brown's Sports & Cycle, for new equipment. Knowing that his father wouldn't approve and that his future was back on the farm, Pete Kelly reluctantly passed on the offer.

Over the next few years, Pete met Frances Owen, a girl from Jarvis, a town a few miles from the Kelly farm. Frances had been attending Loretto Abbey, an all-girls Catholic school in Toronto. Courtship ensued, and they were married at the St. Anne's Church in Walpole on June 29, 1921. The newlyweds moved into the white two-story farmhouse occupied by his grandparents, David and Catherine Kelly. They weren't there long before tragedy struck.

David Kelly, in his 80s but still quite mobile, headed down to the field one day to feed the lambs with a bottle and nipple. On the way out, he yelled over to Pete, working in the apple orchard. Pete waved to his grandfather. Hours went by and, when darkness began to descend, Catherine was concerned that her husband hadn't returned. A search found David lying face down in the dirt near a tree. Nearby stood a large old ram, warily watching them, ready to charge. It didn't take Pete long to figure out that his grandfather had been rammed unsuspectingly from behind and had fallen on a sharp stone, which struck his forehead and killed him. Shortly after this, the widowed Catherine moved out of the farmhouse to Toronto, where she lived until her own death in 1929.

Now the sole proprietor of the farm, Pete was determined to continue the family farming tradition. He had to make it work because, soon after marrying, the children started arriving — first a son, Joe, in 1923, and then Laureen, in 1925; two years later, Frances was expecting again.

While pride in his growing family and in the success of the farm pulsed through Pete's bones from spring until fall, his love of hockey sustained him through the winters. Still young at 25, Pete played local intermediate men's hockey with the Port Dover Sailors. Simcoe and Port Dover had an intense rivalry, and the Doverites had offered him his own cutter so he could get to their games on time. So valuable was Pete to Port Dover that the team would hold up the Lake Erie & Northern Railway commuter train until he arrived from his chores on the farm. Wearing his customary blue peaked cap, he played fair but rugged, and his skills with his stick and fists were both admired and hated throughout the league.

"The whole town of Simcoe used to turn out just to boo Pete Kelly," recounted Ted Reeve of the *Toronto Telegram* years later. "If there had been a Lady Byng Trophy in that league, he not only wouldn't have won it, Pete Kelly wouldn't have even been allowed to look at it!"

In 1927, as Pete worked the farm, and the birth of his third child approached, he followed the sports news. The New York Rangers, Detroit Cougars and Chicago Black Hawks had just completed their first NHL season. The Rangers' Bill Cook won the NHL scoring title with 33 goals and four assists, edging out Chicago's Dick Irvin by one point. Led by Cy Denneny and King Clancy, the Ottawa Senators finished first and won the Stanley Cup despite not having any players in the top ten point-getters. Jack Adams, that pudgy kid Pete had met at the St. Michael's tryout, played his last game with the Senators, and would later move into coaching and management.

On the Kelly farm, Leonard Patrick Kelly came screaming into the world in an upstairs bedroom on July 9. No one could have known how his career would be shaped by that same Jack Adams.

Leonard's group of siblings grew in the next few years to include Frances and Helen, making a family of seven. The farm had an assortment of animals, crops, gardens and pastures.

"For as long as I can remember, we had horses, cows, ducks, geese, chickens — you name it, we had it," Red recalled. "A fox got into the chicken coop one time, and you could hear the squawking going on, a real commotion! Pa ran out. One time it was so cold, Dad got a basket, went and got the piglets out of the barn and brought them into the house to keep warm. He put them behind the stove, and we later fed them all with a bottle that had a rubber nipple on it."

In the early 1930s, the farm's focus changed when Pete Kelly decided to plant tobacco among his 100 acres of mixed crops and pastures. It would turn out to be a major decision: tobacco farming became the centre of their lives for decades to come.

While he helped on the farm, Leonard dreamed about hockey. "Our world was hockey! My brother, Joe, was a pretty good skater. I skated for the first time in our backyard on a small pond in front of the barn," he remembered. "I had bobskates, and soon my feet went out from under me and I landed on my butt. That was the last time I ever wore those bobskates! Then I got my brother Joe's skates. They were a little big, but I wore big socks in them. I sure wobbled around on my ankles at first but then got better.

"Dad also flooded the field behind the kitchen, and we'd play hockey out there. We played summer hockey too, on the gravel road. As I got older, I would put a tarp up between two trees and I would practise shooting the puck. And if we didn't have pucks, we had some other things, and we didn't always have hockey sticks either. Sometimes we'd use a branch or whatever we could get our hands on. We didn't have a lot of money to throw around and get sticks. But we loved our hockey. All summer and all winter, we talked and lived hockey."

As time went by, Leonard continued to skate. Soon he started accompanying Joe to the cedar swamps by Port Dover, where the locals played hockey. Being as southerly as it is, some years Norfolk County wouldn't get freezing temperatures before Christmas. Tired of just skating, helping to clear the ice of snow and watching from the sidelines, one day Leonard decided he wanted to join the game. "I want to play hockey," he said to Joe, who laughed.

"You can't skate well enough yet!" Joe answered. "Hockey's for guys who know how to skate."

"Yeah, scram," said some of the other boys standing nearby.

"I can skate and I want to play!" the younger Kelly insisted.

"Scram," they yelled. "You haven't even got a stick!"

Challenged, Leonard walked over to one of the boys and took a swing.

"Hey, the kid really wants to play," the boy laughed. He then pulled off Leonard's little challenger's tuque and started to run away with it but then paused, noticing the colour of the boy's hair.

"No wonder the kid is so mad!" laughed the older boy. "He's got red hair! Hey Red, you get yourself a hockey stick, even if it's made from a broom handle, learn how to skate, and you'll be able to play hockey with us."

The little boy nodded and took up the challenge, coming back to the swamp whenever he could. Soon he was allowed to join the games.

"I was known as the red-headed kid," he recalled. "When they would pick teams, they would pick me by saying 'the red-headed guy.' When they called me Leonard, nobody knew who they were talking about. I've been Red ever since I can remember. At first I was one of the smaller ones, playing with these bigger guys. I'd get knocked around a little bit, but I soon learned to knock back.

"Joe and I used to walk from the farm along the train tracks by the Lynn River to the swamps. The water froze quicker there. Silver Lake was nearby, too, and we sometimes played hockey there. It had hard ice and was huge, and if you missed the goal, the puck would go forever.

"We played with kids from the neighbouring farms and Simcoe and Port Dover. The Chechawks had a rink at their house, equipment. I remember one of them, his helmet kept slipping down over his eyes. They had good hockey sticks too.

"It was natural ice, and it would be almost Christmas sometimes before we could play, but we'd spend all day there. We'd be frozen, but that didn't matter. We'd come home in the dark, and we would be so cold by the time we got to the end of the tracks and could see the light from the house in the distance. It was so good to get home and stand behind the stove to warm up! Then Mom would have good warm things for us to eat."

Hundreds of miles away in Toronto, Maple Leaf Gardens, opened in November 1931, was the centre of the hockey universe. The games were broadcast nationally on the radio, and the Kelly farm would gather to listen in on the action. That first season of games from the Gardens, the Maple Leafs were a force, led by The

Kid Line of Joe Primeau, Charlie Conacher and Busher Jackson, and they won the Stanley Cup in the spring of 1932.

"Saturday nights we'd listen to Foster Hewitt on the radio from Maple Leaf Gardens," Red recalled. "I would be listening with my ear right beside the speaker — I didn't want to miss anything! Growing up, Red Horner was my favourite player, my hero. He had red hair, so that tied me to him. Then there was Gentleman Joe Primeau, along with King Clancy. I never actually saw them play, but Foster Hewitt would make the games sound so exciting — all the shots barely missed the net, even if they were actually wide by a mile!"

Soon Red was going to school. "My first was about four blocks away," he recalled. "It was a one-room schoolhouse, Doan's Hollow Public School Number 2. Mrs. Hilliard was our teacher, and a good teacher. The smaller grades were in the front rows, higher grades in the back. I failed the first grade. We would walk to school, and sometimes the snow was so high it was just under the telephone wires, and because we were close, we'd be the only ones to make it. The school had a playground beside a hill, and in the winter we would go up the hill and come down on our sleighs, through the gate and go quite a ways down to the corner.

"Then I went to Port Dover Public School for a few years. It was a long walk from home. Joe had a girl's bicycle; he had bought it off a neighbour. One time he came up behind me just outside of town, where the road starts to turn. I had been walking, and he says, 'Do you want a ride?' So I nod and hop up on the handlebars. There was a horn that I had to sit around, place it between my legs. It was in a very tricky, delicate spot. Along we go, and suddenly Joe takes a curve and we bounced. I went flying off and ripped my pants. I had to walk all the way back home to change."

Red was used to having torn clothes. "We used to play soccer and rugby after school and half the time went home with our clothes half-ripped off of us. When they grabbed a piece of you, it was clothes that they grabbed and ripped. Mom never said anything, though. I also got the strap one day — I can't remember why, but a bunch of us got it."

Around this time, a new friend came into Red's life. "Dad got us a pony from a farm down by Jarvis, and we named him Ted. When I first learned to ride him, I'd get on bareback, and if we got going too fast I would be bouncing around and then I would fall off. Ted would just stop, come back around, step over me and wait for me to get back on him.

"He was well trained when we got him, almost like a circus animal. He could smoke a pipe, shake hands. He bucked a bit if you sat too far back on him. He'd come in the house sometimes. He could open every gate on the farm. He'd put his head underneath and lift the rails. He let the horses out all over the country all the time. If there was a latch, he'd use his nose and lift the latch, especially to get at a bag of grain. He would even swim with us. He was just amazing; my best friend."

With Ted as a new means of transportation for the two boys, Red's hockey life entered a new phase in the fall of 1938, when they started playing in an organized league. He was eleven years old. "In Port Dover we played hockey on Saturday mornings. There was a wood-burning stove in the rink where we would change. It was so cold, and we'd ride Ted down and leave him in a lumber shed beside the rink, out of the cold and the wind. Joe would steer the pony, and I'd be sitting behind him, holding on."

For the first time in his life, Red received serious hockey instruction and was properly taught to stickhandle, sometimes around obstacles placed on the ice, weaving around and between them, all the while controlling the puck. Whenever the puck slid off his stick, his feet were there to compensate, an advantage others didn't have.

"In school we played everything, baseball and a lot of soccer. I could really use my feet well in hockey because I learned from soccer that I could do my footwork with the puck. When I was being checked, I'd take the guy out with my stick, push the puck away with my feet and then I'd take off — I'm gone!"

Red learned hockey from coach Sidney McQueen. Whereas at the swamps he could shoot and score as he pleased, in the Dover league he had to learn how to pass the puck and be a real team player. With his growing skating and scoring abilities, this didn't always come naturally. He enjoyed the free-wheeling scrimmage — skating by players, breaking in alone — but passing drills hampered his style. He was competitive. One day, he did some nifty stickhandling and scored, but Coach McQueen wasn't very pleased. "Kelly, you should have passed that puck. This is a team game!" Red took note.

Shooting practices were another challenge. "I want you kids to go in on the left and shoot from fifteen feet out," his coach instructed one time. "Shoot low and shoot for the corners, where the goalie isn't. Got it?"

When it was his turn, instead of shooting, Red deked the goalie and lifted a backhander into the net. He was proud, but McQueen was angry. "You do that again, Kelly, and you'll get benched the next game!"

When the coach told the players they had to score on the goalie before they would be allowed to leave the ice, Red had other ideas — he purposefully kept hitting the post to get extra ice time and to practise his precise shooting. Nobody suspected the delaying tactic, and Red felt a growing sense of ability when he finally decided to score. He was the last to leave the ice, happily.

The farm, the hard work and the influence of his parents and faith formed the basic tenets of Red's life. "Mom and Dad had a strong Catholic faith, and they led by example," Red recalled. "Mom was always cooking for the church. We never missed Sunday mass. The priests were always visiting."

It was not an especially strict household, though. "There was really not much discipline going on in our house. Only one time did my father really hit me — I had done something in the bushes in front of the house, and he gave me a whack on the back of the legs. Maybe I was eleven. He didn't have to discipline us. We obeyed. We all worked hard on the farm, and our parents worked hard; planted potatoes, picked strawberries, tomatoes and corn. But things were tight back then. You did what you could to make a living.

"Dad bought this powerful truck, a REO, from Toledo, Ohio, around 1930. It had a hydraulic hoist and a dump box. Every morning after his own chores were done, Dad would pick up milk cans from the local farmers and drive them to the dairy at Jarvis. We knew Jarvis well because mother came from there, and her father, Joseph Owen, had a garage there right on the corner of Highway 3 and Highway 6. He had racehorses too.

"Then, on the way back, Dad would pick up stones and gravel from Hagersville. Dad's truck had a back gate, and you could dump the stones into a pile. Then he put a little tailgate on the truck, and then in the cab you could trip a switch and the tailgate would open and you could spread the gravel along the road that they were building. It had never been done before, and my dad figured that out. We'd draw water with it as well, for the crops. It was a fantastic truck. I used to ride with him, and there was this place we used to stop to get ice cream cones.

"Dad was an amazing guy. Powerful, not huge, but strong, and he worked hard. He could pitch and shovel gravel into the truck. And before the truck, he had a team of horses. He had two Percheron horses, and the neighbours had larger Clydesdales, but Dad would pitch the five yards of gravel without stopping and then take off with the horses.

"Then, when tilling, Dad would till a row and turn that team around at the end of the row, and the horses knew and would turn around and not touch the plants, they were careful with their feet not to touch the plants. Smart? Oh, yeah! He would work and work but never overworked his horses either.

"I also remember going with Dad with a load of hay. I'm sitting right on top of that load of hay, high in the back box. Sometimes I had to duck under wires too. We're going over the Ivey Dam Bridge, and the load of hay started to shift. Just as we got across the bridge onto land, the whole load spilled right out with me in it. Oh, boy! If that had happened in the middle of the bridge, and the load spilled over the sides into the falls, I'd have been a goner."

If there was hard work on the Kelly farm, there was also a lot of good food and great fun. "My mother was one great cook, and she could sing. The piano was the centre of attraction in our house. Everybody always gathered around there. She was a great dancer, too, and taught us all to dance. We always had music in the house. She led the choir in Port Dover for years.

"They loved to dance, and we always had parties — there was singing, playing of the violin and the old Heintzman piano. We had barn dances, square dances and, when they built the new barn after the old one had burnt, they lifted the piano up in the granary, and it was a heavy piano. It was a job to get it up there. I sat up there and looked down. 'Gals on the left, circle to the right, first couple down the middle, don't be afraid, one over to your partner, do-si-do . . .'

"Also, Grandpa Kelly would come to the farm with fireworks every 24th of May. There was fishing at the river, horseshoes by the driveway and fireworks at night. It was a great time to be a kid growing up on our farm. It was full of life, laughter, love, good times and, yet, hard work."

Like any kid, Red sometimes got into mischief. He liked to ride Ted along the sideroads and frighten other horses, which brought a few complaints. Eventually, Pete Kelly thought it was time to corral his son's energies, so he taught him how to do more complicated duties: handling a horse and plowing the earth; planting the sprouts that had been started in the greenhouse; the August ritual of topping — removing the flowers from the top of the plants to ensure the diffusion of the plant's strength to its tobacco leaves.

Come fall, Pete had his son help with the most laborious of all the tasks on the farm: "priming" the harvest. This involved picking the bottom three leaves from each plant and holding them under one arm while moving to the next plant. The leaves were then hung on a long, small board called a lath, and the laths were then hung in one of four kilns, tall buildings in which the leaves were dried. Red found it truly enlightening to be involved so responsibly for the first time, and it instilled in him a strong work ethic.

In fall 1938, Red's schooling took a new direction when he attended St. Mary's Catholic School in Simcoe. There was a trolley service into Simcoe that the Kelly kids could catch, cutting down on their walking distance.

"When I first went to Simcoe, I skipped grade 7 and went to grade 8," he recalled. "They weren't sure I could handle the workload, so they put me back to grade 7 for the first part of the year, and then back to grade 8 for the remainder."

In front of the high school was a hockey rink with boards, so Red took his skates one day, hoping to play after school before catching the trolley. "I'm skating around, and these kids come onto the ice and they're swinging their tuques full of snow at me. I'm dodging them all. The next thing I know, I'm outside the boards and I'm going to fight this kid. His name was Chin, a big guy. All the kids are around us, and we're nose to nose. I'm looking up at him when all of a sudden someone yells, 'Chin, your mother's coming!' Next they all took off. I was that close to a free-for-all. I didn't go back to that rink ever again."

Under the Catholic school system, his faith grew to become an important part of his life. "I was taught in school by the nuns, and I became an altar boy and used to serve mass at St. Mary's before school. I rode my bike to mass for seven o'clock every morning. The rectory and the church were just around the corner from the school. I got to know my Latin, and I had to answer the priests, the responses. And we'd recite 'The Hands of a Priest' in school."

Come fall 1940, Red tried out for the Simcoe Bantam All-Star team and made the cut, boosting his confidence. As a reward, Grandpa Kelly bought him a new pair of skates for Christmas.

But winter didn't always cooperate with Red's hockey plans. "We only had natural ice, and sometimes we didn't get to play that much because of the weather, or it would be a shortened season. And as good as I thought I was, the lack of skating hurt me, as I had trouble turning to the right. That wouldn't be corrected for a while."

Red and Joe investigated playing in a Saturday morning church league, and though he was Catholic, Red found himself on the Salvation Army team. That didn't bother him; he just wanted to play hockey. The coach was Gerry Karges, a bird dog scout for the Maple Leafs. Red knew him because he sometimes worked on the Kelly farm, as many people did.

By this time, Canada was in the clutches of World War II, and the Simcoe–Port Dover region played its part. The Royal Canadian Air Force built No. 16 Flight Training School southwest of Hagersville. When they practised bombing out over Lake Erie, the sounds could be heard from the countryside. The Kelly farm also contributed directly to the war effort.

"I remember things were scarce," Red recalled. "We grew lots of everything. Our farm had a war contract to send food to the factory. Dad would haul food into Port Dover. Once, when Dad had brought a load of peas to the factory for another farmer, the fellow at the gate refused to unlock the gate because it was closing time. Dad had been working all day on the farm; he was in no mood to play games. Dad said okay and started to unlatch the back tailgate to dump his load right there on the ground in front of the gate. The fellow sure changed his mind in a hurry and let him bring the load in. You didn't mess with Dad!"

By fall 1942, Red was 15 years old and had moved up to midget hockey, on the Simcoe All-Star squad.

Pete Kelly was still playing hockey himself and influenced his second son. "Dad played intermediate in Port Dover. He always played hockey. I would carry his bag in the rink. I used to sit in the stands and watch him play. I'd watch every move he made. He once told me how to score on a goaltender on a breakaway. 'Look him in the eye!' he'd say. 'Don't look down. Look him in the eye. The goalie will have no idea. If you can hit your target, you're going to beat 'im.'"

In his second year of midget, Red's game was improving, and, as his team made the area playoffs, he was starting to get noticed — except by a busy Pete Kelly. "Someone ran into my Dad and asked him, 'Pete, have you seen your boy play hockey lately?' Dad answered no. 'Well, you better go up and take a look at him, he's pretty good!'"

Pete went to a game in Ingersoll, driving some of the players in his big Dodge sedan. It turned out to be a good game to attend. Though Red played defence, he was constantly moving the puck up or taking it up himself, and he scored all of his team's goals in an 8–0 whitewash. His speed put him miles ahead of his opponents. Though he was ultra-competitive, Red was starting to get embarrassed after the fourth or fifth goal. He would get special mention in the papers afterwards.

His father was at Red's next game, against Brantford, a town twice the size of Simcoe. He later talked with pride about his son: "At the start of the game, Red scored, stickhandling through the whole team. After that, Brantford controlled the play and had it all over us, but they couldn't get by Red on defence. Late in the game Red scored again, and we won 2–0. It was then I knew we had a real hockey player in the family."

Red began to think there might be a future in hockey for him. But in the back of his mind, he always had his love for the farm, the physical challenge of the labour, the fresh air, everything about it.

To work the fields, extra labourers were hired in the summer and at harvest time. In the summer of 1943, Red's old coach, Gerry Karges, was back. Karges worked part-time for the gas company in Port Dover, and scouted for the Maple Leafs on the side. Karges believed in Red.

"Karges suggested he could get me into the Maple Leafs training camp in St. Catharines," Red recalled. "We were working together in the field at the time, and I got all excited. I was pretty excited for days. What a dream come true that would be! But in the end, it turned out that he couldn't get me into that Leafs camp. It was a big letdown."

As they say, one door closes and another opens.

"Dad then called Father MacDonald at St. Michael's College, and he was able to get me in. I went in October, a month late for school."

Red arrived just as hockey season was starting, and he was pumped at the prospect of joining the renowned St. Mike's hockey program, which had many levels of competition. But there was still the pull of home.

"I was homesick pretty quickly," he recalled. "I missed the farm, my family, Mom and Dad, I missed my siblings, everything. But I had to get myself ready for the tryouts."

It was a rude awakening.

"I went to the Majors, the A's practice. One practice — cut!

"I went to the Buzzers, the B's practice. First practice — cut!

"I went to the midgets. First practice — cut!

"I remember walking around afterwards in the yard behind the school, totally disillusioned, thinking: *Holy man! No hockey! My hockey career is over!*

"Then my next thought was, *This is going to be a very long winter.*"

● ● ● ● ● ●

CHAPTER TWO

THE LESSONS
of ST. MICHAEL'S

Dejected and disheartened, a 16-year-old Red Kelly had to decide what to do, since hockey didn't seem to be his destined path.

"I didn't have a plan B," Red recalled. "I had only known the farm life, but I was at school now, so I figured, well, I've got to concentrate on getting the best marks I can."

There was an outdoor rink outside his dormitory, and one day he saw kids pour onto the ice for an after-school scrimmage. Realizing he had a free hour before supper, he rushed to put his gear on.

Skating around, he funnelled his disappointment and played with his usual gusto. Watching on that fateful day was one of his dorm scholastics, William Conway. Scholastics were senior students studying for the priesthood, and they were held in high regard by the other students. Conway was also an assistant coach to Father Edward "Ted" Flanagan, coach of the midget team that had turned Red away. Conway was impressed.

"After that scrimmage was over, William Conway took me to see Father Flanagan right away," Red recalled. "He told Father that maybe they made a mistake in cutting me, that he should take another look at me — which he did, thank goodness!"

Blessed with a second opportunity, Red gave it everything he had at practice and made the team. *Thank the Lord for William Conway*, was all he could think afterwards.

Aside from the hockey, Red was affected by the school's atmosphere. Founded in 1852 as a Basilian school, prestigious St. Michael's College operated as a preparatory school, a liberal arts college and a minor seminary. A nearby church was constructed and named St. Basil's. As provincial universities closed themselves off to incoming Irish immigrants in the late 19th century, St. Michael's opened its private doors to them, thus creating a distinctive Irish, Catholic and very pious educational milieu. In 1883, the College became affiliated with the University of Toronto while still maintaining its own separate, theologically based programming and testing. In 1912, Loretto College and St. Joseph's College came under the umbrella of St. Michael's, thus allowing their female students to earn a U of T degree.

The Basilian educational model had always recognized the need for education to coexist with activities and sport. By the turn of the 20th century, St. Michael's was establishing a long history of successful sports teams and had the distinct advantage of attracting the best young Irish minds and talent from around the country in football, basketball, baseball and hockey. It also provided excellent coaching in all sports.

"Playing on that midget team for Father Flanagan was an amazing experience," recalled Red. "I couldn't skate backwards very well early on, and I had trouble turning right, but I got the ice time and the coaching. Father Flanagan then taught me to skate with power. 'Don't let your butt bounce up and down. Skating power is below the waist,' he'd say. I learned to go down the ice with a cup of coffee on my back and never spill a drop and still be able to skate as fast as anybody — or faster! An opponent couldn't tell when I'd suddenly increased my speed. Opponents would have me lined up and then — boom! — I was by them. I used the power, didn't lose the power in letting my hips come up. I practised it, practised it and practised it; over and over and over again. I now had the confidence that nobody was going to beat me."

His grade 11 studies took away from hockey time. "I was the only one in my immediate family to go to St. Mike's. My brother, Joe, didn't even want to go to high school. He was a farmer, worked on the farm. That was his thing. My parents tried and tried, but it was a continuous fight to get him to go to school. He didn't go beyond grade school.

"At St. Mike's, tuition was six hundred dollars for the year. My dad had to foot the bill, and we didn't have a lot of money, so to help compensate, I made two hundred dollars a year waiting on tables in Brennan Hall. The college students were at one end and the high school students at the other. There was always a priest, Father MacDonald, supervising. There was one big kitchen there that served both ends. Wearing a white coat, we would wait on tables at the high school end. Because they were all students, there were no tips. After they were finished eating and were gone, it was our turn, us servers, to sit and eat our meal. There would be six of us, and we'd take turns each night serving ourselves; like tonight would be my turn, tomorrow night somebody else's.

"This one night everybody's gone, finished, even Father Mac-Donald had left. When this happened, we'd often go back and grab an extra dessert. We might not have been supposed to, but . . . So, this one night it's my turn to serve. I brought the dishes back to be washed, and the pies were sitting right on the top shelf. I reached up and grabbed an extra pie, I put it on my little tray, and when I turned around, there was Father MacDonald watching me. He was the bursar. He's looking at me and he's got the thumb and finger pointing out, meaning 'put it back.' I think I went red from my hair down. I was really red! I reached to put it back up on the top shelf, and I guess I didn't quite push it back far enough, and when I turned back around, the dang thing fell, boom, upside down on the floor. He never let me forget that. We had a great laugh after that, but it wasn't too funny at the time. I waited on tables for the whole four years I was there."

Living in residence had its issues too. "The dorms had huge rooms with a bunch of cots, and we'd be supervised by a scholastic overnight. Every night we'd come in and say the rosary with Father Brown before we went to bed. Sometimes pranks happened, and someone would crawl under a bed and reach up and grab you, scaring the stuffing out of you, and that would get us into trouble. Kneeling in the corner was the punishment in my first year in the dorm."

The St. Mike's midget team of 1943–44 — or the "Double Blue," as teams from the school were called — was powerful, losing only once in 35 games while outscoring their opposition 356–38. In the St. Michael's College yearbook, the *Thurible*, their year was summarized:

> *The Irish swept through the group with little opposition. Then they knocked off Miller A.C. and Corpus Christi, the C.Y.O. champs in the T.H.L. play-downs. They took nothing for granted. They were deadly, cold and merciless against the enemy. Then they were ready to meet Sammy Tafts in the final.*
>
> *Tafts had a foretaste of what was coming, when on St. Michael's Night at the Gardens, the Double Blue walloped them 9–1. Some said it was a fluke; but the Midgets proved it otherwise by taking the final in two straight games, 5–1 and 7–1. This showed that beyond a doubt, they were by far the best team in the city. Then in the King Clancy Midget series, the Irish, with the addition of Paul Bracken and Joe Prendergast, swept through with little trouble and when the season ended in the middle of May, St. Michael's Midgets were double champions.*

Kelly garnered an impressive 10 goals and five assists in his last eight games. "The third line of Ed Harrison, 'Red' Kelly and Frank Kirby was a very dangerous one, and by the end of the season, they were pouring goals into the opposing nets," reported the *Thurible*. "'Red' Kelly especially turned in two super games at left wing, bagging four goals and four assists in the finals."

"Father Flanagan was a good coach, especially for the age I was," recalled Red. "He gave one of the best speeches I've ever heard. We had a great team, but this one time we had played a terrible first period and we're getting beat by a much lesser team. Father comes into the dressing room. Everything goes silent. We know we're about to get a blast. Father could get mad.

"Father walks slowly down the middle of the wooden floor: thump, thump, thump. He got down to the end, turned around, and walked back: thump, thump, thump. He then went out the door, slamming it behind him. He didn't say a word. Boy, we fought back like all get out and won that game!"

Besides his studies, hockey and duties at Brennan Hall, Red served as an altar boy, just as he had back home. "We had mass every morning in the basement, though it was different on Saturday and Sunday, but during the week it was early in the morning. We'd have mass there, and I would serve, the whole year. At Christmas time, when everybody else went home, I still had hockey, so I had to stay."

When Red did want to return to the Kelly homestead, he had to find rides. "I hitchhiked from Toronto down to Lakeshore, stood out there with my thumb out in the air, and usually people stopped and gave you a ride. I'd get to Hamilton, then up to Highway 6. At Jarvis, you turned right to go to Simcoe or went straight to Port Dover. Port Dover was the shortest way to the farm."

In early 1944, St. Michael's looked at raising money for the Catholic missions, and boxing matches were suggested. Known as a tough guy, Red agreed to enter the ring; it was for a good cause, after all. The *Thurible* detailed the event: "Perhaps one of the most inspiring sights in the bouts was the dogged persistence and daunt-less courage of young boxers like Tony McGraw, Gerry Masters, and Bernard McAneney. In the second round of Tony's bout with 'Red' Kelly, the latter's left found Tony's chin five times . . . five times Tony went down . . . five times Tony came back for more!"

"When you were on the farm, you were in unbelievable condi-tion," recalled Red. "You didn't have to go to a gym or anything, you got all of the exercise you needed right there. With fighting, well, you just learned on your own to defend yourself. I'd gotten into scraps earlier on and learned how to duck and weave, how to handle myself, whether in school or on the pond, against bigger guys. That was the only training I had before I boxed at St. Mike's. It was a definite advantage, being in great shape for these fights. I won the first fight, against Tony McGraw; and then I won the second one; then the third one, I beat a fellow named Borsecki. He was a dif-ferent type of boxer, could really weave and duck. He was hard to hit, but I managed to beat him. Now, I was going to the finals, against Slugger Zavitsky. My handle was 'Corn Flakes Kelly,' because I ate Corn Flakes every morning for breakfast."

Oshawa's Jim "Slugger" Zavitsky was known around St. Michael's as a tough guy who gave teachers a bit of a hassle. Some of Red's roommates thought he would get walloped. So did a higher power.

Father McIntyre, the school's principal, called Red down to his office one day. He told Red his marks were good enough that he would be allowed to leave early to go home to help on the farm. He didn't have to finish the year.

"Father, thank you all the same, but I can't leave," Red said. "I've got that final fight in three or four days, against Slugger Zavitsky, for the missions. I can't leave until after that fight."

"I see," said the priest. "Well, my advice to you, son, is to go home, right now!"

"I can't go," Red countered. "Everyone will think I'm a coward. I've got to stay for this fight." The priest shrugged and wished him luck.

"The place was jam-packed," Red recalled. "There were supposed to be three rounds, and they had a big chair there for me to sit on, in the corner. They announced Corn Flakes Kelly and Slugger Zavitsky. Slugger immediately came at me and caught me right off the bat, nailed me good, and down I went. He caught me right on the chin, a roundhouse right. He was a skilled boxer, no question. He had boxed outside of school. He had knocked out his last semi-final opponent with one punch.

"I'm on the canvas, but I could hear the count going, and so I just calmly waited until it got to seven or eight, and then I got up. I was okay, but I made dang sure that he didn't catch me with one of those again! It ended up that I eventually won the fight, but it was close. I was the middleweight champion."

Red felt pretty good about it all as he went home for the summer. He hadn't told his parents he was boxing. As he walked up the familiar walkway into the farmhouse for the thousandth time, he approached his mother. She was shocked.

"What happened to you?"

"What do you mean?"

"Well, look at you! Your eye!"

Red looked in the nearest mirror and, oops, yes, he had quite the black eye — he didn't even know he had it. As he told her what happened, and that it was for the Catholic Missions, her anger subsided. Pete Kelly was pleased to hear that his son had won.

Missing upon Red's return home was his pony.

"Ted wasn't around anymore. He used to wander everywhere, get into everything, the neighbouring farms, and well, he wasn't a spring chicken. He was around 33 years old by then. Dad never really told us what happened, except to say that one day Ted never came back home. He had been a great friend."

Legally able to drive now that he was 17, Red bought himself his first car, a 1927 Model T Ford, for $27 from a local man. Now he could get himself around without bugging his parents or using their vehicles.

After a summer of working on the farm, it was back to St. Mike's for year two in the fall of 1944. Red's living arrangements moved from the dorms to what was called the Irish Flat. It was less crowded; he shared a room and a bunk bed with just one roommate, teammate John McLellan. Red was assigned to class grade 12-3 under Father Regan, with teammates Ed Sandford, Les Costello and Thomas Lobsinger. In the *Thurible*, a class poem described Red as "Our Red-headed boarder, the one Leonard Kelly, shines on the ice, but in English is no 'Shelley.'"

Besides attending classes, one of Red's first orders of business was the tryouts for the Junior B Buzzers. "I was always in great shape after the summer," he recalled. "You couldn't help it! You worked, cutting twelve hundred sticks of tobacco a day on which were thirty-two bunches and three leaves to a bunch. Do the math — that's cutting 115,200 tobacco leaves in one day! Then they had to be hung in the kilns, that same day. You'd climb up and hang the sticks here and there, and the guys handed the sticks up to you fast. Your feet rested on a small two-by-four, and you didn't want to slip, because it's a long way down. Just that standing up there kept your legs in shape."

Coached again by Father Flanagan, Red was elevated to the top line with Ed Harrison and Ed Sandford. They were a potent force from the beginning. "The next year, most of us moved up to the Junior B Buzzers," he recalled. "We had a good, solid club — a powerful squad with great players. I came to win. I played to win. I didn't want to lose. You get challenged, and you have to live up to those challenges. You didn't take a step back. Was I fiery? I guess I was. Maybe the red hair made me fiery, but I gave it all I had."

The team won all nine exhibition games, outscoring their opposition 61–24. It was a sign of things to come. In 11 regular season games, the Buzzers were undefeated and outscored their opponents

87–19. The only close game was a 4–3 victory over De La Salle, who finished second in the league. Red was on fire, getting 15 goals with 13 assists, number two in the league in points, behind his linemate Harrison who had 31.

"Their front line of Sandford, Kelly and Harrison was second to none," described the *Thurible*. "Sandford's free style of skating, his deceptive shot and ability to put the puck in the net; the fight displayed by fiery 'Red' Kelly, a nifty stick handler and a very fast skater; combined with the high scoring Ed Harrison, equal in every respect to his brilliant linemates, formed the league's highest scoring line."

"We didn't really care who scored," recalled Red. "The thing was the team won. Hockey's a team game. That's the way it's played. You win or you lose as a team. But Ed Harrison had a great year."

They moved into the playoffs, where each series was a two-game total-goals elimination. The Buzzers beat De La Salle 12–5 over two games. A Toronto Hockey League team, Mecca, was up next, and St. Mike's won the first game easily, 16–5, at Maple Leaf Gardens. The following game, the Buzzers lost for the first time, 2–1, but advanced due to the huge 17–7 goal advantage. Next, the Buzzers outscored the Niagara Falls Cataracts 30–8 over two games. The real test was in the semifinal against the powerful Oshawa B's. Both were hard-fought games, but the Buzzers came out on top, edging them 4–3 and 6–5 to advance to a three-game final against Stratford, who had advanced through a bye.

St. Michael's bid for its first All-Ontario Junior B title in nine years wasn't even close. Father Flanagan's troops squashed their opponents 4–0, 9–3 and 9–1. In 11 playoff games, Red tallied 18 goals and eight assists while picking up only six minutes in penalties.

Then Red was summoned.

"Father Regan, the principal, called me down to his office," Red remembered. "Carson 'Shovel Shot' Cooper was there. He was a scout for Detroit. He told me I was on his list and they wanted me to sign a C Form so that I could go on their protected list. I was tickled pink that somebody wanted me. They gave me a little money for signing, not very much, I think a hundred dollars. I didn't phone anybody. I signed right away. I was afraid they might change their mind. Carson had white gloves on, I'll never forget that. I always wondered what kind of shot he had, given his nickname.

"Most good players at St. Mike's were Maple Leafs property," explained Red. It was often joked that the Leafs had scouts in every parish in the country. During the years Red was at the school, Jimmy Thompson, Gus Mortson, Les Costello, Tod Sloan, Fleming Mackell, Ed Sandford, Ed Harrison and goalie Howie Harvey (Doug Harvey's brother) belonged to Toronto.

As Red returned home from school that spring, World War II was drawing to a close and was on everyone's minds. It had been a gruelling, destructive war, and many families lost loved ones. In the fall of 1945, Red was back at St. Mike's, once again with new living arrangements: he moved up to the top floor and shared a room with Thomas Lobsinger, and each had his own single bed.

He tried out for St. Mike's Junior A team, known as the Majors, coached by one of his hockey heroes, former Leaf great Joe Primeau. "We all moved up to the A's, and then Joe surprisingly moved Ed Sandford and me back on defence," recalled Red. "A little while later, he moved Ed back up to the forward line, but I stayed back. I didn't care; heavens, no. The coach wasn't telling me to sit on the bench; I was still part of the team. Besides, I had been a defenceman back home, and I could still carry the puck up the ice."

Years later, team manager Father Hugh Mallon explained Primeau's decision: "Joe had seen how strong [Kelly] was, how good with the stick, and how smart he was in getting the puck out of our zone."

The Majors had been a hockey force for years, attracting the best and the brightest from all parts of Canada. Their hockey program had been founded in 1906 and quickly earned the reputation for moulding excellent players and developing social and academic excellence. The Junior A team was formed in 1933 and was fed by excellent bantam, midget and Junior B hockey programs. The Majors won the Memorial Cup, the prize for the top junior team in Canada, in 1934 and again in 1945. Though some talent had graduated, there was an expectation that the Majors would repeat as champions, especially since the nucleus of last year's powerful Buzzers team had moved up, including Red, Harrison, Warren Winslow, Sandford and goalie Bob DeCourcy. Notable returnees to the Majors included goalie Pat Boehmer, Les Costello, Tod Sloan, John Blute, Fleming Mackell, Bob Paul, John Muretich, Roy McKay and Ted McLean.

McLean was Red's defence partner. He had been captain of the team the previous season and was in his final year. Four of McLean's brothers had played for the Double Blue, and two of them, Paul and Bill, were killed in the war. After graduating, Ted went into the priesthood.

After a couple of early-season penalties, Primeau gave Kelly advice he would carry with him for the rest of his career. "Joe Primeau taught me how to turn from front to back with my feet together and move with the player. And he said, 'You practise this on your own, before practice starts — you work on this before I come out.'

"He would become a great influence on me," remembered Red. "He also told me, 'You win games on the ice, not sitting in the penalty box. The best laugh and revenge is when you win the game. The satisfaction of giving a poke to someone's head is not as great as winning the game. Don't let those guys get your goat and force you to take a stupid penalty. Stay on the ice. That's where we need you!' Joe stayed a gentleman, would raise and lower his hat, wouldn't rant and rave, never cussed.

"Primeau also taught me how to pass the puck in the air, how to put it over the defender's stick and have it land flat on the ice on your teammate's stick so it doesn't bounce. If it's bouncing, your teammate is liable to miss it. That was an important lesson."

The Majors won three of four pre-season games. During the

Christmas holidays, they travelled to Winnipeg to face the Monarchs, splitting two games. They would face Winnipeg again when the games really mattered.

In 26 regular season contests, the Majors won 24 and lost only twice. Red accumulated 18 minutes in the sin bin but, more importantly, added 13 goals and 11 assists to the offence, impressive numbers for a defenceman.

In the playoffs, they faced the Galt Red Wings in the OHA semifinals. In one game, they showed a never-say-die character: after falling behind 4–0, they roared back to win 5–4; they took the series four games to one. The OHA championship was theirs after they defeated the Oshawa Generals four games to two. In the Eastern playdowns for the Memorial Cup, the Majors swept the Montreal Junior Canadiens in three straight games.

The Memorial Cup Final was hosted at Maple Leaf Gardens. The Winnipeg Monarchs, whose players were predominantly all in their last year, and thus bigger, older and more experienced than the Majors, were a handful for the Double Blue. But Primeau's boys held their own, and after six games the series was tied at three apiece, setting the stage for a deciding game. Game 7, witnessed by 15,803 spectators, was a colossal battle. Play see-sawed back and forth, and, after two periods, the score was tied 2–2.

Monarchs goalie Jack Gibson seemed to spark his team when he caught a Mackell backhand that seemed destined for the twine. And then a rising Monarchs shot eluded Boehmer for the go-ahead goal.

"There was still time left in the game. We tried everything, but their goalie would stretch and the puck would hit his toe," recalled Red. "It would look like a sure goal, but it wasn't. We just couldn't score."

The Monarchs added an insurance goal to seal the 4–2 victory. The Memorial Cup was headed west.

"It goes to show that you don't ever take anything for granted," recalled Red. "You don't give up, and you especially don't give the other team a chance to come back. Interesting thing is, none of those Monarchs ever made it big in the NHL, yet we had quite a few players that did. It was a lesson learned. Winnipeg played as a great team, they had a lot of spirit, and they never gave up. We outscored them in the series 28–25, but they beat us.

"Looking back, we had to learn from losing. If you lose and learn something, then it's not a total loss. That's how you have to look at things, and if we could ever get another chance, by golly, we didn't want to lose again. No way! Unfortunately, sometimes you learn the hard way. I would think about that loss all summer,"

Afterwards, the *Thurible* noted Kelly's presence: "Most popular player with the crowd was St. Mike's red-headed Len Kelly, a rangy and husky enough defence player. Kelly, with his fiery thatch, drew rounds of applause, but he was labouring with a bad leg."

The *Thurible* also had a mini-biography on Kelly: "Blossoming in the tobacco plantation around Simcoe, 'Red' was in full bloom when he arrived here three years ago. His likeable Irish face and rugged physique have long been respected by his opponents in the boxing ring, and on the hockey lanes with the Majors. Planning to buy his own farm after a few seasons in the NHL, Len will raise his own tobacco and a lot of little redheads."

When Red returned home that summer of 1946, he brought along a few teammates, which livened up the farm that summer. "They came with me to work on our farm," Red recalled. "They stayed in the house on the corner, which we also owned, and they joined us for breakfast, lunch and supper, all cooked by mom. There would be twenty of us, every meal. We would have great conversations and discussions, sports and hockey talk, telling jokes, everything. We had a hilarious time.

"We were also very competitive in our family. I think we got that from Dad. One night, after supper, we cleared the kitchen. It was going to be a big night — a table tennis tournament, in the kitchen. We had a big table, and we blocked under the refrigerator and everywhere to stop the ball from getting lost. Then Dad came down the

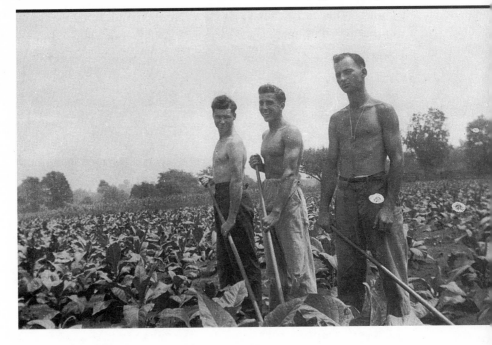

stairs all dressed up in his hockey equipment, pants and all, ready for the big tournament.

"Another time, Jim Cavanaugh, another worker, challenged my brother, Joe, who could really run, to a race. It was a big race, from the house, past the garage, out to the fenceline. It was about one hundred yards. Cavanaugh said he could beat my brother, but my brother beat him. It was all in fun, but serious. A few of my teammates went back to camp in better shape than they had in years."

Through September, much of the sports world was fascinated by Bob Feller of the Cleveland Indians and his race for the single season strikeout record. Feller was scheduled to pitch at Tiger Stadium in Detroit on September 29. Red and his buddies made a spur-of-the-moment decision to head to the game.

"Three other teammates and I hitchhiked all the way to Detroit, through the night," Red recalled. "We get there and the game's sold out. The other guys knew I belonged to Detroit and suggested I use my connections and call Jack Adams, that he could probably get us in there. I didn't want to do that, but they talked me into doing it. I got Jack on the phone and I was explaining who I was, and my situation, but he was having trouble placing me."

"Oh, the big defenceman . . . the redhead?" Jack asked Red. "Are you here for training camp?" The Red Wings had camp at the Detroit Olympia, home to the team since 1927.

"No, I'm not," Red replied. "I've got to get back to St. Mike's to go to school, but I was wondering if there was any way you can get me and a couple of buddies into Tiger Stadium? We want to see Feller pitch."

"Oh, I see, sure," Adams said. "Go to Gate 3 — you'll see the police car there, there'll be an officer there — and just explain who you are and that you were talking to me, that you're one of my hockey players, and you want to see the ball game. He'll look after you. Then afterwards I want you to come to the Olympia. We've got an exhibition game tonight against our Omaha team. You can watch and stay over, and you can come to training camp."

"Okay, but I can't stay for camp, I've got to get back to St. Mike's, but we'll come over after the ball game."

"We saw the sergeant at Gate 3, and we explained everything," Red continued. "He took us in, and we got seats right on the front row between home plate and first base. Fabulous seats, wow! It was like we were important or something! And we saw Feller get the season strikeout record. For the first few innings or so, the Tigers weren't swinging very hard, just trying to make contact, not strike out, but he eventually started mowing them down.

"Afterwards, we went up to the Olympia, and Jack showed us around, into the dressing room, met the trainers, and we saw the exhibition game from up above, that big ice at Olympia, it was all quite impressive. And as I watched the hockey game, I was thinking to myself, *It could be me out there someday*."

Back at school, Red knew the Majors had the makings of a good team.

"That next year, we had a great core of returnees: Ed Sandford, Bob Paul, Fleming Mackell, Les Costello, Ed Harrison, Warren Winslow and Johnny McLellan. Our lineup was further bolstered by newcomers Benny Woit, Harry Psutka, Ray Hannigan, Rudy Migay and goalie Howard Harvey."

Learning that some of his teammates who were Maple Leafs property had made "arrangements," Red decided to use his Red Wings card. "After getting the initial hundred dollars for signing, I wrote Jack Adams. I said to him that the Toronto guys were getting one hundred dollars every now and then. I couldn't have said anything better to Adams, who hated Conn Smythe. Jack sent me one hundred bucks, and when that ran out, I'd send him another letter and he would send me another hundred. I got a few hundred dollars that way."

Primeau's charges made it known early on that they meant business by breezing through the regular season with 31 victories and only three defeats, winning first place by 14 points. In 30 games, Red got an impressive 32 points while taking only 11 minutes in penalties.

In the first playoff series, they met their archrivals from Oshawa, who were coached by another ex-Leaf legend, Charlie Conacher. St. Mike's won the first three games in the series, lost the fourth in overtime, but came back with a vengeance to eliminate the Generals with a decisive 10–3 rout.

The *Toronto Star* reported that the team was getting parental help: "Ed Sandford's father came into the dressing room with a chocolate cake and green icing and you should have seen the scramble! Red Kelly's mother frequently donates baking to the cause as well!"

The Galt Red Wings were next swept away in four games. Detroit GM Adams had taken in the Galt series, and he was impressed with Kelly, telling the local press that Kelly would be "given every chance to make regular place on the Red Wings next season."

The northern champs, the Porcupine Combines, posed even less of a challenge than Galt, and the Majors outscored them 24–5 in the sweep. The Montreal Junior Canadiens received no mercy either, losing by scores of 11–3, 7–2 and a stunning 21–0. There was plenty of hardware: Mackell won the OHA scoring title; Red accepted the John Ross Robertson Cup, symbolic of the OHA Junior A Championship; and Harvey was handed the James Richardson Trophy as the Memorial Cup representative from the East.

The Western champs were the Moose Jaw Canucks. When the team left by train on April 12, team manager Father Hugh Mallon told the *Toronto Star* that they were bringing gallons of Lake Ontario water to drink, and that "the boys aren't overconfident. They know they have to be good since they are in for a real series." He also mentioned that "Red Kelly's twisted knee is responding to treatment and he will be ready for the series opener."

The Memorial Cup final started on April 15 in Winnipeg, and the Majors hammered the Canucks 12–3. Then the series moved further west. "We go to Moose Jaw for the second game, and they wouldn't wait on us in the restaurant downtown," remembered Red. "We were shunned. We beat them pretty good there, too, 6–1. Now we go to Regina, and we were winning 8–1, when the game had something like five or six minutes remaining in the third, and the game had to be stopped when fans started throwing bottles on the ice. The game was called and awarded to us. They didn't have enough police protection in the building. They and we were worried that someone might get hit by the bottles. The crowd got a little ugly there."

Down three to none in the series, Moose Jaw came to play in the fourth game. "The score was 2–2 in the third, and it's nip and tuck," recalled Red. "They had Metro Prystai playing with them, and they had two big guys on defence belonging to Chicago along with Metro. It was kind of like a Black Hawk farm team. One guy weighed about 240 pounds, without an ounce of fat on him.

"The puck gets shot out of our end, up along the boards on the left side, just up over the blue line. I'm rushing up there and this big defenceman was coming from the other way, and I'm thinking, *If I can just tip the puck by him and scoot around him, I'm going to have a*

breakaway. There were a few minutes to go in the game. Well, he thought a little differently. He nailed me!

"I got to the bench and, you know, you never want to let on that you've been hurt or injured, that they had really nailed you. But I will tell you, it was the hardest check that I have ever received in my whole hockey career. I felt it all summer long, in the middle of the chest. It took me a long time to get over that check. I found out later how big he was, that they couldn't buy gloves for him, they had to get them specially made."

At the 10:37 mark of the third, rangy Ed Sandford broke in over the left blue line and fired a shot past the Canucks goalie to go ahead 3–2, and the Majors hung on to win the game. Captain Sandford accepted the Memorial Cup at centre, the third in the school's history.

"The boys were hot tonight!" gushed Joe Primeau in the dressing room.

"They do everything like professionals," the *Regina Leader-Post* grudgingly admitted the next morning. "If they're not the junior team to end all junior teams, they'll do until a better one comes along."

It was a jubilant hockey team that wound its way back by rail from the west. What awaited them took them completely by surprise.

"We got a tickertape parade down Bay Street. That was something," recalled Red. "You have to remember that Toronto had three junior teams at the time — the young Rangers, the Marlboros and us, which makes the fan loyalty in Toronto divided three ways. But when the fans out west threw bottles at us in that one game, it suddenly became the west versus the east. The parade went from the train station up Bay Street to City Hall in convertibles. The whole city cheered for us."

The *Thurible* described Red's hockey contribution that spring: "Red thatch blazing, Leonard Kelly . . . was the nucleus of the Irish defence, the rock around which it was built. On the blue strip, Kelly was poison to impulsive forwards who swooped in on him. As often as not, they found themselves lying on the ice, gazing up at the rafters, as Red skated off with the puck."

Globe and Mail sports writer Hal Walker believed in Kelly's future: "That Kelly sure has hockey brains, no doubt about it. He's ready for the NHL right now."

Red had mixed feelings as he left St. Michael's for the last time. For the last four years, it had been his home away from home. Heading back to the farm that spring, he knew he had an invite to attend the Red Wings training camp later that fall in Waterloo, Ontario. What he didn't know was that a small wager had been made about his future between Red Wings scout Shovel Shot Cooper, who had signed him, and Leafs scout Squib Walker, who had passed on him.

"A new twenty-dollar hat," Walker had said, "that the redhead doesn't last twenty games in the NHL."

Cooper looked at him, extended his hand with a smile and said: "You're on!"

• • • • • •

CHAPTER THREE

A RED WING
TAKES FLIGHT

In the fall of 1947, Red Kelly left the farm in Simcoe and drove the
25 miles north to his first Detroit Red Wings training camp, held at
the new Waterloo Arena.

Red wondered about the reception he'd get from his old enemies.
"We had real battles over the years with the Galt Red Wings, a
Detroit farm team," he recalled. "When I went to my first training
camp, here were all these Galt Red Wings, all enemies. None were
very friendly, except Marty Pavelich. He came up to me right away
and we became fast friends." Born in Sault Ste. Marie, Ontario, in
1927, Martin Nicholas "Marty" Pavelich, played left wing for three
seasons with Galt. When he joined Detroit, some of his teammates
christened him "Blacky" because of his thick black hair; others nicknamed him "Sabu." He started that season with the farm club in
Indianapolis before joining the Wings.

"Marty had an outgoing personality," recalled Red. "That carried
on into Detroit. He was a great guy."

One of Red's early linemates was Billy Taylor, a veteran from Winnipeg who had played junior hockey in Oshawa. "He was a centre, and at camp they put me on his left wing," recalled Red. "We'd go down the ice and he'd pull the left defenceman over towards himself and then give me a perfect pass, a gift pass, right on my stick, real beauties. But I would be so nervous, tense, over-gripping my stick, that the puck would hit it and bounce ahead of me, missing a good scoring opportunity. Billy would send a few uncomplimentary words towards me."

Red found himself among a group of Red Wings that were shaping up to be a formidable force. Gordie Howe was in his second year and was placed on a new line — what would later be called the Production Line — with Sid Abel and Ted Lindsay, conceived under new coach Tommy Ivan and former coach Jack Adams, now solely the general manager.

The warm weather gave ice makers in the new arena problems, but the situation worked out to Red's advantage. "In Waterloo, we only had one workout a day, in the morning, because the ice would get too soft in the afternoon," Red recalled. "It was really hot that fall. So, after the morning workout, I would head home to help out on the farm for the rest of the day. Again, I was in great shape, so I felt the morning workout was sometimes like a rest. Priming tobacco was three times as hard as any hockey workout!"

As camp progressed, Red found himself still on the team. He learned of his fate — erroneously — from an unlikely source. "My uncle Len Owen from Tillsonburg knew someone in the Detroit organization, and they had told him that I was going to be assigned to Omaha," recalled Red. But the Red Wings opted not to send him to the minors. "On the last day of camp, they tell me I'm going to Detroit with the team. Wow that was great news!"

Adams briefed the press on October 10, a week before the season began. "Red Kelly may be carried as an extra defenceman with Jack

Stewart ("Black Jack"), Bill Quackenbush, Doug McCaig, and Leo Reise," he reported. "Tommy Ivan, newcomer Red Wings coach, is about satisfied with the team's condition."

The Wings hosted the Chicago Black Hawks in the season opener on October 15, 1947, and Red immediately made his presence known when he recorded his first NHL point, an assist on Conacher's second-period goal in a 4–2 Detroit victory.

"It was pretty exciting, putting the equipment on, that Red Wings sweater," recalled Red. "Getting help from 'Honey' Walker and Carl Mattson, the trainers, then stepping onto the ice at the Olympia for the first time, in front of that big crowd that seemed to be hanging from the balcony, right down over you."

Twelve games later, again at the Olympia, Red Kelly's first NHL goal came on November 19th, when he beat "Sugar" Jim Henry of the Rangers at 18:17 of the first period; it was the first goal of the season by a Detroit defenceman.

On the road, Red roomed with Quackenbush, who saw the youngster's potential early on. "He's sure to become one of the very best," Quackenbush told writer Paul Chandler. "Among other things, he handles his feet better than any other player I know. He can control the puck with his skates as well as any player can with their sticks."

"Kelly's just about the best-coached player I've ever seen," added Jack Adams after a late November game.

Red's mild-mannered demeanour was beginning to be noticed. In one game, Kelly hit the post and reacted angrily: "Ding darn it, it just hit that pipe, that's all!" His teammates were in stitches, and his non-potty mouth became legendary.

There was a learning curve in the NHL. "You had to learn from your mistakes and quick," Red recalled. "Like the first time I came face to face with Rocket Richard. I had been taught as a defenceman to hold the blue line, and as I turned to take him like I usually did, he went by me like I wasn't even there! He put his arm out with the puck, grabbed my stick with his other hand, pulled the puck ahead and was gone all alone on our net. He scored, too.

"Right away I thought, *I'd better do something different next time, or I won't be up here very long.* The next time the Rocket came down on me, I turned real quick, and went with him, dropped my stick right to the ice to get it below his hand so he couldn't grab it, and as he brought the puck across with the other hand, I got my stick on his stick and he lost control of the puck.

"As the fifth defenceman, I would not be put out in the last minute of play or in a dire situation, penalty-killing or the power play, anything like that. So there were very few opportunities to play, really. When you were on the ice, no matter how short a time you had been on, you came off at the next whistle. You didn't have to wait. When I did play, it was usually with Leo Reise."

Then fate intervened. "At Christmas, Doug McCaig broke his leg, got it caught in a rut. I became the fourth defencemen, and they soon realized they could depend on me. Until you're thrown into that situation, you or they don't really know if you're up to it. Tommy Ivan was similar to Joe Primeau. Tommy knew the game, how you should play as a team, but I really learned a lot from Bill Quackenbush, Jack Stewart and Leo Reise. I learned from playing with all these All-Stars. Tommy Ivan was a great coach, quiet like Primeau. He was also a buffer between the players and Jack Adams, who could get on guys' cases."

Kelly was always on the lookout for any initiation.

"I never got initiated like one rookie I saw. I got off lucky. I watched that fellow get initiated and thought, *Holy moley! I wouldn't have known any different had they picked me first.* But they picked someone else, which worked out for me because, after they'd gotten someone, they couldn't use that trick again. They could only catch one rookie this way. So, after that, we knew better. But they did get me another way.

"We're in Chicago on New Year's Day. We arrived by train. At bedtime, before settling into your berth, your bed, you would put your shoes in a box to get them shined overnight. I got up in the morning and I couldn't find my shoes. I looked all over. They were not there! We pull into Chicago, and it's snowing like the dickens, but I can't get off the train because I have no shoes. The boys were ready, of course, and got me a wheelchair, and I got off the train in that wheelchair. It's New Year's Day and I've got to find someplace to buy a new pair of shoes so I can walk to the game that night.

"I eventually found a store, a Jewish store that was open, and I bought a brand new pair of shoes. I was able to walk to the game that night. Once back in Detroit, I arrived at our next practice at the Olympia, and my shoes were hanging by the laces above the door to our dressing room. Then I realized; they got me. Nobody ever fessed up.

"I wore No. 20 the whole first year. I had been sleeping in the upper berth on the train at first, like rookies do, but when McCaig broke his leg, he was off recuperating. He had been sleeping below me. When he left the team, I just slipped down to his berth, took his spot. Nobody ever said anything to me. I was there from then on."

The shoe incident was not Red's only initiation, but it was quaint compared to the complicated machinations that went into the second. On January 7, Red was charged with making an improper left turn while driving in Detroit. He innocently mentioned the incident to Jack Adams. At traffic court the next morning, Judge John Watts ordered a trial for that same afternoon.

When the case reconvened, Adams and the whole team showed up for moral support and to act as character witnesses; Black Jack Stewart even offered his services as defence counsel. Red was honestly worried when 12 older women were ushered in as the jury.

The proceedings got underway: "The State of Michigan versus one Leonard Kelly."

When Red briefly smiled, the judge chastised him: "Young man, this charge is serious!"

His smile evaporated as his teammates, all in on the gag, tried to suppress their laughter. Stewart had a key role, and was serious, defending his client with all the legal terms he knew. Judge Watts kept cutting Stewart off on technicalities. Red was increasingly worried. The judge looked at Red and said, "You'd better get yourself another attorney. This guy is more like a prosecutor!"

Ignoring the slight, Stewart kept on talking. Finally, Judge Watts had seen enough. He banged his gavel and asked Red and his counsel to stand.

"Leonard P. Kelly, the court hereby finds you . . . guilty of the said charge," Watts boomed. The court room quieted. Red gulped. "I hereby fine you . . . two goals! And you'd better deliver them against Rangers tonight, or I'll have you back in court!"

The court erupted in laughter, howling and foot-stomping. Red could only smile and shake his head. He knew he'd been had, again. When he showed up for the game that night, a fake newspaper was posted on the dressing room wall with the headline declaring: "Kelly — Sentenced! Stewart's Defence Fails!"

Another incident was an eye-opener for the rookie. The team had lost a few games, and a meeting was arranged at the Joy Stables Restaurant that included the owner, James E. Norris, GM Adams and coach Ivan. "They wanted us to do better, so we had a get-together to kind of relax the team supposedly, bring us together," recalled Red. "We were sitting there, talking and eating, and there was an off-colour joke told by Bill Quackenbush. Five minutes later, suddenly Jim Norris stood up, looked at Quackenbush and said, 'What did you mean by that?' and proceeded to angrily come around the table to get at Bill. Norris had to be intercepted by Harry Lumley to avoid an incident. Pavelich and I were sitting beside each other, just rookies, but we were taking everything in, with big eyes and big ears."

With only one minor penalty to his name and 14 points in 40 games, Red was in the discussion for the Lady Byng Trophy for fair play — until an incident on January 28. Kelly and Boston's Fern Flaman fought in that night's 4–2 Detroit victory.

Scribes said Red had blown the trophy along with its $1,000 reward. "When they picked flattened Flaman off the ice," wrote Marshall Dann, "Kelly's only words were a not-so-cool, 'You want more?' Ferdinand obviously didn't, so Kelly rampaged against assorted other Bruins while still in the mood."

Detroit surprised everyone that season by finishing in second place, just five points back of Toronto. Playing full-time for the second half of the season, Red finished with 20 points. His coach was impressed. "One of the things that make Kelly great is that he's a real team player," said Ivan. "I think he is destined for great things. When we decided to use him regularly early in the season, we were criticized. But as I saw, he was making fewer mistakes in those early games than experienced players. I didn't use him too often in serious situations; I didn't want to break his spirit. But slowly I broke him in on those situations and he improved."

In the 1948 playoffs, the Red Wings had the upper hand over the Rangers in their semifinal series. Red popped in two goals in the fifth game — a 3–1 Detroit victory on St. Patrick's Day — and another in the sixth and deciding game, a 4–2 victory. The Wings advanced four games to two.

"Two were arching long shots from the boards," went the story out of Detroit. "He skated off the ice from one of the New York games with two black eyes and a mashed (broken twice in the same game) nose, his prizes for getting in front of a flying Ranger stick. But he played a whale of a game and his Irish eyes sparkled behind his scars of battle. True to the tenets of a star defenceman, Kelly likes it best where the going is thickest and the sparks fly wherever his red head is bobbing."

King Clancy, the league's referee-in-chief (and former star player), called Kelly "the best rookie defenceman the league has ever seen."

Black Jack Stewart went further with the praise: "Red will be the next defenceman to win the Hart Trophy awarded to the league's most valuable player."

On the eve of the Stanley Cup Final against the Maple Leafs, Red's growing prowess was noted. "Much of the early chatter of the Wings concerned young Kelly, the ex–St. Mike's redhead who has been popping pucks past [Chuck] Rayner of late at an astonishing rate," reported the *Toronto Star*. "Wings rate Kelly as one of the best puck carriers in hockey today. He doesn't part with the biscuit until he sees a colleague in position to take a pass. This is so extraordinary in the current scene of hockey; it has brought Kelly overnight from the status of a rookie to an accomplished star."

In the final, Red Wings rookies Kelly and Pavelich, played impressively well, but Toronto swept the Wings in four straight games, on the strength of a lineup that included the legendary Turk Broda in goal, and stars Syl Apps, Max Bentley and Teeder Kennedy.

At the conclusion of the playoffs, it was announced that Red had come in third place in the Calder Trophy voting for rookie of the year, with 14 votes. The winner was his teammate Jimmy McFadden, with 48 votes, and second place went to Pete Babando of the Bruins. "Jimmy McFadden was a little older when he got to the NHL," Red recalled. "He was about 26 or 27 years old when he came to us from Buffalo, but he had a fabulous first year."

The Red Wings placed three players on the NHL First All-Star Team: left winger Ted Lindsay, and defencemen Bill Quackenbush and Black Jack Stewart. The latter two proved invaluable in tutoring Red for the big leagues. "I had a front row seat in the classroom — Defence 101," said Red.

Stewart grew up on the family farm in Pilot Mound, Manitoba. He was scouted while playing junior hockey in Winnipeg and joined the Red Wings in the 1938–39 season. Adams called him the strongest hockey player he had ever seen.

There was security in having Black Jack around. "I called him 'Dad' because he always looked after me," recalled Pavelich. "I remember one night against the Rangers, I got into a scuffle with a guy by the name of Pat 'Boxcar' Egan. Egan fell on top of me and was about to really hit me when Stewart skated in close and said, 'Egan, if you lay a hand on that kid, I'll put you into the balcony.' Egan looked up at him and instantly backed right off. With Stewart around, we all thought that we were eight feet tall."

After another gruelling Simcoe summer on the farm, it was off to the 1948 training camp. When Jack Adams gave him a new sweater one day with a new number — four — Red was taken aback. "Oh I'm happy with No. 20," he said. "I don't know why I've been given this new one."

"Twenty, that's two numbers, that's too heavy," Adams quipped. "You only want one number." Red accepted it, well aware of the meaning behind the gesture, that the four starting defenceman got the lower numbers. It was a little thing, but a big thing. Doug McCaig, the previous owner of No. 4, was traded to Chicago on October 25.

As a team, the Red Wings were clearly in the ascendency and occupied first place for much of the 1948–49 season despite major injuries to Howe and Lindsay. McFadden suffered from the sophomore jinx as his output fell, but other players like Abel, Quackenbush, Stewart and Red picked up the slack.

Living arrangements changed for Red that second year. In his first season, he lived with his Aunt Clara and Uncle Doug Owen, near Seven Mile Road in Detroit. His brother, Joe, did as well, playing intermediate hockey in Detroit with a team called Metal Molding. Aunt Clara was a teacher and Uncle Doug was a Sears salesman. The next year, Red lived at Ma Shaw's rooming house, where many a Red Wings player stayed over the years.

"She used to report to Adams, but that was all right because we behaved, generally. We used to bring her with us quite a bit when we went out. She was like a chaperone," recalled Red. "The funny thing about Ma Shaw was that she never cooked. We never ate there; ever. Harry Lumley loved lobster, and so we went to this lobster place on

Grand River all the time. He'd eat lobster like you wouldn't believe. For breakfast we'd always go to this Greek place just around the corner. We had to foot the bills to eat while at home in Detroit, but thank goodness not on the road."

For his first two years on the road, Red roomed with Bill Quackenbush. "He was the veteran, so it was the unwritten rule that I would close the window in the morning when it got cold, get the cab when we needed one," he recalled. "During the game he was my defence partner and would yell to me, 'Go get 'em, Red!' and I'd go in the corners and battle. I learned a lot from him, because nobody got by Bill Quackenbush."

Born in Toronto, Quackenbush had permanently joined the Wings in the 1943–44 season. In his seventh NHL season, the veteran's elite defensive skills were more to do with positional and strategic manoeuvres than power and brawn.

On the ice, the Red Wings defence had a system. "Our defence and forwards worked together as a team," Red remembered. "We felt that if the guy had the puck behind our net; who cares? Leave them there! We had to worry about the guys in front of the net that he might pass it to. Only if he came out from behind that net, a little too far, when he might be able to score, then you worried about him. Even at that, from the side, Lumley had him blocked. But at a certain point, then you had to stop him from coming across any more. But I was taught not to run back there and leave the guy wide open in front. If we could score three goals, we'd win ninety per cent of the games, and Lumley was a huge part of that."

With things going well in the NHL, Red was given star treatment back home: on January 20, the area honoured him with a Red Kelly Night at the recently constructed Talbot Gardens arena in Simcoe. Prior to the exhibition game between his Red Wings and the Hamilton Tigers, he was given new luggage from the towns of Port Dover, Simcoe and Woodhouse. At ice level, Red presented his mother with a bouquet of roses from the Detroit organization. He

tallied four assists in a 9–4 victory over the senior league team. Both teams paid their own expenses, and the proceeds from the 2,500 in attendance went towards new arena seating. Many hundreds were turned away disappointed, unable to get tickets for the game.

"That was the first and only game where both sets of grandparents attended," recalled Red. "And especially Grandpa Kelly, it would be the only time he ever saw me play. It might have been just an exhibition game to the others, but I was sure playing hard in front of all my friends and family."

The next day, a big bus carrying the Red Wings drove the five miles down the country roads from Simcoe to the long driveway of Pete and Frances Kelly. They toured the silos, barns and fields, and saw for themselves where Red took his first hockey steps with bobskates on the pond in front of the barn.

"Then we all piled into the dining room," Red recalled. "Mom served us all quite the lunch, quite a spread. Feeding twenty-five or so hungry men was nothing to her. They were quite impressed, and Mom and Dad were sure proud. Of course, Mom was such a great cook! We left from there and travelled to Toronto for a game the next night."

In an article published in Detroit, Adams extolled the virtues of players that could play both defence and offence. "We've got boys who can shift around and still do a terrific job!" Adams boasted. "Take Bill Quackenbush, for instance, the best defenceman in the league. Bill used to play centre and when he combines his forward ability with his beautiful defensive play, there's no stopping him. Then there's Len Kelly, another top defenceman. When our first line of Ted Lindsay, Max McNab and Gordie Howe was broken up by injuries, we threw Kelly up in the line and he played with the best of them!"

The country break from the schedule must have been tonic for the Red Wings, as they won eight of their next nine games to remain in first place, and clinched first place by beating Toronto on March 9. With 10 games still left in the schedule, it was the earliest a team had ever sewn up the top spot.

In the six-team NHL, there was always last-minute jockeying in the standings just before the playoffs. Leafs owner Conn Smythe sent Adams a letter after the playoffs commending the Red Wings for not letting up at season's end, thus setting themselves up to face a tougher opponent, the Canadiens. It should be noted that in the last games of the schedule, the Red Wings took a hard-fought 2–1 victory over the Canadiens while Toronto surrendered 7–2 to the Bruins, which enabled Boston to sneak into second place over the Canadiens by one point, thus ensuring that the Leafs would face the Bruins, and not the Canadiens, in the first round.

"At the end of the year, we were way ahead, and we could have picked our opponent by losing a couple of games," recalled Red. "But instead we played it all out, winning everything we could win.

That put us up against Montreal, instead of losing a few and then facing an easier team like Boston or New York. Toronto got Boston; I think that's who they wanted."

The Red Wings were the team with the most potent offence by far, and they knew they had to adjust to playing defensive playoff hockey. Though Montreal had finished 10 points behind them in the standings and were eight-to-five underdogs, the Habs' defensive style had allowed 19 goals fewer than the Motown crew.

The tone for the series was set in Game 1, when it took three overtime periods for the Red Wings to win 2–1. In Game 2, the Wings were leading when a third period penalty to Red, a rarity, proved disastrous. At that time, a player served the full duration of his two-minute penalty, regardless of how often the opponents scored. With Red in the box, the Habs scored twice to go ahead 3–2, and eventually won 4–3 in overtime.

At the Forum in Game 3, Montreal won 3–2, but the Wings battled back to win Game 4, 3–1, on two goals by Howe and one from Red.

Adams singled Red out as the star of the series so far. "Every night has been a good one for him," Adams praised. "He's been worth more to us than even Howe and Lindsay!"

The series stayed even as the teams split the next two games. Pete Kelly drove to Detroit to watch his son, and Detroit finally vanquished the Canadiens 3–1 in the seventh and deciding game at the Olympia. Both teams appeared exhausted as they exchanged warm handshakes after a hard-fought series. The belief was that the Wings were spent.

"No, those Wings are tired," said Montreal's Ken Reardon. "We've worn them to a frazzle." Reardon was correct. The Leafs, seeking their third straight Stanley Cup, had beaten the Bruins in five games and were well rested. Toronto swept the tired Detroiters aside in four straight games, again.

In one game, Red was singled out as a superman. "At times it looked like it was Kelly against Toronto," went one story. "Ivan played Kelly at his regular defence post, as a penalty killer, on the power play, at left wing and at centre. Red played the entire last period as a forward and made some of the Wings' most threatening rushes, then fore-checked."

Detroit had five All-Stars, with Abel, Stewart and Quackenbush on the NHL First All-Star Team and Lindsay and Howe on the Second.

Quackenbush treated himself to a new car before the summer of 1949. "Bill had just bought himself a new DeSoto convertible," Red recalled. "He took Lindsay and me, and we drove to Hollywood, California, for a couple of weeks before we went our separate ways. We had a great time.

"The deal was whoever was driving and ran out of gas, it was your responsibility to walk and get gas, so we were all cognizant of that. I was driving when we went up to see the Hoover Dam. At the top the gas gauge was kind of low, so I shut the car off and glided all the way down. It was a very long stretch. At the bottom I started the car back up and we reached a gas station a few miles further on.

"We took Route 66 up to Arizona and the Grand Canyon, where you could take a mule ride down into the canyon, have lunch down there and then come back up. The little path down was narrow and the drop was dead steep. Bill's mule tripped once and fell to one knee and he almost went over the edge. He went white as a ghost and didn't say a word for the rest of the way down.

"It was a great trip. When we got back, I headed to the farm. Little could we have foreseen that it would be our last time together."

Detroit's general manager hated losing, especially to Smythe. When he found out about some side trips Quackenbush had made during the playoffs, he acted. "During the Toronto series, we stayed in Hamilton at the Royal Connaught Hotel, and we were driving in for the games from Hamilton," recalled Red. "Then we'd drive back and forth and wait there for the next game. Adams later found out that Bill had slipped away and gone golfing on our off days. Adams wasn't too happy about that." On August 16, Adams traded Quackenbush, who had just won the Lady Byng as the most gentlemanly player, to Boston, along with Peter Horeck, in exchange for Pete Babando, Clare Martin, Lloyd Durham and Jimmy Peters.

Back home, Port Dover followed Simcoe and took its turn in June by hosting a Red Kelly Testimonial Dinner at the town hall, attended by Jack Adams and Tommy Ivan.

"The nicest thing I can say about Red is that I wish I had 15 players like him, and I would have no worries with the Red Wings," Ivan told the crowd. "Of all the players I have coached over the years, there is none as fine as Red." ·

For his third training camp, in the fall of 1949, Red prepared for another contract-negotiating session with Adams. His old scout, Shovel Shot Cooper, gave him some advice.

"Remember you're a very big part of this team, a very big part! You know what I mean?" Without saying it outright, Cooper was suggesting Red ask for more money than he was offered. The 22-year-old Kelly was thankful for the advice from someone he truly respected.

"Shovel Shot signed all the Detroit stars," Red recalled. "He certainly got a lot of talent out from under the nose of Toronto. I don't think he was given enough credit. I really don't think so. Maybe that's why he gave me that advice that time, to ask for more money at training camp, to stand up and not let them walk all over me with the contract. Something must have been going on, because it wasn't long, a few years later, that he was gone from the organization. Did I get more money? Maybe a bit, but not much more. I was just happy to play hockey."

As the season began, the NHL Board of Governors decided to paint the ice white in order to see the puck better and also voted to increase the length of the regular season schedule from 60 to 70 games. It would help the NHL coffers.

"It didn't mean a thing to us, except that now we played an extra ten games," recalled Red. "They didn't give us any extra money for it, not a dime! What could we do but accept it? The owners made all the money."

The league's minimum player salary at the time was $6,500 per season over 60 games — $108 per game. Add the extra 10 games to their workload, and the wage dropped to $92 per game.

Red was surprised when he was handed his sweater with an *A* on it, meaning alternate captain. It was just another of those little things that was kind of a big thing. The redhead just shrugged, and the Red Wings started the 1949–50 season on a tear by winning eight of their first nine games, led by the Production Line. But Red's play was also so exceptional that coach Ivan made headlines when he gave Kelly the highest of praise.

"I hate to go out on a limb like this but I've got to say he's the greatest all-around player in the league today!" Ivan told Red Burnett of the *Toronto Star*. "When we're shorthanded, he goes up front from his defence position to kill the penalty. Then back he goes for his regular turn alongside Jack Stewart. If someone gets hurt up front, up goes the redhead to fill the pinch and he usually takes over in better fashion than the fellow he replaced!"

It clearly demonstrated Red's growing confidence with the puck and his new defence partner. "Whenever they asked me to play up front, I did it. Usually it happened if we weren't scoring, or we ran into trouble, losing, or somebody was hurt," Red recalled. "So they would throw me up there. It used to be said that defencemen were supposed to stay back, but I went with the puck, got it out of our end. The best way to pass it up, to get it out, was not send the puck around the boards but on my forward's stick. If you passed it to your teammate along the boards then he has to dig it out, and by that time his checker could be right on top of him. So I would put the puck right on his stick as he's moving. That was the key. I was definitely an offensive defenceman. I used to carry that puck no question. Get the puck out of our end.

"And if I could take off as fast as I could, bang, we've got them caught. With two or three of their players caught up ice, we'd have the other team outnumbered going the other way. I knew I could make that play, as long as the puck was ahead of me. I didn't hang around there. I made the play and got right back to my position. I was a defenceman first and foremost. And I had a good stay-home defence partner in Leo Reise."

Red's 1949–50 hockey season was going great when, on December 11, he was chosen for his third Schaefer Award as the most valuable Red Wing in that night's game. He would garner a few more before he was finished. Also that December, Red and Lindsay returned to St Michael's College to donate to the memorial fund and be present at the blessing of the cornerstone at the site of a new facility. While there, he also donated the Red Kelly Trophy for the most valuable player of the minor midgets. Lindsay and Ed Sandford of the Bruins also donated trophies.

The Red Wings cruised to first place for the second year in a row, this time by a healthy 11-point margin over Montreal, and Lindsay, Abel and Howe finished one-two-three in league scoring. Red played in all 70 games and led all defencemen with 15 goals and 25 assists.

Once again it was Toronto versus Detroit in the playoffs, but this time in the semifinal. The Wings had beaten the Leafs in 8 of their 14 encounters during the season, outscoring them 46–21.

The Wings-Leafs semi was a battle from the get-go. With a second period 3–0 lead in the series opener at the Olympia, Toronto had the game well in hand. Teeder Kennedy, Toronto's captain, was carrying the puck up the left boards out of his zone just as Howe swooped across from the side to intercept him.

"Kennedy was skating with the puck along the boards, and Howe was coming up behind, about to overtake him," recalled Red. "Gordie went to take him with his body, and Kennedy pulled back and his stick hit Howe just as Howe went in, and Howe crashed head first into the boards."

Howe crumpled to the ice unconscious, his head a bloody mess. He was wheeled off on a stretcher amid a hush in the Olympia. After what seemed like forever, there was a hockey game to finish — but the Wings were an emotionally distracted mess, more concerned about their star player. Tempers flared, and the Leafs captured an easy 5–0 victory.

At the nearby Harper Hospital, doctors drilled a hole through Howe's skull to drain accumulated fluid and relieve pressure on the brain. For hours his life hung in the balance, and hourly updates on his condition were broadcast over the radio. When doctors upgraded Howe from critical to serious condition, the hockey world heaved a collective sigh of relief. And for the Wings, there was unfinished business amid the accusations of foul play, the butt-ends, sidesteps and apologies given and taken away.

"Detroit critics feel that the Red Wing players, upset by the loss of their likeable right wing star, will be in no shape to halt the Leafs," wrote Burnett in the *Toronto Star*.

"This series is far from over," retorted Ivan. "We will be back and we won't look like we did tonight. We'll roar back and win this for Howe."

The Wings were still a potent force without Howe, but his absence necessitated some line-juggling. Marcel Pronovost, then a defenceman on the Omaha farm club, was called up just in time for the playoffs and filled in up front.

With the Wings having a score to settle, the second game took an ominous turn in the last period, when fights and stick-swinging broke out everywhere. "Everybody was fighting," recalled Red, who fought Vic Lynn. "Fans and chairs were on the ice. It started just to the left of their net, and Gus Mortson reached out and with his hand caught Lindsay under the chin, his feet went out and he went down. One of their players then carried the puck up the ice and one of our defencemen nailed him coming out from the other way; the referee blew the whistle and gave us a penalty but didn't do anything about the Lindsay trip. That's when it all started. Then everybody was fighting — even the two goaltenders were at centre ice. Fans were on the ice."

After the dust settled, the Red Wings evened the series with a 3–1 win.

In Game 3 at Maple Leaf Gardens, Turk Broda shut out the Wings 2–0, but Howe's teammates roared back to tie the series with a 2–1 overtime victory. The teams exchanged shutout victories over the next two games to send the series to a seventh and deciding game at the Olympia.

"I remember Howie Meeker saying to some of our guys that we'd be back home fishing pretty soon before the sixth game," recalled Red. "But we won it, and we're returning home. Before the seventh game, we stayed at the King Edward Hotel in Windsor, but I couldn't sleep. In fact, nobody slept that night. We all lay there with our eyes wide open, staring at the ceiling."

In the third period, with the teams tied at 0–0, Red shot at an open net with Broda out of position, but hit the post. In the last minute, Broda deflected a Kelly blast just barely wide with his glove. In overtime, the Wings prevailed when Leo Reise's shot bounced off Bill Barilko's stick and fell behind Broda for the series-winning goal.

The Wings were now off to the 1950 Stanley Cup Final against the fourth-place Rangers, who awaited them on the strength of an upset win over the second-place Canadiens, four games to one.

With a circus booked at Madison Square Garden, the Rangers had to play all their games on the road. Games 2 and 3 were set for Maple Leaf Gardens, and the rest for the Olympia. Backed by the great goaltending of Hart Trophy winner Chuck Rayner, the Rangers, under coach Lynn Patrick, gave the Wings all they could handle and then some. Don Raleigh got two overtime goals for the Rangers, as they went up three games to two. Detroit came from behind to win Game 6, 5–4, on an incredible go-ahead goal by Abel, who was proving to be a real sparkplug.

"Against New York, Black Jack Stewart told Abel that if he didn't wake up and hit Bag of Bones Don Raleigh, Black Jack would hit Abel," recalled Red. "He was serious and was Abel's roommate. Abel said that he slept with one eye open!"

It was down to one game for all the marbles. The Rangers had come to play and took a 2–0 lead before Abel and Babando tied it for the Wings with goals 22 seconds apart. Before the end of the second period, the teams exchanged another goal each to head into the third deadlocked.

Third period play see-sawed back and forth, and both goalies were outstanding. The teams played 20 scoreless minutes to send it to one overtime, and then another. At 8:31 of the second overtime period, Babando took a pass from George Gee, came over the blue line, cut to the middle and backhanded a shot through a mess of players in front of Rayner, hitting the back of the net.

The Olympia exploded in joy as the players threw off their gloves and rushed onto the ice to congratulate Babando at the Ranger blue line. Hats and debris littered the ice. After the customary hand-shakes, the Stanley Cup, sitting nicely on a small table, was handed to team captain Sid Abel. Abel pushed the table around the ice for the fans to see. Looking on, Lindsay had another idea.

"Next thing you know, Lindsay picked up the Cup off the table and carried it around the ice," recalled Red. "I believe it was the first time that that had ever happened. It was the first time I saw it. The fans were screaming, everybody was happy. A tradition was born.

"Afterwards, Rangers goalie Chuck Rayner and some of their older players came to the hotel and drank champagne with us. That surprised us! We had no qualms about that, they had also earned it. It had been a great series. It made it an even better celebration to drink with them.

"Later, we had a party at the Book Cadillac Hotel, but they had no food at all — just buckets of champagne, lots of champagne! We were all a pretty hungry, as none of us had eaten since one o'clock that afternoon, so a few of the fellas got pretty sick. One of the scouts, Carson Cooper I think it was, fell flat on the table. We partied again a few days later; a dinner one of the fans threw us. But that was it. There was no parade, city hall ceremony, anything like that."

Winning meant more money, somewhat.

"Instead of $3,000 for the league, playoff and Stanley Cup wins, we received $2,365," Red recalled. "Where did the rest go? They divvied up the money among the players, trainers, officials; Adams and Ivan probably got some as well. It was a decision made by management.

"When I look back, it sometimes cost us more money to play in the Cup Final because we had to pay an extra month's rent and expenses. If you played fourteen extra games, two full series, that's a lot of games, right? Figure that out to what they paid you during the regular season and the fourteen extra games; did we really get paid extra? We sometimes wondered!"

In the NHL of the 1950s, a Stanley Cup victory over the full 14 games netted each player $169 per game, compared to the $96 per game they made during the regular season — if they made the league minimum salary of $6,500. For the owners, it was a cash windfall because playoff ticket prices were much higher, increasing profits.

Red got another, unexpected cash bonus of $1,000 when the NHL announced that he had been selected to the Second All-Star Team along with fellow Wings Reise and Howe; Abel and Lindsay were selected to the First Team. He also came in second in Lady Byng voting, behind Edgar Laprade, and was tenth in Hart Trophy voting as the league's most valuable player — though only winners got any money.

As Red travelled back to the Simcoe farm that spring of 1950 to help his family with the crops, he had a great sense of accomplishment. He had done very well personally, his star was on the rise, and the team had done something that every Canadian boy dreamed of — they had won the Stanley Cup.

But in Detroit, "Trader" Jack Adams considered his options. He had stayed with the same roster after winning two separate Stanley Cups in the 1930s, and both teams rewarded him with last-place finishes the year after. "Never again will I stand pat!" he had vowed to himself.

He would be true to his nickname.

• • • • • •

CHAPTER FOUR

THEM'S
the BREAKS!

In the spring of 1950, Red Kelly wasn't thinking about anything other than returning home. The change in lifestyle after a hockey season was immediate.

"As soon as I was halfway across the Detroit–Windsor Bridge, exactly halfway across, it was like night and day," recalled Red. "You took a big breath, exhaled and everything changed. Your whole mental state just relaxed. Life was no longer a big rush, like during the hockey season. Returning to Canada and life on the farm was just so relaxing. The work was hard but it was simple, honest. At night you lay on the grass in the fresh air and looked up at the stars, the moon, and listened to the crickets. A lot of nights I went to Port Dover and the large Summer Garden because I loved to dance. There were dances there every night of the week during the summer. A bunch of us workers on the farm and the neighbours would go."

If there was ever a definition of a summer town, Port Dover was it, coming to life every July and August with an influx of tourists who came to lie on its fabulous beaches and live the cottage life. The Summer Garden hosted such famous bandleaders as Guy Lombardo, Tommy Dorsey, Duke Ellington and Louis Armstrong. Into the 1950s, the Big Band Era started sharing the Sunday night limelight with a strange new music called rock 'n' roll, including up-and-comers like Ronnie Hawkins and Gordon Lightfoot.

"The Summer Garden was a fabulous place to dance," Red remembered. "It was an octagonal building and had a large circular wooden dance floor. It was a great dance floor and had excellent music. And there was never a shortage of dance partners."

Sports filled much of Red's time away from the farm and the dance floor. "I was on the go all the time," he said. He played lacrosse on the nearby Six Nations Reserve. "They really had some great lacrosse players," Red recalled. "I used to think I could handle a lacrosse stick, but I had nothing on those guys." On the diamond, he played for a senior men's team in Port Dover and managed a girls' softball team for a time and boys' baseball teams for a couple of years.

News out of Detroit in July wasn't positive. After having been assured that the elbow surgery for young netminding prospect Terry Sawchuk had gone well, Trader Jack Adams put into play a plan he'd been working up for some time. The Black Hawks were desperate for a goaltender. Adams offered Hawks president Bill Tobin a deal involving Sawchuk. As Adams had hoped, Tobin was spooked by Sawchuk's recent elbow surgery and demanded Harry Lumley instead. On July 13, Adams agreed to a mammoth nine-player deal, the biggest trade in NHL history at the time. Tobin acquired the proven Stanley Cup–winning goalie Lumley plus defencemen Black Jack Stewart and Al Dewsbury, centre Don Morrison and left winger Pete Babando, whose overtime heroics were apparently already forgotten.

On the record, Adams claimed he'd been reluctant to make the deal, but secretly he was pleased with his acquisitions. Along with forward Gaye Stewart, Adams received a player he had always wanted, Metro Prystai, and a defenceman among defencemen, Bob Goldham.

And most of all, he had made room for Terry Sawchuk, known as "Ukey" or "Uke" to his teammates due to his Ukrainian heritage.

At this stage in his summer life, Red dated a few local girls, though nothing serious developed — except once. "I was coming home late one night after having dropped this girl off, Joyce Manion, in Caledonia," he recalled. "She was a classmate and friend of my sister Laureen at Notre Dame in Waterdown. I fell asleep at the wheel and went into a big ditch between Hagersville and Jarvis. It rocked the car and woke me up. I had a hold of the steering wheel with both hands and I saw the hydro post coming and I hit it dead on, went right through it and came back onto the road.

"The rad had been driven back into the motor. I severed that hydro pole like I cut it off with a saw. It was still attached at the top, hanging by the wires, but the bottom was loose. That was close. I didn't look forward to waking up Dad and telling him I had totalled his car!"

He came out of it all unscathed, and, before Red knew it, it was time for the 1950–51 season. "I was feeling good after three years in the league," he said. "But you never get complacent, never overconfident. You're always trying to better yourself. I always signed a one-year contract. If I did better, then I could get more money the next year.

"Going into my fourth year, I was still making the league minimum wage but getting extra money from bonuses and awards." The teams were expected to match bonuses for each playoff round and for post-season awards, which Adams would complain about during contract discussions. "We had too many All-Stars! They almost held it against you, if you can believe it."

Black Jack Stewart's departure was an adjustment. "At that stage he was playing some good hockey and had been a big presence on the team, a real team guy," recalled Red. "He could lift the team by things he did, but I don't think they ever quite replaced him. He played hurt, under all kinds of conditions. He sometimes had trouble bending over to tie up his skates! That's the kind of a team guy he was. To treat him like that at the end, I didn't think that was very good."

Bob Goldham was a different kind of defender. "He was a great shot-blocker. He wasn't a very fast skater, but he was rangy. He really helped the defence."

As the season was set to begin, Red was called into Adams's office in the Olympia. "You're looking pretty good out there, kid!" Adams said, pushing a contract across the table towards Red, who looked at it long and hard but hesitated to sign. The delay caught the general manager by surprise.

"What's wrong, kid? Aren't you satisfied with our offer? What we're gonna pay you?"

"Oh, it's not that, the money's fine, but . . ."

"But what?"

"Well, I'm playing hockey away from the farm, and my brother, who helps my father on the farm, will be playing intermediate hockey in an Ontario-Michigan league, and so my father's going to miss our help sometimes, and . . ."

"And?"

"Well, there's this tractor we could use, a Farmall, it would really help my Dad a lot, because we're away. These tractors are hard to get because of the shortage of parts from the war, and . . ."

"I see. So, if we can get you one of these tractors, you'll sign?"

"Yes, sir!"

Adams smiled and called for the team's financial assistant, who had a cottage in Leamington. He instructed him to find a tractor, at any cost, for the Kellys.

"They got that Farmall tractor down by Leamington," Red recalled. "It was only two or three years old. It had the motor in front but off to the side, so you could see where you were driving. It could cultivate, fertilize, had a hoe behind it, a three-in-one operation. It had the disks, all the attachments. It was marvellous! The farm needed a tractor. I signed for $6,500, the league minimum then, but I got Dad the tractor. Adams would brag about getting that tractor

for me, but he never mentioned the fact that when they found it, I had to pay for it. But I didn't care, the farm needed that tractor."

On October 8, Detroit hosted the NHL All-Star Game. It was the fourth year for the contest, with the Stanley Cup champions facing a team of NHL stars. Detroit became the first champion to beat the All-Stars, 7–1, thanks to a hat trick — another first in All-Star history — by Ted Lindsay.

A few weeks later, Red put the rest of the league on notice that he was starting where he left off the year before. On October 22, Detroit was trailing the Canadiens 2–0. Montreal goaltender Gerry McNeil was cruising along confidently, having blanked the opposition for 158 straight minutes. But before McNeil knew what happened, Kelly had blasted two long screened drives from the point past him to tie the game and end McNeil's streak. Jimmy Peters gave the Wings the 3–2 win. "If Gerry McNeil, Montreal's rookie netminder, didn't know about Kelly before," wrote Marshall Dann, "he found out Sunday night at the Olympia."

The Wings flew out of the starting gate in an attempt to catch the Leafs, who'd opened with a 2–1 loss to Chicago but then went on an amazing 11-game undefeated streak. Rookie Sawchuk and the defence were more than up to the challenge, and after 12 games Detroit had the league's lowest goals-against average, at 1.67 per game. Sawchuk's unique gorilla crouch was also gaining attention.

Against Toronto in mid-December, Red was at his best. "Even Al Rollins' magical goaltending couldn't stop Detroit's attack led by Red Kelly," went the story in the *Detroit Free Press*. Red opened the scoring in the first period on a screen shot that eluded Rollins. The Leafs tied it, but then "Kelly came right back to put Detroit in front to stay. The red-headed defenceman took Jimmy Peters' pass and went in on Rollins for a close shot."

"The redhead went through the entire Leaf team in that deceiving way of his in which he combines kicking the puck with stick work," added a Toronto report that likened Red's second goal to a Howie Morenz moment. "When Kelly reached the Toronto defence, our old friends Bill Barilko and Bill Juzda barred his path. Kelly skated right at them, then veered toward Barilko. He seemed to disappear. Kelly was in. So was his shot." Kelly continued his one-man show 30 seconds later with a nifty pass that Prystai rapped home.

As the Wings arrived in Montreal on December 23, the *Montreal Star* praised Red as "the best utility player in the league . . . the way he is playing, he will get serious consideration for all-star honours in March." Red kept up his pace by drilling home the first goal and assisting on the next two as the Wings tied the Canadiens 4–4.

It was clear that the Red Wings possessed a powerful offence, an excellent goaltender in Sawchuk and an equally strong defence to protect him. Some Wings players joked that they should get Sawchuk a rocking chair after a game in which he went a span of 22 minutes without facing a single shot.

As the Wings prepared to host Toronto on January 9, the *Detroit News* suggested that the Leafs concentrate on Kelly. "The Maple Leafs will be out to stop big Gordie Howe, little Ted Lindsay, 'Meatball' Metro and the rest of the Red Wing snipers when they come into Olympia tomorrow night . . . but that red-headed kid Kelly back on defence is the Wing they'll really be watching. Kelly is the boy who played everything but goal, for the Wings against Boston last night. He was up on the forward line, played at his regular position on defence, then took a whirl on the power play and was back out again when Detroit was shorthanded through a penalty."

Some teammates voiced concern. "Ivan would play me so much the other guys would say, 'He's going to wear you out!'" Red recalled. "But that's the most important thing to a hockey player; that they play you. I never thought about it. I could handle it, was always in great shape. I didn't smoke or drink, and because of that, I had a great wind. It also mattered who you hung out with. There was no doubt that some players over-drank, and I think it shortened some hockey careers. They liked to hang out in places, watering holes. The problem was also that we had a lot of free time between games and practices."

"Back in those days, we wasted a lot of time," Jimmy Peters added. "We could have been trying to better ourselves with education or courses or something. Instead we'd go someplace drinking beer, or to a pool hall between games."

But not everyone did.

"Some of us choose to go dancing. It was great exercise," Red remembered. "We would also go bowling, so that kept some of us busy doing things other than drinking. I hung out with Marty Pavelich, and we both liked to dance. We would go stag to different dance halls around, and we would have a ball.

"Sometimes we would have a team party on a Monday night, after a weekend of games, and I would end up dancing with all the wives whose husbands didn't like dancing. But it would be great to get together. Another guy who liked to dance was Gordie Howe. He would go dancing with Marty, Meatball and me."

Red explained Prystai's nickname: "He roomed at Ma Shaw's with us, but he sometimes hung out with friends over by Hamtramck, and they had great food over there. They would have card parties, and they apparently had great meatballs, and that's where he got his nickname. He liked to bowl, too."

In a January 21 article, *Detroit News* writer Paul Chandler asked the 10 eligible Red Wings bachelors their wish list for a potential mate. "I'll marry anytime now," Red answered tongue-in-cheek. "I'm just waiting for the right girl. On the average there's no difference between Canadian and American girls. Brunettes or blondes are fine but I can't get along with another redhead. We always clash. I want a wife who's a good cook but I hope she's good looking too."

As February began, the Wings were in first place with 28 wins, 11 losses and nine ties, setting an incredible pace; yet the Leafs were hot on their tail.

In a match at Maple Leaf Gardens on February 10, won 2–1 by the Red Wings, Red was again singled out by the Toronto press. "Red Kelly was the heart of the Wings machine," observed Red Burnett. "He was either carrying the puck, taking it from a Leaf or passing it to a mate. You'd see the redhead leading a charge one moment and the next taking it from a Leaf at the other end. He did everything but play goal and was out there for over 40 of the 60 minutes. The dashing Irisher started both Wings goal-getting plays."

The Wings returned to Toronto on March 7 and beat Leafs goalie Al Rollins 3–0 for Sawchuk's eighth shutout of the season. The win spread the Wings' lead over the second-place Leafs to eight points. Despite a 7–0 shutout of Chicago on March 11 and a 4–0 shutout against Boston on March 15, the Vezina race for top goaltender went down to the wire and the final two games of the season, with Sawchuk having allowed one goal fewer than Rollins. (At that time, the Vezina Trophy was awarded to the goalie with the lowest

goals-against average; in the 1980s, the rules were changed and it
went to the goalie "adjudged to be the best" according to a vote
among NHL general managers). And while Howe was in a league
scoring battle with Rocket Richard, Red had his own NHL record
to shoot for, made possible after he got three points in a Detroit 4–1
win against the Rangers on March 21.

"Keep an eye on Leonard Patrick Kelly, rated the NHL's best
defenceman," wrote Lewis Walter. "With 52 points, Kelly has already
gone 11 past the former Red Wing record set by Bill 'Flash' Hollett
in 1945. If Kelly could pick up five more points . . . he would tie the
all-time NHL record of 57 set by Walter 'Babe' Pratt."

In a pre-game ceremony before the season finale, the Detroit
Hockey Writers Association handed out its awards. "For the first
time in history, the Red Wings 'most valuable' and 'most sports-
manlike' player is one and the same man, Leonard Patrick Kelly

of Simcoe, Ontario," went the story in the *Detroit News*. "Highest scoring defenceman in Detroit history, Kelly's value was measured perhaps more about his all-around adaptability than by his scoring ... on the power play ... penalty-killing ... and forward when power was needed up front. Kelly served more time on the ice in minutes than any teammate except the goalie. Kelly is a standout candidate as the National Hockey League's 'most valuable.'"

Red and his teammates played stingy hockey in a 5–0 win over Montreal, but he fell three assists short of Pratt's record, while Rollins edged out Sawchuk for the Vezina. Still, Red's season tally of 54 points was not too shabby, and the Red Wings' 44 wins and 101 points were NHL records, while the shutout, Sawchuk's 11th of the season, was a high for the modern era. Now the team turned its thoughts to the playoffs.

Their opponents in the semifinal were the rookie-filled Canadiens, who had finished in third place, 36 points behind the league champions. What could not be ignored, however, was that the Canadiens had entered the playoffs with only one loss in their last 10 games. Montreal coach Dick Irvin could afford to make light of his team's underdog status.

"We're along for the ride," Irvin said, "everything to win and nothing to lose. The burden is on the mighty Red Wings, and what a disgrace it would be if they should lose."

The Canadiens brought their A game to the Olympia. Although Detroit kept the Montreal attack to a lone shot in the first period of Game 1, it was 2–2 through regulation time. Rocket Richard scored the winner in the fourth overtime and did so again in Game 2, this time in the third OT, as Montreal took a stranglehold on the series.

With their backs against the wall, the Wings went into a frenzied Montreal Forum and showed character as they won the next two games, 2–0 and 4–1, to even the series.

In Game 5, the Wings took a 2–1 lead, and then a shoving match between Lindsay and Richard erupted into fisticuffs. Without warning, Richard levelled Lindsay, who fell to the ice, out cold. The Canadiens caught fire and won 5–2. After the game, Irvin turned the knife.

"Give me my rookies when the going gets tough — they've got the spirit," he boasted. "Detroit can have its stars. When Richard threw the punch and Lindsay went down, it took all the fight out of the Red Wings. Who's doing the chasing now?"

Montreal smelled blood. The Wings were not about to go down without a fight and hoped the home-ice jinx would hold. Both teams played clean end-to-end firewagon hockey. Referee Bill Chadwick did not call a penalty all night. Montreal led 3–2 with 45 seconds remaining.

The 14,448 fans were on their feet, roaring and screaming as the Wings made their way into the Canadiens end and pulled Sawchuk for an extra attacker. The Habs frantically attempted to keep the Wings at bay and got a whistle with just six seconds left. Elmer Lach won the faceoff against Abel, fed the puck back to Doug Harvey, and the Red Wings season was over. When the Wings reached their dressing room, they found Adams holed up, unable to stand the pressure of watching the final few minutes.

In the Stanley Cup Final, the Leafs won a truly memorable series, beating Montreal in five games, all of which were decided in overtime.

For some Red Wings, there would be some consolation after the heartbreaking loss, as Howe took home the Art Ross Trophy for the top scorer, and Sawchuk won the Calder as the top rookie. Red joined Howe, Sawchuk and Lindsay on the First All-Star Team, netting himself $1,000, and then, on April 30, he was awarded the Lady Byng for another grand. As well, Red finished third in voting for the Hart Trophy, behind Rocket Richard and winner Milt Schmidt of Boston.

As Red headed home for the summer, the Stanley Cup loss haunted him, as it did his GM. Sitting in his office at the Olympia, Adams studied his roster. He knew he had the core of a team with dynasty written all over it. But Adams was always looking for ways to fine-tune his lineup. On August 20, he sold six players to Chicago in the greatest cash deal to date: $75,000. Gone were George Gee, Jimmy McFadden, Clare Martin, Clare Raglan, Jimmy Peters and Max McNab. But Trader Jack wasn't done. He sent Gaye Stewart to the Rangers for small but tough Tony Leswick.

In the fall of 1951, the big story out of the Red Wings' 17-day training camp was Sawchuk's weight — he reported in at a staggering 212 pounds and was placed on a no-starch diet. Red reported in great shape after his summer working on the farm, as usual.

Red participated in his third straight All-Star game in Toronto, after which the Wings opened the season with a 1–0 shutout against Sugar Jim Henry and the Bruins at the Olympia. It was Detroit's 13th straight season-opening win.

Few teams in history could boast the firepower the 1951–52 Wings had at their disposal. In front of Sawchuk was a defence crew without peer. "Benny Woit was the fifth defenceman, who didn't see all that much action," remembered Leo Reise. "He'd play maybe six, seven shifts a night. Red Kelly was a great defenceman who could really carry the puck. Bob Goldham could really block shots. Marcel Pronovost was my partner and was a great puck carrier, and I stayed home more at that point in my career."

Pronovost recalled how the season and the team were shaping up. "Our team had every element: phenomenal goaltending, amazing defence and experience up front. And overall, this was still a very young hockey club."

"The key to our success was our third line, really," recalled Red. "We had the Production Line — Abel, Howe and Lindsay. Then we had the Checking Line — Leswick, Pavelich and Skov. They would check any team's top line. Then the third line was Prystai, Wilson and Delvecchio. We hoped they would come through with goals. Each team's checking line would try to hold each team's power line.

Often if the third line could come through with goals, it would make the difference."

Play was noted to be rougher in this NHL season, and Red was singled out as one of the toughest hombres to think about tussling with. In an article published on November 14, it was noted: "The Byng Bowl went last season to Red Kelly, a former boxing champion at St. Michael's College . . . . Young Mr. Kelly seldom resorts to the use of his dukes on the ice. The impression appears to exist around the league that there are few, if any, players who would attempt to knock even one 'l' out of Kelly. We saw Vic Lynn, then with the Leafs start something he couldn't finish with the redhead . . . . Kelly peeled off the gloves, put his stick down (neatly) and proceeded to give Mr. Lynn one of the neatest whippings he'd (ever) had."

As the season progressed, Red continued to play an exorbitant amount of ice time and was notching points with his usual aplomb. In November, the Wings lost only once, outscoring the opposition 37–29.

Sometimes, off the ice the Red Wings split naturally into two distinct groups: one comprising Howe, Lindsay, Pavelich, Kelly and Reise; the other made up of Wilson, Prystai, Delvecchio, Pronovost, Skov, Leswick, Woit and Sawchuk. "But," recalled Wilson, "on the ice and in the dressing room, we were one group. That was one of the main reasons for our success. We had a good captain and we were a close-knit team."

Pronovost recalled one example of team togetherness that occurred in Boston after a 5–5 tie in December. "Tommy Ivan called for a one o'clock curfew. But all the guys decided to go out for Chinese food. So we all went out to this Chinese restaurant. We just get served our food at a quarter past one when Tommy Ivan walks in the door. He looked around, saw that everyone was together, a couple of guys had a beer but we were behaving, so he came in, sat down for some food himself and then picked up the bill. What could he say to us?"

The Red Wings streaked to the regular season finish line with

100 points, 22 ahead of second-place Montreal and 26 ahead of Toronto, their first-round playoff opponents.

The Wings had heard the whispers that they weren't a playoff club; that they folded when the chips were down. And they were facing the defending champions in the first round.

Game 1 at the Olympia was a chippy affair. Sawchuk and his tough defence shut down the vaunted Leafs attack and claimed a 3–0 win. Game 2 saw Conn Smythe looking for inspiration as he called upon the legendary Turk Broda to take Rollins's place in the Leafs net, even though Broda had only played 30 minutes and eight seconds all season. The Leafs and Broda did play an inspired game. Action see-sawed back and forth. Throughout the game, Red played centre in place of the injured Abel along with his usual defence slot in emergency situations. Wilson put one past Broda at the three-quarter mark of the first period to put the Wings up 1–0. It stayed like that until the final minute of play. The Wings were pressing, with Red on the top forward line with Howe and Lindsay.

"The puck goes down into their corner," Red recalled. "I get there first, and I know Howe would be coming up behind me, so I went to move it back to him. But Jim Thompson came in and hit me from behind, nailed me right into the boards. I really hurt my hand."

Detroit hung on for the 1–0 win but it cost them their best defenceman, who was "in a state of shock." The *Toronto Star*'s Milt Dunnell added, "The redhead has been just about Detroit's top man to date. Without Kelly, the Wings would be hurt."

Though press reports disclosed that Red had a sprain, X-rays taken the next day revealed a fracture in his left wrist. He seemed to be done for the season.

Back at Maple Leaf Gardens, the Broda experiment backfired as the Red Wings pummelled him in a 6–2 loss that ended his Hall of Fame career. Rollins was back in the Leafs net for Game 4, but the Detroit juggernaut could not be denied, and the Torontonians were swept aside by a final 3–1 loss.

The Wings had to wait nine days for the finals to start, while the Canadiens and the gritty Bruins battled it out. The Wings practised and tried to stay fired up at their hotel in Toledo, Ohio, away from the distractions of their daily lives. For Red, the layoff was supposed to help his wrist heal.

The tough Boston-Montreal series went seven games and was won on a determined effort by Rocket Richard. Having missed part of the regular season due to injuries, the Rocket was knocked out of the final game after a second-period collision with the Bruins' Bill Quackenbush. With four minutes left in regulation time and the score tied 1–1, the shaky, stitched-up Richard returned and skated through four Bruins and fought off Quackenbush to beat Sugar Jim Henry for the eventual winner. The picture of a bloodied Richard shaking hands with a black-eyed Henry, who is bowing respectfully, is one of the most evocative hockey photographs ever taken. Even Montreal coach Dick Irvin sported two shiners, a result of a flying puck into the Canadiens bench that struck him between the eyes during Game 5.

A booking conflict with the Hollywood Ice Revue at the Olympia meant that the first two games of the final would be played in Montreal. The Wings were ready to settle old scores from the year before.

The first game, on April 10, pitted a tired Canadiens squad against the rusty Detroit gang. Sawchuk made at least five outstanding first-period saves to keep the game scoreless. Leswick opened the scoring three minutes into the second, assisted by Pavelich. Howe's playoff scoring drought continued when he failed to put the puck in a net left vacant by an out-of-position Gerry McNeil.

After Leswick scored his second goal of the night at 7:57 of the third period, Montreal's Tom Johnson finally put the Habs on the scoreboard three minutes later. When the Forum's public address announcer declared that one minute was left in the game, Irvin pulled McNeil for an extra attacker, only to have Lindsay score into the empty net. When it subsequently came over the loudspeaker that the timekeeper had made a mistake and that there still remained another full minute to play, Irvin was incensed. He claimed the timekeeper had forced him to pull his goaltender early. The game ended 3–1 Detroit, after which the Forum announcer admitted, "I don't know what I would have done if a Montreal goal had been scored in the last minute!"

In Game 2, the Wings regained their form, while the effects on the Canadiens of nine games in 19 nights were evident. Montreal's last gasp came as Elmer Lach tied the score 1–1 with just under two minutes remaining in the opening period. They would not score again in the playoffs. After Lindsay put the puck behind McNeil at the start of the second, Sawchuk was golden. While Howe couldn't seem to score, he did knock Habs defenceman Dollard St. Laurent out of the series by standing his ground against the charging Montrealer and inflicting a lacerated eyeball.

Red Kelly had dressed for both Montreal games but didn't see action until the Wings were two men short. "I had to wear a cast," he recalled. "They put a cushion on my hand and wrapped and taped it, but I couldn't put any pressure on my hand. I couldn't really do much, only handle the stick with my good hand, but I'm on the bench.

"We get two penalties and have two men in the penalty box. Ivan taps me on the shoulder to go out on the ice. Holy moley! So don't I go out there, and the puck comes to me, but I can't shoot because I can't put pressure on my hand, so I used my good hand and my knee and I flipped the puck into the Montreal zone, and we somehow killed that penalty off. They didn't score on us. I came off the ice and didn't play any more after that. Back in Detroit I didn't even dress."

A tumultuous roar greeted the Wings as they skated onto the Olympia ice — for the first time in 15 days — for Game 3. The seating rose in two steep tiers giving spectators a feeling of being over the ice. Though its seating capacity was officially 14,200, it would swell during the two upcoming games to well over 15,000. For a price, it was said, the fire marshal conveniently turned his head the other way.

"The Olympia was a great place to play hockey," remembered Lindsay. "The people in the first four rows of the balcony were the best hockey fans in the world. The fans at the Olympia always gave us such a boost. They were so loud, and they were right on top of you."

Howe broke out of his slump by beating McNeil on a screen shot four and a half minutes into the game. Then, at the nine-minute mark of the second period, Lindsay lofted a 70-foot blooper towards the Montreal net. The puck took a bounce and McNeil couldn't catch it. Howe got his second goal of the playoffs in the third. Sawchuk recorded 26 saves, and the game ended 3–0.

Cup fever was at a peak as the Red Wings, sans Kelly, came onto the ice for Game 4. Every indication was that the Wings were ready to wrap it up. With fatigue setting in on the Habs, they concentrated on shutting down the Howe line.

Montreal had the better scoring opportunities early on, but Sawchuk was up to the task. A save on Floyd Curry from five feet out seemed to indicate that he was unbeatable. At the 6:50 mark of the first period, Prystai took a pass from Delvecchio and put the puck in for a 1–0 Wings lead.

When Skov scored from Prystai at the end of the second, it was clear that the uncanny assignment Ivan had given them before the game was paying off. "Tommy came up to us — me, Prystai and Delvecchio — and said he wanted us to win the game for the team, and we were the checking line!" recalled Wilson.

It was also during the second period that a sign from above — more precisely, the upper balcony — might have sealed the fate of Richard and company. An octopus was thrown onto the ice, its eight tentacles representing the eight total playoff wins needed to win the Cup. Octopi have hit the ice during Detroit playoff games ever since.

"I remember when the arena staff came out onto the ice that first time to pick up the squid, they didn't quite know what it was," recalled Red. "Then it moved and really startled them and they jumped. That was funny!"

In the third period, Prystai scored unassisted. The crowd cheered wildly, anticipating the sweep. Sawchuk made back-to-back stops on Dickie Moore that had the rookie banging his stick on the ice in frustration. At the buzzer, pandemonium erupted. Irvin could not stomach the loss and hurried to the dressing room without offering any on-ice congratulations. Detroit was the first team to win the Stanley Cup in eight straight games.

Red, who hated watching from the sidelines, happily took to the ice with his celebratory teammates as Abel was presented with the Cup.

As he prepared to go back home for another summer, news out of the NHL office lifted Red's spirits even more: "Red Wings Put Three 100 Percenters on NHL All-Stars: Kelly Is Unanimous Choice for Second Straight Year. Regarded as the best all-around player in the NHL today, he has been the top scoring defenceman in the National Hockey League for the past three seasons," read the news.

The accolades, and the $2,000 to come with the honour, eased the pain in his left wrist. The cast meant he could not be as helpful around the farm that summer.

But that also meant he had time to go and see someone he had just met, a girl who lived far away in Colorado.

• • • • • •

CHAPTER FIVE

SEASON *of* THEIR DISCONTENT

In May 1952, love was in the air for Red Kelly.

"Back before the playoffs began, it had been arranged by Ray Gaynor, the stage manager for the Hollywood Ice Review, for Gordie (Howe) to meet Barbara Ann Scott, the Olympic figure skating champion, who was in Detroit with the skating show at the Olympia," Red recalled. "A planted story in the newspaper had stated that Gordie and Barbara Ann were engaged, when in actuality they had never met. Gordie was to go to Carl's Chop House, a steak place, to meet her. Gordie was rooming with me at Ma Shaw's, and he didn't want to go alone. He asked me to go with him, and I said no at first, but he then bugged me enough that I finally relented and went along.

"It turned out that Barbara Ann was not there, but the manager asked us if we wanted to meet another star of the show, Andra McLaughlin, who was there with her mother and her little brother. We said okay, and we went around the corner to where they were at a table. I was sort of a passenger, because Andra was interested in finding out about Gordie. I merely watched and listened."

Andra McLaughlin was a 17-year-old athletic blonde from Manhattan and a former member of the world champion U.S. figure skating team of 1948–51. She was described in the January 1952 issue of the *Bee's Magazine* as "the greatest entertainer skating has yet produced, with a personality that floods up to the highest seats in the house." Her solo dances in the Revue were "The Hula" and "The Charleston."

"I was supposed to give a report back to Barbara Ann about Gordie," recalled Andra. "After they left our table, I talked about what I would tell her about Gordie, but my mother said to me, 'Yes, he's nice, but I kind of liked that shy red-headed fellow who was with him.' The next day, Red called our hotel to see if my younger brother wanted to go see the Red Wings hockey practice in Ann Arbor, because our ice show had displaced them from the Olympia. My brother said yes.

"My mother then told me, 'Take your brother down to the lobby when Red comes to pick him up, and take a good look at him.' I sure did, and there must have been a connection because, a few days later, Red called to see if I would like to go to a party. He had also invited my mother along — I guess he figured we needed a chaperone, as I was only 17 at the time. My mother didn't want to go to this party, so Red brought Ma Shaw along.

"It was after an ice show, and I still had some of my makeup on, so I looked older, I guess, because someone asked me if I wanted a drink, and before I could answer, Red said, 'She'll have a soft drink or milk.' He was such a gentleman. I was greatly impressed. He almost treated me like a little sister. We saw each other a few times, went for ice cream and went dancing, he came to see my show and then my show left town and he was involved with the hockey playoffs. So that was that, I thought."

But Red Kelly was a determined redhead.

"He called later that spring and came out to see me in Colorado, where we lived. He drove all that way. He was wearing a cast on his

left arm. My friends thought he was just a fine young man, so polite and respectful. He made quite an impression. Then his mother invited me to come to their farm in Simcoe. I said sure. I looked it up on a map and mistakenly saw Simcoe County, which was much farther north in Ontario.

"I flew down, and Red picked me up at the airport, and we drove through the evening and arrived at the farm in the middle

THE RED KELLY STORY

of the night. His mother had waited up for us, and she showed me to my room, and she was so delightful. I remember hearing a wolf howling through the night, and I was frightened because I thought I was so far north. The next morning, Red's father explained that I wasn't that far north and that the howling was just a dog across the street. We had a good laugh about that."

Her future in-laws made as much of an impression as Red did.

"I didn't know what to expect, but they were wonderful, just so dignified, polite and respectful of family, each other and their faith. They said grace before meals and meant it, and I met all his family, his sisters, and I just fell in love with them. I was so impressed with the farm and everything about them, including Red. His parents took me on a tour of the area, the town of Simcoe, and they treated me like gold. The whole time Red was such a gentleman! I almost didn't want to leave, but then I left to perform in summer theatre and then more skating and touring and that was that."

It was not, though their romance could not be hurried.

"Andra was certainly on my mind, in my thoughts, when she left," recalled Red. "I was quite taken. I saw her skate in the ice show, and she was really something. She was a natural, and she loved what she did. She could touch people, no matter where they were sitting in the audience, even up in the rafters. I loved watching her. Our lives were busy, and we went our separate ways, but I thought of her a lot after she left."

The 1952–53 Red Wings had a title to defend, and Jack Adams boasted about his champions that summer: "For balance, for depth, for anything you want to call it, this is the best Red Wing team I've ever had in my 25 years in the NHL. I'll let the figures speak for themselves."

His words seemed to imply that he was contemplating breaking his cardinal rule and might leave his lineup intact. He did not. In August of 1952, Adams traded Leo Reise, a two-time All-Star, to the Rangers for forward Reg Sinclair, some cash and an amateur defenceman.

Terry Sawchuk's weight was of concern at camp again, but this time for the opposite reason. His teammates were taken aback by his gaunt appearance. "The year he came into camp skinny as a rake, we thought that he was sick or something," recalled Johnny Wilson.

On October 5, the Olympia hosted the sixth annual All-Star Game. In his fourth straight appearance, Red played on the First Team against the Second Team. The score was an uneventful, tight-checking 1–1.

The Red Wings got off to an uncharacteristically slow start. Adams shook things up when he removed the *C* and *A* from his captain and alternates. He felt the league referees were ignoring their questions, so he tried to make a point. League president Clarence Campbell was not amused, and the letters were returned.

On October 25, the Wings — one of the first teams to fly regularly — flew into Montreal through a bad snowstorm. The experience was traumatic, as the pilot had to make five attempts through the blinding snow before he was finally able to land the plane. Most of the players were white-knuckled and on edge as they disembarked.

"The guys were pretty shook up," Red recalled. "It didn't bother me much. *If we go down, then we go down,* I thought. *What are you going to do?* But the guys were really sweating bullets, were really upset. Then we got onto the bus, and doesn't it go into a ditch. We were stuck there for quite a while after the landing debacle. We were not in a great mental state by the time we got to the Forum. We weren't ready to play hockey."

The Canadiens took full advantage to hand the Red Wings a 9–0 shellacking. The Wings were never in it. Marcel Pronovost recalled that night, as his mother was attending her first NHL game: "The Canadiens wouldn't let us have the puck! The game wasn't 10 minutes old and it was 4–0; after that, it was downhill all the way. It was one of those nights when everything went wrong, just everything. At the 10-minute mark, my mother asked the usher to give her a chair so she could sit in the hallway — not because she was embarrassed, but because she knew that when Montreal got so far ahead, the game was going to get out of hand with fights. She didn't want to see any fights."

It was a slow start for Detroit, winning only 4 of their first 13 games. Adams was looking for scapegoats, and told writer Lewis Walter that there was lots of blame to go around.

"The team hasn't been playing as a unit," Adams said. "Some games we've played good defensively, but our offence didn't click; other games it was the reverse. This team's age averages 25 years. These players just can't go from stardom to hockey's skid row in a season. Kelly looked drawn and peaked but says he isn't tired . . . Woit seems to be pressing a little now . . . Goldham, our oldest player, will take a little longer to hit form . . . Reg Sinclair, acquired in the Reise trade, hasn't popped in one in 12 games . . . Skov, Leswick, Pavelich and Prystai aren't scoring."

"Adams had some reporters in his pocket," recalled Red. "Sometimes I'd read about the games, but I remember one night we're in Montreal the night before our game, and we had a chance to see the Canadiens play Chicago. I sat up in the press gallery and listened to what was going on, how these reporters were seeing the game. It drove me crazy. I was eager to watch all the players, how they moved every which way, but these reporters missed half the plays. They'd be talking and laughing and would miss most of what actually happened on the ice. Then they'd ask each other and me what had happened, and these were supposedly the top sports writers. I was shocked by their poor observation habits."

By early December the Wings finally got their act together and began inching up in the league standings, and a couple of back-to-back wins over the Maple Leafs launched them into second place, just ahead of Montreal and behind the surprising league-leading Black Hawks.

On December 4, James E. "Pops" Norris, owner of both Detroit and Chicago, was jolted by a stabbing pain in his chest as he worked at his desk at the Norris Grain Company in Chicago. Before an elevator carrying Norris to a waiting ambulance could reach the ground, he was dead. His 25-year-old daughter, Marguerite Ann Norris, took over the Wings, and her brother James D. Norris took over the Hawks.

Marguerite was no slouch. It was noted that she had a business background, having managed the farm segment of the Norris empire, to go with her love of hockey. She had been working at Dun and Bradstreet, a financial and credit-information giant in New York. As the first female hockey club president, Marguerite was introduced to the media and NHL brass in Detroit a few days after the printed news release. Hockey writers found themselves jockeying with fashion writers and photographers to get a good shot and quote from the new darling of the hockey world. Hockey had never seen the like.

"The Norris chassis was done up in a black crepe sheath dress that made a nice foil for Margy's plump, rosy-tanned cheeks and blond hair," wrote a fashion writer present.

Her Wings went on a roll, heading into the Christmas season on a 12-game undefeated streak. Incurring a small bone fracture during a Christmas Eve practice, Sawchuk relinquished his net to young

Glenn Hall from the Edmonton farm club, who more than ably filled in for a few games.

On February 18, Neil MacCarl of the *Toronto Star* wrote how Kelly had a chance to set a new mark for defencemen, as he had amassed 16 goals in 55 games, getting him close to Flash Hollett's 20-goal mark from 1944–45.

Praise for Red's chances came from his old St. Mike's coach, now at the helm of the Maple Leafs. "He's got a good chance," predicted Joe Primeau. "But it's always toughest to get the final one or two to break a record. He played left wing as a junior and he has always been a good goal scorer. I think that experience as a forward helps him. He's a good skater and can carry the puck well and when he gets a break he can go all the way."

A March article by sports writer Bill Furlong brought more plaudits for Red's skill and demeanour. "He's as good a defenceman as there is in the league," coach Tommy Ivan told Furlong. "He's terrific on the power play, he can kill penalties with the best of them and he's got a good, hard shot. But his main asset is that he can come out with the puck from a defensive zone as good as or better than any forward in the league. Kelly is in his sixth year with the team now, and I've never heard him curse. Kelly can put as much feeling into 'shucks' or 'ding dong' as any man on the team can put into a curse."

"Len Kelly is the type of player all managers dream about," added Conn Smythe. "He's a star on the Wings' forward line and a greater star on defence; he's a player equally valuable as a killer of penalties and on the power play. He gives a coach a one-man bench . . . An exemplary player both on and off the ice, Kelly is the most valuable player in the National Hockey League today."

The article explained that Kelly has "an advantage over most defencemen because he has split vision, a phenomenon which allows him not only to see the puck and the puck carrier but also other details of action around him, in greater detail and wider focus than the normal player." A sixth hockey sense? All the great players had it.

And the accolades kept coming. A wire story out of New York quoted both Rangers coach Bill Cook and general manager Frank Boucher saying that hockey's greatest player was not Howe, almost certainly everybody's choice, but Kelly.

"I'd say Howe was the greatest player in the game today," said Cook. "But over this season, I feel Kelly has been the Wings' most valuable man. He's always out there . . . power play, short-handed . . . regular defence . . . up to centre. I've never seen anyone to equal him when it comes to bringing the puck out of his own end."

"I agree with you that Kelly should get the Hart, but I don't agree with you that Howe is the best player in hockey," countered Boucher to Cook:

> I'm definitely a Kelly man! Detroit stayed on top and I say it's because of Kelly. He is the key to the defence, the standout player in the NHL. Not only should he get the Hart, but he rates right up there for the Lady Byng. It wouldn't surprise me if Kelly wasn't a unanimous selection as an all-star defenceman for the third straight year. You've got to go all the way back to Eddie Shore to find one in his class. Shore was more spectacular than Kelly because of the way he skated. He was a weaver — something like a broken field runner in football — and he was a showman. But I doubt if he was any more effective.
>
> Remember, this is the fifth year in a row that the Red Wings figure to take the pennant and in that space of time they traded away two outstanding defencemen in Bill Quackenbush and Leo Reise. Yet as long as they've got Kelly, they don't seem to be weakening their defence. The redhead attacks like a great forward and defends like an even greater defenceman. There's nobody like him for taking the pressure off his own team and in a few seconds applying it to the other guys.

By the final weekend of the campaign, the Wings had locked up first place, Sawchuk had easily captured the Vezina, and Howe, who had set a new single-season point record, was gunning to tie or surpass the 50-goal record held by Rocket Richard.

In the 69th regular season game, the focus was on Howe: he played extra shifts, but the Black Hawks shut him down. On March 22, in an ending worthy of a Hollywood screenplay, Richard and his Canadiens came into the Olympia for the season's final game. Again Howe double-shifted all night, but little Gerry McNeil stopped all five Howe shots, and Bert Olmstead delivered on coach Irvin's directive to "go where Howe goes." When the game ended, Irvin rubbed it in by raising the Rocket's arm, the way a boxing referee would signal the winning fighter. Sitting in his dressing room, the Rocket commented after the game: "Safe for another 70 games. I'd have hated to shake his hand in Detroit. I wouldn't mind in Montreal — but not here."

Kelly also fell short of the mark. "Kelly Hero of 1–1 Tilt: Declines goal tying record," read the headline by Lewis Walter. "The real hero of the night was Leonard 'Red' Kelly, who gave away the goal which would have tied Flash Hollett's NHL record for defenceman."

"I remember taking that long screen shot and it went in, but I was pretty sure Meatball had touched it," recalled Red. "They announced it to me, but I went to Metro and said, 'Meatball, you touched that puck didn't you.' It was more of a statement than a question. He put his head down and said, 'Well, I might have . . .' He had touched the puck but didn't want to own up to it. I went to the referee and then the timekeeper, and Meatball got the goal. Twenty goals would've been a magic mark, but I didn't want a goal that I hadn't scored."

As the Wings prepared to meet Boston in the playoff semifinal, all observers expected a mismatch. The Wings had 10 wins in 14 meetings against the Bruins — most of them lopsided. But under the radar was the fact that the Red Wings had limped into the play-offs with only one win in their last six games.

The first game in Detroit *was* a mismatch, as Detroit shelled the Bruins 7–0. The Wings attacked aggressively in Game 2, but Bruins goalie Sugar Jim Henry was heroic, stopping 45 of 48 shots in the 5–3 victory. Sawchuk, on the other hand, seemed unnerved and tired after Fleming Mackell beat him about eight minutes into the first period. In Game 3, Bruins winger Ed Sandford scored first. The Wings fought back on a second-period goal by Leswick, then Sawchuk and Henry closed the gates the rest of the way, forcing overtime.

"In the overtime, we went at them, threw everything but the kitchen sink at Sugar Jim. You never saw a skate mark outside of the Boston blue line," recalled Red. "Then Jack McIntyre broke out into the right corner. He shot from the corner, and the puck just went by Ukey. He just stood there. They win 2–1. Ukey had a tough series. What are you going to do?"

"We all felt bad for Terry," Johnny Wilson recalled. "He was in a rut like we all were. We tried to help him to forget. We said, 'Come on, Uke, we'll get 'em next game,' but we all felt terrible."

"Sure, Terry should have stopped McIntyre's goal," recalled Lindsay. "But we shouldn't have even been in overtime, and even then we should have scored way before Jack had that shot on Terry. But it was typical of the way that series was going."

As if the Wings weren't having enough trouble with the upstart Bruins, rumours began circulating for the sale of the Detroit franchise and the trading of star players Howe, Lindsay and Kelly to Chicago. The Norris family's financial interest in the Detroit, Chicago and New York hockey teams had for years been a befuddling and murky issue for the NHL. Now here was Jim Norris Jr. making news, at the expense of his sister, trumpeting his 50 per cent control of Chicago and 25 per cent ownership of Detroit. It was all part of an ugly, public family tug-of-war as their father's estate was settled.

"I didn't know Jim was sniffing the stuff these days," snarled Jack Adams, who was working with estate administrators back in Detroit. "At that rate they might as well buy the whole club and close up Olympia." He alleged that Boston writers were writing "maliciously" to hurt the morale of the Wings.

In the fourth game at the Boston Garden, Sawchuk was clearly fighting the puck. Soft goals were getting by him, and he seemed unable to cope. Sawchuk's strength had always been coming up with the big save when the Wings needed it most, and that appeared gone. Henry turned in another virtuoso performance, and, although outshot, coach Lynn Patrick's Bruins emerged with a 6–2 win.

Prior to Game 5 in Detroit, it was clear to all concerned that Sawchuk was not himself. "Only Lefty [Wilson] and Jack knew it, but Terry was not well for a couple of those games against Boston," broadcaster Budd Lynch revealed. "He wasn't feeling good and he was hurt, but nobody knew except the three of them. And all three thought that Uke would bounce out of it anytime and have a good game."

Back at Olympia for Game 5, the Wings staved off elimination with a 6–4 win. Howe even got a goal on a breakaway to reassert himself a bit. Still, Boston mounted a charge late in the game and was the more confident team as the series headed back east.

Game 6 in a sold-out Boston Garden opened with a pair of Bruins goals in the first period. Sinclair pulled the Wings back to within one midway through the hockey game before Mackell broke down the left wing and let go a rising 50-foot floater.

"You could have almost read the label on the puck, that's how slow it was going," Lindsay recalled. "Sawchuk just watched the thing float by him into the outside corner of the net."

The Sawchuk muff fired up Lindsay, who banged a six-footer past Sugar Jim to make the score closer, but, four minutes later, Leo Labine again put the Bostonians up by two. Still fighting to avoid elimination, coach Ivan pulled Sawchuk with a minute and a half left in regulation time and the Wings went on the attack, throwing the puck around in a frenzied attempt to tie it, but time ran out.

"My biggest thrill in hockey was upsetting Detroit in the 1953 series," said Sandford, who netted six goals in the series. "We weren't supposed to have a chance. But we used the 'shadows,' Woody Dumart on Howe, and Joe Klukay on Lindsay, and we beat them in six games."

"I just missed it, that's all," a dejected Sawchuk said of Mackell's fluke goal. "I thought I had it but it dipped."

"Who's to blame? Not Terry!" said Ted Lindsay years later. "Who the heck looked for blame? None of us looked for blame on anyone. It wasn't his fault. I shoulda scored more goals than I did."

"It was just one of those series. Sugar Jim stood on his head. Sawchuk was fighting the puck but they wouldn't take him out of the net," recalled Red. "I know it wasn't the defence. We would keep the shots from far out on the blue line so they wouldn't reach the net. Gordie was in love, not sure of his relationship with Colleen. He was definitely not himself, and the old guys from Boston, Milt Schmidt, Dumart, the others; they checked Howe's line to a standstill."

"After that last game, we all went over to Jack Sharkey's bar across the street," Budd Lynch recalled. "We knew Jack Sharkey, and he put us at the back and gave us free beer, and I passed out cigars. We stayed there until one o'clock in the morning to unwind.

"Suddenly Fred Huber, the Wings publicist, shows up to tell us that Marguerite Norris is throwing us a champagne party back at the hotel. We sure hustled our buns over there. She had ordered these very beautiful trays of food, and there was tons of booze, and she thanked each player individually, which was a nice gesture in a very tough hour for them. It was a very late night!"

The next morning, the team walked the three blocks to the train station. In a moment of comic relief, the Wings put five-foot-five Leswick into the overcoat of Red Wings photographer Roy Bash, who stood six-foot-five. "All you could see was this overcoat going down the street," Lynch recalled. "God, we laughed. We had to laugh at something."

"It was a very long ride home on the train, a very, very long ride," Red remembered.

For the Bruins, Henry's magic disappeared in the finals against the Canadiens, who easily defeated Boston in five games to capture the Stanley Cup.

Red Wings players again dominated the 1952–53 NHL All-Star Teams, with Sawchuk, Kelly, Howe and Lindsay making the first team and Delvecchio the second. With only eight minutes in penalties through the season, Red was awarded his second Lady Byng Trophy for sportsmanship. He finished third in the voting for the Hart Trophy as well.

There were larger issues brewing in Motown. The Detroit ownership issue again reared its ugly head right after the Wings returned home, forcing a clearly riled Marguerite to make a strong public statement.

"I shall remain as President of Olympia and the Red Wings — probably for many years to come," she said from her seaside cottage in Connecticut, where she had gone after the Boston series. "There is no thought of selling Olympia and the Red Wings. We are not going to sell Gordie Howe, Ted Lindsay or Red Kelly as the rumours have it. I'd like to keep this team together until we prove how good we really are, after this last Cup disappointment. We'll be NHL and Stanley Cup champions again . . . all those rumour stories are just bunk."

If anybody wondered whether Howe's mind had truly been torn between hockey and love during the Boston series, it was confirmed 10 days later, on April 15, when he married Colleen Joffa. Red was an attendant, along with Pavelich and Lindsay. Marguerite Norris was there, as were Adams and Ivan.

As the Howe wedding party left the ceremony at Calvary Presbyterian Church and headed to Detroit's Statler Hotel for the reception, it was a happy time, a chance to forget the unpleasant memories of Sugar Jim, Dumart, floating pucks, the noisy Boston Gah-den and the impending issues over the Norris estate.

• • • • • •

CHAPTER SIX

THE GREATEST
ALL AROUND

When the 1953 Red Wings training camp opened in Sault Ste. Marie, Michigan, Jack Adams announced that the team's goaltending job was up for grabs. Detroit had Glenn Hall ready to take over for Terry Sawchuk. The challenge drove Sawchuk to a great camp, and Hall was sent back to the Edmonton farm team.

"Hall was a great goaltender and so was Sawchuk . . . you could see that from the beginning," recalled Red. "Hall had the butterfly and Sawchuk would stand in the crouch. Both could get up to their feet quickly from being down."

Hall was not the only Detroit prospect. "We had a flock of young juniors at training camp with us," coach Tommy Ivan said after the team had returned to Detroit. "And you should have heard them talking after watching Red Kelly control the puck with his feet enough times so that they knew it wasn't just luck."

Others on their way to the main roster that year, graduates of the team's strong development system, were Earl "Dutch" Reibel, Al Arbour, Keith Allen, Jimmy Hay and Bill Dineen.

On October 3, Red went to Montreal to participate in his sixth straight All-Star Game in just his seventh season. Participating was a badge of honour. It was also meant to bolster the pension fund.

"At that time, 25 cents from every ticket was supposed to go towards our pension fund, but I don't think it happened at all," recalled Red. "Eventually all of us players had to put in $900 a year to start up the pension. There was also a need to help the older guys, like Dumart, Schmidt, Bauer, who had been playing for a long time and who only had a few years left to play but had just started to contribute to their pensions. So the fund gave them some type of pension when they were done. It wasn't much, but it was a start. Eventually, the league paid for the whole thing and you didn't have to contribute or put money in. Nine hundred a year was a fair amount out of our paycheques back then — about 10 per cent, sometimes 15 per cent, of our salary."

Players took the All-Star affair seriously and gave it their best effort. During this year's game, after having been elbowed in the mouth on a few occasions by Montreal's Bert Olmstead, Red had had enough. At the 12:52 mark of the third period, he took matters into his own hands. "I liked my teeth and wanted to keep them," Red recalled. "We got into a fuss, pushing, shoving and swinging."

Both players received majors for fighting, the last recorded fight in an All-Star Game. The All-Stars defeated the Stanley Cup champion Canadiens 3–1 on two goals by the Rangers' Wally Hergesheimer and an empty-netter by Alex Delvecchio. Rocket Richard spoiled the All-Stars' shutout bid in the third period.

Amazingly, Adams hadn't shaken up his lineup with any trades in the off-season, and the Wings rewarded him by jumping out of the gate quickly, losing only 3 of their first 11 games. Red had a great start with five goals, and his five assists put him fourth in the NHL points parade, behind teammates Gordie Howe, Ted Lindsay and newcomer Reibel. "Ranking up among forwards in scoring isn't exactly new for Kelly," wrote Marshall Dann. "He has been the No. 1 scoring NHL defenceman, both in goals and points, the last four seasons. It should be no surprise that several rival coaches have called Kelly the best hockey player of his era — rating him more valuable than even Howe, Lindsay, Terry Sawchuk or Rocket Richard."

Through the season's second month, the Wings lost only once, and Red put together an incredible string of points when he tallied two goals and three assists in a 9–0 clobbering of the Black Hawks on November 28 and then had another goal and two more assists against the same team the next night, for eight points in two games. He was named the *Hockey News* player of the week.

By December 17, Red was still humming along with 10 goals and 16 assists for 26 points, still fifth among NHL point leaders. In an article by the Associated Press that same day, Boston coach Lynn Patrick was asked which player he'd take for his team if he could, Gordie Howe or Rocket Richard.

"Neither!" Patrick answered. "I'll take Red Kelly! Kelly is the best all-around performer in our league. Sure Howe and Richard are good, but Red is not only great on defence, he can score too! In my opinion, he's the big reason Detroit has won five straight championships. When Kelly rushes up the ice, it's something to see. He sparks Howe, Ted Lindsay and the others. When we play the Wings, we go out to stop him. We feel there's a better chance of winning that way."

"Lynn Patrick's or anybody else's quotes didn't affect me at all," Red recalled. "I was just happy to be playing in the NHL. There were a lot of great players in the NHL, and each game was a battle to the finish line. You could never quit till the final play. Your ego doesn't play for you on the ice. You have to give it everything you had, to play in the NHL, and you had to give everything you had to stay there."

At the halfway point in the season, Red garnered headlines for outpolling everybody in the first-half All-Star voting, with 89 of 90 points. There was talk of Red receiving a brand new award, the James Norris Memorial Trophy, to be awarded to the best defenceman. It was named after the deceased Red Wings owner.

When it was implied that the Leafs' Tim Horton was "the new Red Kelly," Adams jumped into the debate. "If Horton tries to clear that hurdle he may strain himself so he can't play next year for the Leafs," Adams said. "He may be the young Kelly in the same sense that a youngster with a new Christmas cowboy outfit is the Lone Ranger. But that is as far as it goes now. Our boy has the real silver bullets!"

Dink Carroll of the *Montreal Gazette* compared Red to Doug Harvey of the Canadiens. "We have heard it said that he was on the ice for many of the goals scored against his team, but he would have to be if only because he is out there so much. He plays about 45 minutes of every game, takes his regular turn on the ice, kills off penalties, and is on for the power play . . . there can be no quarrel with the choice of Doug Harvey for the other defence spot on the First (All-Star) Team. There are nights when Doug can do anything that Red Kelly can do, but he doesn't have them as frequently."

In an article for *Weekend Magazine*, Andy O'Brien called Kelly a coach's dream player. "Coaches think first in terms of defence and . . . he is the best in the world." In a personal letter to Red with a copy of the article, O'Brien told him, "You oughta be in Hollywood instead of working for a living."

As the month of February began, the Red Wings took part in a unique event that provided a nice break from the grind of the regular season. After the 1952–53 season had finished, the Wings had been involved in a promotional tour with the Stroh Brewery, and Adams and Lindsay found themselves in northern Michigan.

"We end up at Marquette Prison, full of lifers and the remnants of the Purple Gang, which was the Jewish mafia in the U.S.," recalled Lindsay. "One thing led to another, and the next thing you know there's talk of the Wings going up to Marquette to play a game against a team of prisoners."

A rink was constructed in the prison yard, and a team calling itself the Pirates was formed. They practised until they felt they had improved enough to take on the Wings, and then sent word to Adams that they were ready. At 12:40 p.m., on February 2, 1954, the Wings filed through prison's steel doors.

Lefty Wilson remembered it well. "It was so cold, Carl [trainer Mattson] and I cut up a bunch of old hockey socks and taped the tops to make tuques for everybody. But it was a great." The Wings won 8–2, but hijinks certainly outweighed serious play.

"It was colder than all get out, but there were prisoners all along the sidelines," recalled Red. "They had listened to our games and knew the Red Wings players. There were killers in there, it was a tough prison. There were members of the Duke Ellington band out of New York, former band members who had killed somebody, and they were lifers. They were tough guys. There were members of a gang from Detroit who had obliterated another gang, and the guy who did most of the shooting was a mild little guy behind the counter now, dishing out clothes there. When they told us that he had done all the shooting, holy moley! It was hard to believe. He looked like a minister, had these glasses on. You wouldn't think he would hurt a fly. He was convicted of killing them all.

"The hockey game was in the yard, and we had tuques on, it was fun. The engine of the plane froze and we couldn't leave the next day until noon. It was fascinating to be in there, in that surrounding, and to hear some of the stories, what happened within the prison."

Marcel Pronovost couldn't help but laugh when he remembered the trip years later. "One of the inmates along the boards wanted to give me two bucks to bodycheck one of the prison staff who was playing and often used to send him into solitary confinement."

"We had lunch with the inmates and the prison team afterwards," Wilson recalled. "It was great being with them. They presented us with this trophy, like a bucket." The inmates presented the Red Wings with a cup that had at one time been a refuse bucket, used in cells without sanitation facilities. It was labelled the Doniker Trophy, and the names of all the Red Wings, the inmates of the prison team and the date of the game were inscribed on it. Adams good-naturedly hoisted it to cheers from inmates and spectators alike after the game.

Back in the hockey world, the Wings clinched the NHL title with five games left in the season. Red was cruising along with 14 goals, and another 7 would put him in the record books for a defenceman.

Despite first place being wrapped up, Sawchuk and the Wings were in a battle for the coveted Vezina Trophy. It was an award that had as much to do with defence as goaltending. Harry Lumley and the Leafs were leading in the Vezina race with two games to go.

In Montreal on March 20, the Wings were pounded by the Canadiens 6–1, while the Leafs fared no better getting beaten 5–2 by the Rangers. As chance would have it, the Leafs and Wings, Lumley

Jack Adams hoists the "Doniker Trophy," given to the winning team at the conclusion of the Marquette Prison game between inmates and Red Wings, on February 2, 1954. The trophy was fashioned using a prisoner's urine bucket.

and Sawchuk, would face each other in the season's final game, a Sunday-night tilt at the Olympia.

"We're down to one game to get Terry the Vezina," Red recalled. "We needed six goals for him to tie Lumley and the Leafs, and seven to win. Right from the puck drop we pressed! We were determined."

Lumley realized he was in for quite a night when Howe ripped a shot that deflected off a skate past the startled Leafs goalie. Bill Dineen made it 2–0 Wings just four minutes later. Wilson knocked in a Dineen pass with his chest, but referee Red Storey called the goal back, maintaining that Wilson had directed it in with his arm.

In the second, Leswick banged a wobbly rebound into the Leafs cage to cut Lumley's Vezina lead to only three goals with almost two full periods to go. At the opposite end, Sawchuk was quite inactive. The Leafs converted very few rushes into scoring chances, and Uke could only watch.

"We were really pressing, trying like hang," Red continued. "Then the Leafs' Jim Thompson skated from behind his blue line and lobbed the puck into our end before heading to the bench. It was a real floater that bounced towards Sawchuk. The Olympia had a high roof, so you could lob pucks pretty high. Ukey was unsure about the timing and the bounce, so he stayed back in his net to play it. After the puck bounced, he swiped at it with his glove and missed it, and the puck was in the net. Thompson pretty well watched the thing from the bench." It was only Thompson's second goal in almost four seasons.

It set the stage for the third period, which began with Lumley up by four goals. The Wings came out determined, and just two minutes in, Wilson scored, then Lindsay potted two in a row with seven minutes to go. The Wings swarmed around Lumley's net. "We poured it on," Red said. "We were in their end the whole time, pushing, pushing. Throwing everything we had at 'em! Tommy Ivan even pulled Sawchuk for the last minute — and we were up 6–1. That's how much we wanted that Vezina for Ukey."

Sawchuk's teammates threw the puck around in a desperate frenzy as the seconds wound down — three, two, one. The buzzer sounded and the Olympia seemed to let out an anguished groan. The Leafs swarmed a happy Lumley, who had allowed 11 goals in two games but came out a winner.

"What a way to lose $1,000!" Sawchuk lamented to the press afterwards.

"We tried hard for Terry," recalled Red. "We all really gave it everything we had, just everything. In the end, he ended up losing it on that fluky Thompson bounce that he missed. He always had trouble with those."

Kelly had had another great year, putting up his best totals in three years with 16 goals and 33 assists, good enough for sixth place among league point-getters. True to form, he got only 18 minutes in penalties.

The Leafs and Red Wings were paired off in the semifinal. Smythe's charges felt secure in the knowledge that they were no slouches, as they had finished only 10 points behind the Wings and 3 behind the Canadiens. But Detroit had scored 39 more goals for the season.

"They have too many guns for us," Smythe conceded after his Maple Leafs were shut out 5–0 at the Olympia in the opening game. But Toronto bounced back and took the second game 3–1.

Game 3 was only 10 minutes old when Red grabbed the puck near centre ice at Maple Leaf Gardens, flew past Ted Kennedy and an anchored Leo Boivin and broke in alone on Lumley. He cut across the net to his right, made a fake that forced the goalie to fall on his knees and backhanded the puck past the outstretched left leg of Lumley into the net; 1–0 Detroit. "Lum tried to be cute and make me shoot, but I crossed him up, cutting over and using my backhand," Kelly told the press. The Wings took the game 3–1. An unusually cheery Smythe assessed the result: "They're the best team in the world and we're a trifle green." A pencil sketch of Red appeared in the *Toronto Star* with the caption, "Red Kelly: Detroit's All-Star Everything!"

At the Royal York hotel prior to Game 4, six-foot-five, blond-haired Bruce Norris, Marguerite and James Jr.'s brother, turned heads and had people wondering about his identity. When he walked over to Jack Adams, who took him over to the desk to sign in, someone asked head scout Johnny Mitchell, "Is that a young rookie you've brought up to use tonight?" His appearance on the Red Wings scene would have repercussions for years to come, especially for his sister.

Game 4 was tied at one apiece with less than four minutes remaining in regulation time. The Red Wings were pressing when Wilson passed the puck back to Red, who was breaking in. He took a quick stride and fired a hard, low shot that appeared to be going wide of the net.

"Toronto defenceman Tim Horton wasn't even in line with the goal," recalled Red. "I let the shot go real quick, and it hit Tim right

Detroit Times Photo

Four veteran stars of the Red Wings looking ahead to another National Hockey League season are (from left) Capt. Ted Lindsay, Gordie Howe, Red Kelley and Marty Pavelich, all of whom have served on the six teams that brought the NHL trophy to Detroit. It's a man-sized job.

on the toe and deflected to his right, a flop shot, into the net! We would laugh about it later, but he wasn't laughing at the time; I was. I hadn't given him much warning."

"It was estimated later that it would have missed the net by seven to 10 feet," wrote Lewis Walter. "It should have hit me in the head," lamented Horton. "Sure it was lucky," added Tommy Ivan. "Luck is usually with you when you win. We were in the Toronto end . . . firing at the net . . . pressing for the kill. We made our own luck."

Kelly's goal was the game-winner, and the Detroiters led three games to one heading back to the Motor City. There, they finished off the Leafs with a 4–3 win in double overtime.

Their Stanley Cup opponents were Montreal, who had swept the Bruins in four straight. Despite being hampered by injuries all season, the defending champs had stayed close to the Wings in the standings. Besides Rocket Richard, the Canadiens offence also included Bernie "Boom Boom" Geoffrion and Bert Olmstead, placing second, fourth and fifth in the league scoring race. Also on the team were the fiery Dickie Moore and a pair of rookies who would one day need no introduction, centre Jean Béliveau and goalie Jacques Plante.

"You could see the Canadiens getting stronger with each year," Wilson recalled, "We knew we'd have our hands full. But hey, we weren't chopped liver. That '54 regular season title was our sixth in a row." The Wings felt the Stanley Cup was theirs to lose, not Montreal's to win.

Plante was in the Montreal net for Game 1. Though he'd played just 17 games during the regular season, the rookie had done so well down the stretch that he had wrestled the playoff assignment from veteran Gerry McNeil.

The Detroit defensive game was at its finest in Game 1 as the Canadiens didn't get a shot on Sawchuk until the nine-minute mark. Lindsay deflected a Reibel shot past a helpless Plante for first blood. In the second, with Skov in the penalty box, Geoffrion took a pass in the crease from Doug Harvey and stuffed the backhander past Sawchuk on his stick side. Reibel regained the lead for Detroit in the third period, sailing a long shot from the right point that went over everyone's head, over a screened Plante's shoulder and into the Montreal cage.

With Pronovost in the penalty box in the third stanza, Red was on the ice for his usual penalty kill. He and Pavelich worked a classic give-and-go play, and Red backhanded the puck past a falling Jacques Plante for the insurance goal. The Detroit defence was dominant, limiting the Canadiens attack to just 18 shots during the 3–1 Detroit win.

In Game 2, a first-period shoving match between Béliveau and Skov threatened to turn into a free-for-all and had referee Red Storey struggling to maintain order. Later in the period, Howe was penalized, and 17 seconds later, Leswick joined him in the box. Detroit would play the next 1:43 two men short against the powerful Montreal power play. Moore scored on a pass from Geoffrion; Sawchuk argued vehemently that he was interfered with, but to no avail. Twenty-one seconds later, the Rocket ended his 1954 playoff scoring drought with a blast past Sawchuk's stick side; he struck again 31 seconds later with a backhand. A second-period screen shot by Delvecchio brought the score to 3–1, where it remained for the rest of the game.

Game 3 switched the series back to Montreal. The Wings took a 1–0 lead when Delvecchio took a Sawchuk rebound up the length of the ice and put the puck by Plante after a give-and-go play with Howe. With three minutes to go in the first, Red pushed the play into the Montreal end and passed the puck to Lindsay who, while falling, slapped the puck high over Plante's glove for a 2–0 lead. Plante was clearly struggling. Wilson fired a 50-foot wrist shot between Plante's legs, and Prystai later scored on a wraparound that left the future Hall of Famer flat-footed. The Wings won 5–2.

Game 4 was a physical, defensive affair in which nerves still seemed to get the better of Plante. In the second period, with Richard in the penalty box, Wilson launched a long backhand from the top of the crease that Plante missed through his legs. The game-changer came when Howe was given a major penalty for drawing blood against Harvey. Red was out for the full five minutes, and the powerful Montreal power play managed only three shots.

"We had a great, strong defence in Detroit, and our pairs were so well suited for each other," recalled Red. "Marcel Pronovost was a powerful skater, hitter and had a great shot, while his partner, Bob Goldham, was not a fast skater, rangy, but a great shot blocker — a real stay-home defenceman. His and Marcel's style complemented each other perfectly. Benny Woit was the same stay-at-home partner to cover for me."

The Canadiens lifted Plante for an extra attacker, but, with seven seconds remaining, Red slid the puck down the ice into the empty net to secure a 2–0 win. The Wings were one win away from capturing the Stanley Cup.

Canadiens coach Dick Irvin switched back to McNeil in goal to start Game 5, and he was up to the task, staying even with Sawchuk for three scoreless periods.

"Despite the hard close-checking, the game was one of the most spectacular of the playoffs," observed the *Toronto Star*. "It was a gruelling affair in the summer-like heat of Olympia Stadium before 14,583 howling fans but it was brilliantly executed from start to finish."

At 5:45 of overtime, Montreal centre Kenny Mosdell skated the length of the ice, spun himself around in front of Goldham, and fired a backhand that left Sawchuk guessing — wrongly. The series was now three games to two, for Detroit.

In Game 6, Montreal used its depth, sending out four forward lines to Detroit's three, and it paid dividends as the Canadiens won 4–1 at the Forum.

The Olympia was rocking on April 16, with 15,791 fans shoehorned into the arena, the largest crowd ever to see a hockey game. From the puck drop, the Wings poured on the offence, outshooting the Habs 12–5 in the first period, with McNeil making a number of great saves. But it was Montreal that struck first when a Floyd Curry screen shot found its way behind Sawchuk.

At 1:17 of the second, Red got the equalizer in the dying seconds of a Wings power play with a quick, low shot that made its way through a maze of players. "The Wings had a one-man advantage," wrote Harry Staples, implying that Red was the difference, power play or no. It was such a tight-checking game that at one point a frustrated Rocket Richard illegally swatted the puck into the Detroit net with his glove. The third period was scoreless.

For only the second time in league history, the seventh game of a Stanley Cup Final would be decided in overtime. The last time this had happened — in 1950 — it had been a Red Wing, Pete Babando, who had produced the heroics.

The Canadiens got the first chance to end it, but Sawchuk made a great stop on Bert Olmstead. "We were checking heavily and had the Habs bottled in their end," recalled Red. "Pavelich, Skov, Leswick were really pressing them; they were the checking line, and we defencemen were pressing as well. Doug Harvey had the puck behind his net and he threw it around the boards. Leswick was about 10 feet inside the blue line by the boards and got the puck. Harvey realized he had given the puck away and rushed in front of his net. Leswick shot it, and Harvey went to catch it, and the puck hit the top of his glove and deflected over McNeil's shoulder and into the net."

McNeil stood frozen in disbelief as the Olympia crowd screamed and the Wings mobbed Leswick. As they had done after Detroit's 1952 win, the Canadiens, led by coach Dick Irvin, headed straight for the dressing room without congratulating the victors.

"The Habs quickly left the ice. Those were dynamite games and we had real, emotional battles, very emotional," recalled Red. "The crowd also really got on Dickie Moore, who was also very emotional. When you live or die by one goal, those were tough games and there wasn't much difference between winning or losing . . . a bounce of the puck one way or another. It could be hard to take."

Gaye Stewart went to the Red Wings dressing room to offer his congratulations to his former teammates. "I guess I should apologize for some of our fellows," he told the press. "They felt like I did and wanted to come out on the ice to shake hands all around, but we were restrained from higher up."

At centre ice, Tommy Ivan took off his fedora, wiped his brow and shook his head in disbelief. NHL president Clarence Campbell walked onto the ice to present the Cup to captain Lindsay, who stood with an arm around Jack Adams. Three youths carried a large banner around the ice that read "The New World Champions."

"Winning the Cup also meant extra money," Red remembered. "Sid Abel used to say, 'Boys, winning is the difference between drinking canned beer or bottled beer.' If you won, you got the bottles; lose, you got the cans. We topped our small salaries with awards and winnings, and a good year could almost double it."

The first woman executive to ever receive the Stanley Cup, Marguerite Norris was on the ice and alongside Adams and Ivan. "Marguerite was great as far as we were concerned," Red said. "She treated us very well. She'd buy us small gifts or trinkets during Easter or Christmas. There was never any doubt that she always appreciated our effort on the ice and never hesitated to tell us so, even when we lost. But I don't think Jack Adams liked having to answer to a woman, quite frankly. Chauvinistic? Well, I'm sure he thought women shouldn't be in an executive position in hockey, especially *his* hockey team. Marguerite was more than capable in our eyes. She was a great lady."

In April, Red was chosen by the *Hockey News* as the league's most valuable player, a great honour — but one without money, since it was not the official league award; in Hart Trophy voting, Red finished second behind Chicago goalie Al Rollins. In All-Star voting, Red garnered 177 of a possible 180 votes to place on the First All-Star Team, far outpolling anybody else at any position; he was joined by teammates Howe and Lindsay.

On April 29, it was announced that Red was the first winner of the James Norris Memorial Trophy as the league's best defenceman. He had received 76 out of a possible 90 points, while Bill Gadsby received 28 points and Doug Harvey 22. The next day, Kelly copped his third Lady Byng Trophy. His total awards and Stanley Cup earnings were pegged at $6,000.

"Winning those awards and getting the bonus money was great, but it didn't change anything," recalled Red. "I was still working on the farm in the summer, going up and down, priming that tobacco."

But there would be an exotic trip too — to Korea.

• • • • • •

CHAPTER SEVEN

A PATRIOTIC
SEASON

When the hockey season was finished, Red went home to Norfolk County and used his hockey connections to make the Port Dover Lions Club's Hockey Night something extra-special. The evening was dubbed a salute to the provincial semifinalists Intermediate C Sailors hockey club, of which Red's brother, Joe, was a member. High-profile attendees included teammate Metro Prystai and foes Lou Jankowski (Chicago), Ron Stewart (Toronto), Paul Meger (Montreal) and Leo Reise (New York). The locals never dreamed that their small community would host such an array of NHL talent. All the players answered questions and spoke of their starts in minor hockey.

Former Ontario Hockey Association president Jack Roxburgh heaped special praise on a hometown hero: "You have produced many fine hockey players including our own Red Kelly, not only has he put Port Dover on the map in a hockey way but shortly he leaves for Korea to represent Canada . . . no finer tribute can be paid to a fine hockey player, athlete and citizen of this community."

In the spring of 1954, Red had accepted an invitation from the Canadian Department of National Defence to be hockey's ambassador on a four-week trip to military installations in Japan and

Korea, where Canadian troops, under the umbrella of the United Nations, were acting as peacekeepers.

On the tour with Red were Canadian football star Ken Charlton of the Saskatchewan Roughriders and newsmen Hank Viney, Lloyd Saunders and Bob Hesketh. Viney kept an extensive diary of the trip, while Hesketh published periodic columns for readers back home.

Flying to Vancouver on May 10, Red met up with the entourage, and, after receiving medical shots and getting briefed, the group flew to Anchorage, Alaska. Landing in Tokyo on May 14, Red was immediately struck by the teeming mass of humanity on the crowded streets and the different type of cars he saw. It sure was a long way from the farm. He played tourist, getting a ride on a two-wheeled human-pulled taxi called a *jinrikisha* and renting a bicycle to explore street markets.

On the morning of May 15, he had a rude awakening. "It was around 7:30 in the morning when the bed started shaking, everything moving. I had never experienced an earthquake," he recalled. "It was quite exciting but unnerving. Everybody was talking about it, though the locals were used to them."

The next day they arrived in Seoul, South Korea, and were driven two hours south to Maple Leaf Park, home of the 25th Canadian Infantry Brigade. They met soldiers and showed films of the Stanley Cup playoffs — though the projector didn't always work. In these cases, Red improvised and answered questions. He was received like a conquering hero.

"Kelly is the real star of the show, the star attraction, the one everyone wants to meet," Viney wrote in his diary. "We've had a day on which we've met hundreds of troops and that's what we're here for."

For Red, the gathering at Maple Leaf Park had special meaning. "A few months before this, during the winter, there were troops, the Black Watch, stationed in Wallaceburg, Ontario. Four or five of us Red Wings got into a car, went over and played hockey with them. They'd gotten a real kick out of that, and so had we," recalled Red.

"So now we're in Korea and these very same soldiers were stationed there. They sure remembered that pickup game, and so they really looked after us. They threw us a big dinner party and had music outside the tent. Then they put us on mock trial and charged us with a heinous crime! We were convicted and had to drink this concoction that would knock the socks off your feet. It was powerful! But it was part of the ceremonies, the trial."

On a typical day, they ate lunch with an army unit, had supper with another, did a radio show and then went on to another gathering to show Stanley Cup movies and answer questions.

On May 26, Canadian brigadier general Jean Victor Allard, with his dog in the front seat, drove them to Castle Rock, the point where Genghis Khan's conquests ended, located at the border between North and South Korea. Red put his foot over the dividing line and stuck out his tongue.

"I was amazed when we went to the dividing line, with barbed wire and the lookout towers, and we stared across at the North Korean troops on the other side, who were all dressed in white uniforms," recalled Red. "What I really found interesting was to look at the terrain; the hills in this area were huge. If you ever had to fight your way up the first hill, they would be shooting down from the top, and then if you happened to take that hill, boom, you were faced with another hill, and another one after that. And what would one really gain? The climate, the hills, the terrain were really something.

"The roads were dusty, and you'd see the Koreans working in their fields, their rice paddies. Oxen pulled two-wheeled carts; you could smell them a couple of blocks away. There was a bag around by the tail to catch the droppings, and they'd run around and also catch the urine, no question they used that stuff up in the fields. They worked right up to their thighs in these rice paddies. After seeing that, I thought I would never eat rice again."

Brigadier General Allard was an impressive figure and had spent a decade in Russia. "I had dinner with him, and he described life

Korea 1954

in Russia, what their hockey program was like and how they were getting ready to challenge the North Americans one day," recalled Red. "The general had offered to bring an army team into Russia to play them, but they said they weren't ready — but maybe in a year or so. He said he was going to fortify his team with Sergeant Richard, Corporal Howe, Private Kelly. We laughed about that."

At a gathering of 500 soldiers that night, Red did colour commentary over the hockey movies, and drew howls of laughter when he kept referring to himself as "that No. 4 there."

Back at Maple Leaf Park, Red met and befriended a young orphan named Johnny, a boy rescued from the streets of Seoul by the Canadian soldiers. They had brought him back to camp, cleaned him up, fed him and kind of adopted him. Hesketh reported on the meeting: "Red met Johnny like the rest of us that first morning he was there. Johnny knew only a couple of Canadian words and Kelly was no Korean conversational whiz. But you can tell when some people hit it off right away and that was the way it was with Johnny and Red. Johnny had never seen a hockey game in his life and probably never will. He didn't know Red Kelly from [Korean president Syngman] Rhee. But there is something about this Kelly that most people, particularly kids, discover as a contagious friendliness. It was that way with Johnny."

"We called him 'Boy-san,'" recalled Red. "He and I hit it off. He was around a lot. One day he washed our clothes down by the water with rocks. He got them so clean, but that didn't last long — clean clothes were not an option in a camp environment."

On May 26, Red gave his mother, Frances, a thrill when he called her from Kure-gol, Korea. In a voice she could hear clearly from so far away, he told her he was well, and thrilled with the trip, calling it, "a wonderful experience." Two days later, Red and company were allowed their first shower in many a day.

The next day, back in Japan after a cold Air Australia flight, Red donned some borrowed hockey equipment and a pair of ill-fitting skates to put on a two-hour clinic for 70 young Japanese players at the Nikkatsu Sports Center arena in Tokyo. He noted that his students were "fine skaters and pretty good stickhandlers, but need polish and experience in making plays." That afternoon he visited the offices of the *Mainichi* newspaper, which had sponsored the clinic.

On June 8, Hesketh compared Red to a famous actress: "Red Kelly is creating more of a disturbance here than Marilyn did, although he is not in as good a shape. Kelly is busily amazing a bunch of black coated college kids by showing them a movie of the Stanley Cup playoffs. They are watching with wide eyes and mouths to match, though none can understand the commentary. Kelly has gone over quite large. It's impossible to describe the atmosphere here, like a new world. [At the Sports Palace] every time Kelly would throw a

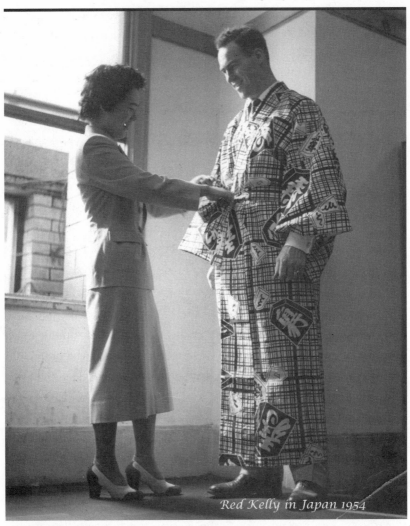

Red Kelly in Japan 1954

block the air would be filled with 'ah-so's.'" When an exhausted but satisfied Red returned to the farm, he estimated that he had shaken thousands of hands, answered as many questions and signed even more autographs.

After a few weeks home, a letter arrived from the Norris Grain company. "Dear Red, Jack Adams sent me a copy of the letter Mr. Campbell wrote you ... regarding your trip to Japan," wrote Detroit's Bruce Norris, now a co-owner of the Red Wings. "I certainly think that you did a very good job and are most certainly a credit to the sport as well as to the Red Wings. I would also like to say how happy I was that you won the Norris Trophy which I know would have made Dad very pleased indeed. Have a nice summer . . . see you in the fall."

The Kellys had gotten used to the work on the farm being interrupted by visiting fans and the press. Reporter Bruce Davenport from *Canadian Tractor Farming* did a cover piece showing Red driving the famous Farmall tractor. Red was actually plowing and planting *his* 40 acres of land — a few years before, he had purchased land across the road from his parents' place. His lot included a house, which he rented to his newly married sister Frances.

The Kelly farms sprawled over 200 acres that included a red garage, a large barn, four kilns and two spacious greenhouses, while the arable fields included 36 acres for tobacco, with the rest used for hay, corn and other crops, and pastures for the 25 Holstein cows, a pony, a colt and two horses to graze on. Red was especially fond of the pony.

"Someday, when Red Kelly's name becomes legendary . . . there will be many stories to tell," wrote Davenport. "But they will have to be told by people who knew him and saw him play, because the hardest thing in the world to get Red Kelly talking about . . . is Red Kelly."

Writer Margaret Scott also visited Red on the farm and did an exquisite two-part series for the November and December editions of *Hockey Pictorial* magazine titled "The Private Life of Red Kelly." Clearly enamoured with Red, the Kellys, the farm and its hospitality, Scott wrote: "Within minutes you'll realize that the Kellys are a clannish lot . . . big enough to include others. Their friendliness spills over and the stranger is drawn into their midst on a tide of homespun hospitality." Barely mentioned was Red's hockey career; Scott's focus was life on a tobacco farm.

As the leader of the crew of pickers, Red always set the pace for the day. "As soon as Leonard goes [to training camp] we notice the speed [of the fall harvest] drop," Red's mother told Scott. "He has

Red photographed on the family farm near Simcoe, Ontario. "Priming"
or harvesting of the tobacco plant, the main staple of the Kelly farm,
was a test of fitness and endurance and contributed greatly to
Red's always arriving at camp in the fall in excellent condition.

the interest of the farm at heart and sets a good pace, so we can beat the frost. There's always a sharp decline when he goes."

After Red helped the local ball team from Jarvis win a game 4–2 by knocking in two runs, Scott was along for the ride home, and she captured the essence of Red's summers. "After the game, it's homeward bound along quiet roads, a journey through a peacefully sleeping Simcoe and a turn to the left to a farmhouse with yellow lights gleaming through the window. It's a peaceful slumber in an indescribable quiet, shattered only by the moo of a cow and the bark of a small dog named Jiggs."

There was unrest in Motown as Red returned for a new season. Coach Ivan was gone, now the general manager of the league's perennial doormats in Chicago. The move had been engineered between two branches of the Norris clan; James Norris Jr., president of the Hawks, sought and received Ivan's release from his sister, Marguerite, president of the Wings.

Ivan was replaced behind the bench by Jimmy Skinner, who'd just had a successful season coaching the junior team in Hamilton and had coached the Windsor juniors for five years before that. "It took me two or three times to believe Jack when he said I was the next coach of the Red Wings," Skinner recalled. "I took a plane down there the next day for a press conference. But I was green as the dickens. I didn't know what to think of it all."

Skinner was in a tough spot, taking over a team that had won six consecutive league titles and three Stanley Cups in five years. Fortunately for him, the Red Wings were essentially the same squad that had captured Lord Stanley's mug the previous spring. Many players, Lindsay among them, believed it really didn't matter who coached the team. "Everybody on that Red Wings team and most players in the NHL were professionals," Lindsay recalled. "We were all the best at what we did. By the time we got to that level, a coach couldn't teach us anything else. We were all self-taught. The game wasn't that complicated; we could almost change the lines ourselves, and with Skinner, we sometimes did."

Perched near the Detroit bench, Adams used to bark orders at the more timid Skinner, a situation that wasn't good. "Things were certainly different on the bench, Jimmy would get a little flustered," recalled Red. "That affected us, as sometimes he would put the wrong guy out there at the wrong time."

The season was only six games old when Red and his teammates hosted the Bruins at Olympia on October 21, and history beckoned. In a scoreless first period, the Wings were on the power play.

"Lindsay fired the puck into the corner and I cut in behind the Boston defence," Red told reporters after the game. "The puck hit the boards and came out past the goal line to me. I couldn't see any openings so I aimed for the side of [Sugar Jim] Henry's pads. The

puck slid in off his glove about three inches inside the far post." Goal number one.

Red missed part of the second period after injuring his hip in a collision with Lorne Ferguson, but returned in the third; the score was 2–2 with a minute gone in the third period when he came back onto the ice. "Alex Delvecchio really worked," Red said. "He dug the puck around the net and was falling over when he threw it out to me. I saw it coming and slapped it. Lindsay was standing in front of the net, and it went between his legs. I don't think Henry saw it." Goal number two.

Six minutes later, the Wings were killing a penalty and Red was on the ice to defend. The Bruins were desperately throwing the puck around in the Detroit zone when a Boston defenceman mishandled a pass and it caromed out to centre ice. "I saw the puck going . . . towards the centre," Red explained. "Ordinarily, you wouldn't take such a chance going after a puck, but there was nobody in front of me. I drove down left wing. Don McKenney came across, trying to cut me off. I was 20 feet in front of the net when he hit me, but I shot simultaneously. Henry had come out of the goal just a little bit, and I had just a little piece of the corner to aim for. I fired the puck along the ice. That's the toughest to stop. I was probably lucky to get it away." The puck was in the net — a hat trick!

The crowd gave Red a seven minute standing ovation, the longest and loudest the Olympia had seen in years. As he skated to centre ice for the next faceoff, the cheers continued, and he kept his head down, his emotions in check. In his 464th game, Red was the first Detroit defenceman ever to get a hat trick, and the first by a defenceman in the NHL since 1929, when forward passes had just begun to be allowed. It was also the first hat trick by a Red Wing in three seasons. "It's funny how they come at times," Red remarked to the press in the dressing room after the 5–3 Detroit victory, which pushed them into first place. "I've had lots of twos, but this is the first hat trick I ever got."

The win lifted the team until a jackhammer ripped through it in the first week of November, when the NHL owners met in New York and Maple Leafs owner Conn Smythe pushed all the clubs to help out the lowly Bruins and Black Hawks. He initiated the cause by sending part-time defenceman Leo Boivin to Boston. His manipulative move worked, as the ever-popular Metro Prystai was traded to Chicago before the meetings adjourned. The move did not go over well with the Detroit press or its players.

"Is bigtime hockey not a legitimate sport or just a family syndicate?" Marshall Dann railed in the *Detroit Free Press*. "That is the question fans and observers are asking . . . in the wake of the trade . . . Prystai was shipped away as Marguerite and Bruce Norris, sister and brother . . . rushed to the aid of the Chicago team, owned by James D. Norris, another brother. The whole affair was handled in such a fashion that it seemingly couldn't help but shake the confidence of players in the organization . . . not to mention the irritation and downright disgust for Detroit fans."

"We immediately thought they were trying to break up our team," recalled Red. "Sending one of our players away, we were upset about that. It seemed sometimes like we were giving up players to Chicago because they could never make the playoffs. It was upsetting to have just won the Stanley Cup and then they trade a player from our team away."

Some players attempted to contact the Norrises, but without success. The situation brewed as the Maple Leafs came into town for a November 11 game. With Smythe blamed for the trades, the Detroit players were in a very sour mood. Bruce Norris came into the room to speak to the players before the game, but his explanation did no good. Red, representing the players, conferred with Marguerite before the game. The taste in everyone's mouth was foul and lingered as the game approached.

"We weren't going to go on the ice that night, no way," Red recalled. "The people were in the stands, but we didn't care. They eventually talked us into going out, but we didn't want to. We were mad at ownership, Smythe, the league for taking one of our players to help another team. Really? Chicago had won only 2 of 13 games, but that wasn't our fault! The Norris family had a monopoly. That was our immediate reaction to that trade. We hated to see Meatball go."

The surliness continued on the ice as the Leafs won 1–0, their first win in Detroit in three years. A few Wings even climbed the wire mesh to get at hecklers in the first row.

"The Metro Prystai deal to Chicago was hatched in Toronto last week," said Jack Adams, who hadn't learned of the deal until it was done. "Everybody knew about it but Detroit! We learned about it Wednesday and they expected our kids to play hockey! I've quit. I'm all through! There'll be no more road trips, radio, TV, special committees or other extra-curricular activities for me! I slugged for 28 years building up hockey and selling it to the people here and Smythe wrecks it with one blow."

Toronto won the rematch at Maple Leaf Gardens two nights later by the same score. The Red Wings were not happy campers, but there were brighter moments to come, especially for Red.

In a December 1 game at New York's Madison Square Garden, Howe scored two goals to become the seventh player in NHL history to reach the 250-goal plateau. Not to be outdone, Red also notched two goals in the 6–1 victory to reach the 100-goal plateau, the first defenceman in NHL history to do so. It was his 283rd point, which placed him sixth all-time among all Red Wings greats. Red had also only missed 12 games in seven seasons.

The Red Wings were battling for first place with Montreal at the end of January. Just as important to Red, Andra was back in Detroit with the Ice Revue for three weeks of shows. Though Andra had never really been far from Red's mind, their conflicting travel schedules kept personal contact minimal. Theirs was a long-distance relationship, conducted almost exclusively by mail.

"Red and I courted by correspondence. With our busy lives, we hardly saw each other," Andra recalled. For example, when she returned home from a tour of Europe, Red was in Korea. "I would write to him, and I wanted to know how the hockey season was going, and I would say, 'Send me some hockey news.' So what would Red do? Exactly that — he would send me copies of the *Hockey News*! Oh, my! He was not a big writer."

It was one thing to correspond, but to have her around for three weeks was, for Red, the equivalent of drinking Love Potion No. 9. He and Andra spent quality time together between her rehearsals and visited with Red's sister Laureen, who lived in Detroit. Andra watched the Wings host three games at the Olympia at the end of January and was photographed chatting with Red between periods. Not long after her arrival, they were driving down Grand River Avenue when he wondered aloud whether they should just get married. The notion caught her by surprise.

"I never dreamed Red was serious!" she told the press later. Oh, but he was, and she answered yes. It didn't take long for the word to get out. "Kelly to Desert Bachelorhood With Pretty Skater — Lucky Gal!" was one of many headlines.

"Because Andra's contract with the Ice Revue has another year to go, they plan to wait a year to be married," wrote Marshall Dann. "Miss McLaughlin, who will leave the ice show when she marries, said: 'Marriage will be a full time job for me. I don't believe in weekend marriages! I plan to raise a bunch of little redheads!'"

When the Wings went on an extended road trip, Red let Andra use his car, which allowed her and her roommate Gundi Busch to see the city. She returned it to Ma Shaw's sparkling clean, polished and full of gas.

A month later, a story and picture of the couple appeared in the Detroit press, with Andra quoted as saying, "When we're married, there'll be only one skater in the family." She told reporter John Walter that she planned to retire from skating. There was talk of a wedding after the hockey season.

Adams expressed frustration with the Wings players growing up — Lindsay, Delvecchio, Howe, Sawchuk, Skov and Wilson had recently married, and Pavelich and Kelly were engaged. Adams lamented to Lewis Walter of the *Detroit Times* that his Wings lacked drive. "One reason is that the players are going through a phase. We made the greatest record with a team that breathed, ate and slept hockey, like a Notre Dame team lives football. The players, most of them young and unmarried, lived together and lived hockey. In the past year or so that has been changing. It was inevitable. The men have been marrying, buying homes. Many have babies and more on the way."

The Red Wings rebounded from a mid-season slump as Hall replaced Sawchuk for a few games and the Motown crew started to win, really win. By mid-March, the Wings had only one loss in their past 15 games, putting them just two points back of first-place Montreal.

A game between the Canadiens and Bruins in Boston on March 13 altered all the playoff paths. Maurice Richard had his sights set on his first-ever Art Ross Trophy for the scoring championship. During the rough game, he was cut by a Hal Laycoe high stick, resulting in a vicious free-for-all. In the melee, the Rocket punched linesman Cliff Thompson. It was actually his second offence — he had punched another linesman earlier in the season, resulting in a $250 fine. Discipline would be stern.

On March 16, NHL president Clarence Campbell announced that the Rocket was suspended for the three remaining regular season games and the playoffs. The entire province of Quebec screamed foul, while throughout the rest of the league it was felt that Richard had gotten his just rewards.

The same day, Detroit beat Boston 5–4 to pull into a tie for first place with the Habs. As fate would have it, the Wings — for whom Richard's absence seemed all too convenient — were scheduled to play the Canadiens in their last two games of the season, the first of these falling on St. Patrick's Day, at the Forum. Campbell, who attended all the Habs games, stubbornly insisted on attending this one as well.

"We had won a squeaker in Boston a few nights before, and we couldn't lose that game. We were going for seven straight league championships. We needed to win," recalled Red. "When we came into the Forum that night an hour before the game, it was like a mob in the lobby and we had to worm our way through. The fans didn't bother us, they recognized us, but there were a lot of black jackets around, police. You could feel the tension in the air.

"The game started, and we had them down 4–1. Then Campbell came in partway through the period. And you instantly could hear the rumble, a murmur that swept through the arena. We knew something was happening and it wasn't on the ice. Campbell came into his seat with his girlfriend. She had a big hat on like an umbrella. So they sat right behind the goal at the end where I was defending.

"The murmur grew louder and louder, and then the period ended. I'm on the ice and, as I'm heading off back to our dressing room, there was a real commotion. I looked up and over behind the net, and I could see four or five guys swinging, and I could see Campbell, he's got his arm trying to protect his girlfriend's hat. They were throwing tomatoes and cabbages at him from up above. That's the last thing I saw as we went off the ice.

"We go to our dressing room, and all of a sudden our team doctor comes running in and says they've thrown tear gas out in the arena, and he's crying. They put wet towels at the bottom of the door to stop the tear gas from coming in. We don't know what's going to happen. We had our skates off, and at that moment we just wanted to win this game. It was 4–1 for us but two periods still to go. So we waited and waited."

A note eventually arrived from Montreal boss Frank Selke stating that the game had been awarded to Detroit and ordering the Wings to clear the building.

"We had to get dressed as fast as we could. The bus was at the back of the arena. They told us not to talk or look at anybody, just go single file over to the bus, and then we would leave for the train. We all got on the bus; there were people all around the bus. We normally turned right at the back of the building to leave the Forum, and then right again, to go in front of the building, but we had to go a different way to get to the train station.

"At the train station there were some crowds, but they couldn't believe what was going on downtown. We heard the crowd was rioting downtown, breaking windows, overturning police cars, they were just wild. We knew French Canadians and fans of Montreal were very emotional, they could get excited, and we hoped nobody got hurt."

Stores were vandalized in the area around the Forum, many arrests were made and dozens sent to hospital, including many police officers. On Friday morning, Richard took to the radio to ask for calm.

On March 19, Montreal regrouped to beat the Rangers, pulling them even with the idle Red Wings. First place would be on the line the next night in Detroit, in the last game of the season. Also on the line was Sawchuk's third Vezina. Scores of police were on hand, and everyone entering the Olympia was searched. The atmosphere was tense.

The Canadiens quickly fell behind on goals by Reibel, Leswick and Lindsay. Halfway through, it was announced that the Rangers had defeated Toronto, 3–2. A Sawchuk shutout would earn him the Vezina, but none of his 11 shutouts to date had been against Montreal.

"When we knew that Terry had a shot at the Vezina," Pronovost recalled, "we all dug down deeper, and because it was against the Canadiens, we dug a little deeper still."

With a 6–0 lead and the seconds winding down, the crowd was standing and cheering as the Wings stayed close to the Canadiens and the defence formed an impenetrable wall. At the final buzzer, Sawchuk began jumping up and down and the Wings poured onto the ice to celebrate his third Vezina and their seventh consecutive league championship. "Red Kelly and Marcel Pronovost have been our big men during our stretch drive," observed Adams.

Despite claims by Conn Smythe that his Leafs were the team to beat in their semifinal, Detroit swept aside Toronto in four games. The final win was a 3–0 shutout. Red and fellow defenceman Bob Goldham were singled out as the keys to victory. "Their performance on defence has been a source of confidence and inspiration to their teammates, easing goalie Terry Sawchuk's job and making it possible for Howe, Reibel and Lindsay to score," reported the *Detroit News*. "Next to the two goalies, Kelly was on the ice the longest of anyone at 36 minutes and 25 seconds."

"Red played one of the greatest games of his career," said Adams. "He never once lost control of the puck in his own end after he got it."

Meanwhile, the Canadiens disposed of Boston in five games to put themselves into the Stanley Cup Final for the fifth time in as many springs. Montreal coach Irvin singled out Red Kelly in the advance hype: "The only mistakes he makes are when he scores against us, which is too often!"

In the third period of Game 1, Floyd Curry gave the Habs a 2–1 lead. With Dollard St. Laurent off for tripping, Lindsay fed Vic Stasiuk in the slot to tie the game. After three great Sawchuk saves, Marty Pavelich broke loose and beat Plante on the glove side. Lindsay's empty-netter sealed the 4–2 victory.

Irvin made a goaltending switch for Game 2, starting 21-year-old rookie Charlie Hodge in place of Plante. The two had alternated in the Boston series, but the strategy backfired as the Wings surged to a 4–0 lead after the first 20 minutes. In the second period, Howe banked a shot off the boards behind and to the right of Plante, who was now in the Montreal net. The puck bounced back out to a rushing Lindsay, who slammed the puck through Plante's legs. The Red Wings linemates had mastered this play in practice. The Wings stretched their lead to 7–0 after the second. At 12:32 of the third period, Kenny Mosdell spoiled Terry's shutout bid, but the Wings prevailed, 7–1.

Back at the Forum for Game 3, the Frenchmen were flying as Geoffrion, vilified by Montreal fans for edging out the idle Rocket in the scoring race, won them over by firing in two goals 12 seconds apart. The game featured great saves by both Plante and Sawchuk, but the game's outcome was typified by Hab Jackie Leclair's golf shot from a poor angle that eluded a surprised Sawchuk standing too far back in his net. Despite being outshot 37–26, the Habs won 4–2. It was a similar story in the fourth game: it was Plante's night as the Wings outshot the Habs 40–30 but lost the game 5–3. Heading back to the Olympia, the series was tied at two wins apiece.

Though Howe's hat trick in Game 5, a Detroit 5–1 victory, gave him a new record for post-season points with 19, Red was the one who made the headlines for his first-ever misconduct penalty. He and Butch Bouchard exchanged punches after Bouchard slashed him on the ankle. The benches emptied and, after Kelly and Bouchard had been separated and sent to the penalty box, the fight resumed — in those days, both teams shared the same penalty box. "According to Kelly, a shove from Bouchard and some unkind words about Kelly's ancestry led to the second scuffle," read one report. Each of them was finally sent to his dressing room after receiving 17 minutes in penalties.

"You can get a broken ankle easily, if you are hit hard with the stick," a still irate Kelly commented after the game. "And Butch Bouchard gave me a good whack! I didn't have the puck and wasn't figuring in the play."

"We got into the fight, but neither of us landed any blows," Red recalled. "Butch was a big man, not normally a fighter, but he could handle himself. You had to handle yourself . . . It's a little different fighting on the ice than it is fighting on the ground."

Back in Montreal for Game 6, the Habs came to play, and home ice advantage again prevailed as Montreal blasted the Wings 6–3, setting up a deciding game.

The largest Detroit crowd of the season, 15,500 fans, packed the sports palace on Grand River Avenue for the decisive game. Both Plante and Sawchuk were unbeatable during the first period. Then, at 7:12 of the second, Red pushed the puck deep into the Montreal zone and fed a nifty pass back to a charging Delvecchio, whose shot beat Plante to put Detroit up 1–0. At the end of the second period, Howe deflected a Pronovost shot to send the Wings to the dressing room with a 2–0 lead.

Three minutes into the third, Delvecchio broke through the Montreal defence, firing a high shot over a diving Plante to pad the lead to 3–0. With five and a half minutes to go, a Geoffrion point shot knocked Sawchuk's stick out of his hand, and Floyd Curry knocked home the rebound to make the score 3–1. The defence tightened up for the rest of the way, and at the final buzzer, teammates streamed from the bench and mobbed Sawchuk.

This year, the Canadiens did not storm off to the dressing room. Instead they exchanged handshakes with the Wings. There was a moment of comic relief as the Wings players and officials gathered at centre ice for Clarence Campbell to present the Stanley Cup. The public address microphone became tangled on its descent from the rafters, and, to the delight of the crowd, six-foot-one Glen Skov was boosted onto the shoulders of two teammates to untangle the wire. The players stood listening to the NHL president, their arms resting on each other's shoulders.

In the weeks that followed, there was criticism from the Canadiens camp that the Wings only won because Montreal didn't have the Rocket. "The Rocket's absence may or may not have made a difference," Pronovost recalled. "I believe in his absence the Canadiens actually turned it up a notch; some of their players played better than if the Rocket had been there. It will always be a 'what if?' In our defence, down the home stretch at the end of the season we were by far the winningest team, even before the Rocket's suspension. We entered the playoffs very strong."

The Wings were on top of the hockey world as they celebrated at the Sheraton-Cadillac Hotel. They had won seven consecutive league titles and now four Stanley Cups in six years.

Red was named to the First All-Star Team for the fifth year in a row, and finished third in Lady Byng voting and second to Doug Harvey in the Norris Trophy voting.

Red had planned to head for Florida and then maybe visit Andra in Colorado, but when he found out that she was vacationing in Hawaii, he flew there to surprise her. "I was there on vacation with my brother Chuck, who had just gotten out of school, and the phone rang in our room, and it was Red," Andra remembered. "I said to him, 'Boy, we have a good connection. It sounds like you're right around the corner!' He said, 'I am!' And he was!"

Her mother, also named Andra McLaughlin, wasn't keen on the courtship. When Chuck let slip to his mother back in Colorado that Red was also in Hawaii, Mrs. McLaughlin was upset. "Our engagement would be on and off again quite a few times," Andra recalled. "We had lots of correspondence. We were both hesitant, but it was mostly my mother. She had been in show business, a dancer in the Ziegfeld Follies. She was Czechoslovakian, and she loved what I was doing. She didn't want me to give up my career. That was the problem. As soon as she found out that Red was in Hawaii with me, I was on the way home. Red finished the vacation there with my brother."

The *Toronto Star* noted on May 17, 1955, that the Kelly-McLaughlin union was going to be delayed "following a vacation in Hawaii, where he and bride-to-be Andra McLaughlin, the ice show star, decided they will not marry until next spring. There had been some talk of a wedding this summer."

For Red, working the tobacco fields, driving the familiar Farmall tractor and relaxing with his family was straightforward compared to the complications of his long-distance love life and the machinations of Trader Jack Adams.

• • • • • •

CHAPTER EIGHT

UNRAVELLING
of a DYNASTY

If Jack Adams had vowed never to stand pat after a Stanley Cup victory, he sure outdid himself as the 1955–56 season approached. It helped that he had the full support of the new Wings president Bruce Norris, who had ousted his sister Marguerite in a family power struggle. Marguerite, humiliated, hurt and now powerless, stayed on as the team's vice-president in name only.

On May 28, Adams sent Glen Skov, Benny Woit, Tony Leswick and Johnny Wilson to Chicago in exchange for Dave Creighton, Jerry Toppazzini, John McCormack and Bucky Hollingworth. Five days later, Adams sent his All-Star goalie, Terry Sawchuk, along with Marcel Bonin, Lorne Davis and Vic Stasiuk, to Boston for Ed Sandford, Réal Chevrefils, Norm Corcoran, Warren Godfrey and goalie Gilles Boisvert. Sandford would be dealt to Chicago in October so the Wings could repatriate Metro Prystai.

Marcel Pronovost remembered the Bruins deal: "That Boston trade was a catastrophe for us. Adams got nothing in return for Sawchuk. He traded away home-grown players who had Red Wings tattoos on their butts. He got players in return who weren't that dedicated to the organization."

To fill Sawchuk's skates, the Red Wings promoted goaltending sensation Glenn Hall from the Edmonton farm team. As for the rest of the players acquired from Boston, Red concurred with Pronovost. "Jack brought some new players in — Ed Sandford, Warren Godfrey — but the deal didn't make out so well," he said. "There were some problems with Chevrefils and some of the others. In the end, the deal looked like Boston got the better of it. Those guys never panned out."

With Sawchuk in net, the Bruins blazed out of the starting blocks before cooling, while the Wings, with only nine players from their Stanley Cup roster of the year before, struggled.

Red was uncharacteristically chippy as the season got underway. In one of the first games, he got into a dandy fight with Toronto's Eric Nesterenko. "I'm not playing much differently from what I ever did," Red told the press. "That Nesterenko and I never got along too well. In this case I was going for the puck in the corner. Nester was behind me and I suspected he'd have his stick high, so I side stepped and sure enough, he went crashing into the boards. I could have hoisted him into the seats!"

In his next game, against the Bruins, Red had a skirmish with Leo Labine as the Bruin went to take the feet out from under him. Knocked off balance, Red flailed, and his arm caught Labine near the eye, cutting him.

"It was completely accidental on my part, but the blood was showing on Leo's eye, so there was nothing the referee could do except give me five minutes, and the game had just started," Red explained at the time. "Ted Lindsay and I were kidding at the start of the season. He told me he was out to win the Lady Byng, so I told him I guessed I would go after his title as one of the bad men in hockey. The way things are going, I may be closer than I thought!" His penalty minutes were now at 27, one minute fewer than he'd earned during the whole previous season.

The Red Wings won only 6 of their first 24 games, scoring a mere 54 goals while allowing 49 goals against. Concern set in. When the Rangers plastered them 7–3 in New York on December 4, Red was deemed to be the solution to the goal-scoring woes.

"Red Kelly Moves to Forward Line in Red Wing Shuffle!" went one headline out of Detroit. Lindsay was moved off the first line, and Red played left wing with Dutch Reibel and Gordie Howe. "I'm hoping Red can give us a little more offence," coach Skinner explained. "We need more goals and if he can get them then we've got to use him there even if our defence is weakened."

In his second game up front, Red potted both goals in a 4–2 loss at the Montreal Forum and netted another in a 2–0 win over the Rangers in the next game. Though the switch to forward seemed seamless for Red, it wasn't.

"Before I got the hang of it, I kept running into Gordie," Red told the *Hockey News*. "Then I began to get the feel of moving over to right wing when he cuts to the left. When he is carrying or Dutch is feeding him, I keep my eye on Gordie. When he moves, I go the other way. I guess it's a lot like dancing partners. At first I worried about whether I was breaking in fast enough to stay with Howe and Reibel. Then I realized that they could time my moves whether I was ahead of them or behind, so I quit worrying about that."

The verdict was soon in. "Many hockey observers are convinced that he (Kelly) deserves the Hart Trophy as the player most valuable to his team," suggested writer Lewis Walter.

"The Red Wings have made only one important move which contributed to their bounce from the basement," wrote *Toronto Star* columnist Milt Dunnell. "That was the shift of Red Kelly to left wing, from his accustomed beat at the blue stripe. The redhead's presence on the firing line has helped give the team greater balance."

"Kelly is having the time of his life up there on the line," added George Van of the *Detroit Times*. "At last count he had six goals. Only one other Red Wing is ahead of him, Alex Delvecchio has eight. Kelly loves to skate. He is a mountain goat for being sure of foot, or skate. As a forward he gets more chance to use his skates handling the puck. He hasn't a peer in hockey in this respect."

When he had scored his 11th goal, the talk around the league was that his switch to forward would cost him his usual All-Star spot on defence, and thus the $1,000 bonus. He dismissed that talk. "I've had more than my share of bonus money already," he was quoted as saying. "Besides, I like playing left wing. I've always hoped for a 20-goal season and I couldn't make it when I was playing defence. Maybe I can make it as a forward."

"Red was always our highest scoring defenceman, and the logical player to move to forward," said Adams. "He's as good as any other left wing in the league right now. But he won't get any All-Star support because he played defence for the first month and it took him a few games to get used to the switch."

Amazingly, Red was still chosen as the All-Star defenceman alongside Montreal's Doug Harvey at the season's halfway mark. The choice of Kelly, though understandably automatic, dumbfounded some experts.

"The two best defencemen in the NHL are Harvey and Kelly. There's no argument about that," lamented Boston defenceman Hal Laycoe. "But when you're voting for the All-Star defence for the first half of the season, I don't see how you could vote for Kelly. He spent too much time up at left wing. Harvey deserved to be picked but Bill Gadsby of the Rangers should have been his partner."

Red went back to the farm for a rare winter weekend visit and took along teammates Bill Dineen, Marty Pavelich and Metro Prystai, along with staff from the *Detroit News Pictorial*. He demonstrated his tobacco-leaf-picking skills, played pond hockey and carved the turkey for a large gathering of 20-plus in the Kelly kitchen. The meal was finished off with mother's famous apple pie.

Not there was Andra.

"Look, no ring," Andra McLaughlin answered with a smile while waving her hand towards *Detroit Times* reporter George Van, who had asked her about the state of their engagement. "But he's still the only one. You see, we've both got our careers. He called me last night! Still the sweetest guy in the world . . . and isn't it great his being named on the All-Star again, as defenceman even though Jack Adams has him playing forward and he's going great . . . so are the Wings."

In a *Sports Illustrated* article just before the start of the playoffs, writer Herbert Wind described the redhead as "a revelation on left wing. . . . One picture or, more accurately, one series of pictures remains clearly in my mind. It is Kelly back-checking with that effortless finesse of his, breaking up one enemy rush after another before they could even get started and generally creating the impression that progress up his side of the rink was virtually impossible, a road temporarily closed to traffic."

When Pronovost was injured, Red was moved back to his usual defence spot as the season wound down. As a precursor of things to come, the Red Wings dropped five of six points to the Canadiens in a three-game set that saw les Habitants clinch first place.

In the first round of the playoffs, Detroit faced the Maple Leafs and beat them at home two straight heading back to Toronto. An injury to Tod Sloan of the Leafs in the second game prompted one irate Toronto fan to phone Lindsay with a threat to shoot him. Lindsay answered the threat by scoring the tying and winning goals in Game 3 and then hoisting his stick up to the crowd in a shooting gesture.

The Leafs won Game 4, but the Red Wings were not to be denied as they won the fifth game to eliminate the pesky Leafs — but not without a play that was, for Red, a jaw-dropper. A hard stray shot off the stick of Toronto's Sid Smith ripped into his mouth, broke three teeth, cut him savagely and broke his jaw. Blood was everywhere as he was taken off the ice in great pain, done for the night at least. At the hospital, his jaw was wired back together, and he received 21 stitches inside and outside of his mouth.

Prior to the Stanley Cup Final series against Montreal, Red was advised not to play. He would have none of it. He pleaded with management and was outfitted with a specially designed face guard that protected his jaw and was strapped onto his head for stability. Since the finals coincided with Easter, the mask was dubbed his "Easter Bonnet."

"I wore this four-pound mask on my head with a guard out front so I could play," recalled Red. "I was wired up. I had broken my jaw, and I couldn't eat. I lost several pounds. The only thing I could eat was to drink through a straw — milk and soups. The mask was wired in front so I couldn't get hit from the front. It protected the chin and everything; it was a very cumbersome outfit."

Red's injury pulled at Andra's heartstrings. "I was in Colorado Springs," she recalled. "The paper would never print the NHL scores in the paper, only college hockey. After I met Red, I wanted to always know how he was doing, and so I would call the local paper, and the sports editor there was a man named Tom McLaughlin, an elderly gentleman, a friend of my father's. I would say, 'I know Red Kelly. How is he doing?' and he would tell me.

"So, one night I hadn't called him yet, but the phone rang and it was for me. It was Mr. McLaughlin, and he said, 'I thought you'd want to know that fella that you met, Red Kelly, he had a very serious accident in his hockey game tonight.' I said, 'Really?!' And he said, 'Yes, it's pretty bad, awful. I thought you might want to know.' He didn't really tell me much of what had happened.

"And I said, 'Oh, my!' I was shocked, because I always thought of Red as indestructible! He was not a rabble-rouser of a hockey player. How could this happen? Here I was a thousand miles away in another world, a figure skating world."

She changed her travel plans, adding a stop in Detroit before going to Ottawa for a scheduled ice carnival appearance. "I just had to see Red for myself to see how bad he had been injured. I had to be very clever, because my mother felt that my skating should come first above all things, especially before being with professional hockey players. When she kissed me goodbye in Colorado Springs that day, she had no idea of my secret plot. I got to the game just as the players were coming onto the ice, and I sat in Mr. Adams's box."

She was a day late for the Ottawa show. "I missed the dress rehearsal, but that was worth it because I loved Red. And he needed someone to take care of him."

Red loved the surprise awaiting him in Jack Adams's box. "We would walk up beside his box to go onto the ice. I came out, and there she was," he recalled. "I had a black eye and cuts; my face was black and blue."

The Canadiens came back from a two-goal deficit in the third period, scoring four goals in four and half minutes to steal Game 1. "We just ran out of gas," explained Skinner afterwards. "But I'm sure the three days' rest before the next game will help us catch up."

When Red came out of the dressing room to see Andra after the game, his injured appearance cast a spell on her.

"He looked like Quasimodo, the Hunchback of Notre Dame," she wrote years later.

> *I fell hopelessly, helplessly, head-over-heels in love with him. His face was black and blue, green and yellow, one eye was closed, the other dripping, one side of his face cascading down over his wilting white shirt. His teeth on one side were all crooked and going every which way, his jaw broken and wired shut, and I decided he needed me. He needed me, well, he needed someone and it might as well be me!*
>
> *This big, strong and mighty hockey player became so vulnerable, so apologetic about his dramatic appearance, so like a little boy, that I made the decision to do everything I could to take care of him for the rest of my life. But that was not going to be easy. We came from different worlds. The 1940s and '50s were a time of glamorous ice shows and hockey games that had not been seen before or since. Red*

and I were experiencing our career dreams simultaneously
and they were fabulous years but for us to ever get together
was either going to be by sheer good luck or absolute deter-
mination. It would turn out to be conniving determina-
tion that night in Detroit. From then on we did a lot of
rearranging of schedules to see each other a few minutes
here and a few hours there. We would have big phone bills
and many letters sent.

In Game 2, the Montrealers easily beat the Wings 5–1. Detroit fought back to take the third game at the Olympia, 3–1, but the Canadiens were not to be denied as they took the next two games to capture the Stanley Cup. At the victory party back in Montreal, Canadiens GM Frank Selke called Red "the best hockey player I have ever seen."

Despite spending 26 games up at left wing, Red still finished only two votes behind Bill Gadsby for the second spot on the First All-Star Team.

In the off-season, writer George Carver visited Red as he vacationed at a friend's cottage near Belleville on Lake Ontario. Red was a picture of fun and relaxation; wearing a gold-flecked bathing suit, he waterskied and danced on the beach. When Carver asked him about a Lindsay trade rumour, Red scoffed, "Nah, Ted will never play with another club," explaining that Lindsay had a nice home and flourishing business in a Windsor suburb; he was a Red Wing from the tips of his toes to the top of his head.

Adams wanted to place blame, and targeted the team captain. At the next training camp in the American Sault in the fall of 1956, Adams summoned Red to his office.

"Red, we want you to be the next team captain, for a year."

Red balked, shaking his head. "If you take the *C* away from Ted, you're gonna hurt Ted. And if you hurt Ted, you're hurting the team. I don't want any part of it!"

*Relaxing poolside in Hollywood, Florida, in the mid 1950s with
homeowner and fan Truman Cullen, Red sits in front with teammates
Metro Prystai, Bucky Hollingsworth, Gordie Howe and Dutch Reibel.*

Red left the office.

A short while later, he was again summoned back.

"Red, you're an alternate and the C has been removed from Ted.
Nothing is going to change that. We're going to have a new captain
for a year," Adams said, choosing his words carefully. "If you don't
take it, it's gonna go to somebody else, but we would like it to be you.
Everybody respects you."

Adams watched him carefully. Red took a deep breath and
sighed. "Okay, I'll take it, but only for a year. I don't particularly want
it. I think it's a bad thing, a bad move. You will certainly have hurt
Ted, whether he shows it or not. And that's not good for the team!"

The change was met with approval in Red Wings circles, but
Red knew the real reason for his appointment. "Lindsay was trying

to get the players' union started," explained Red. "Adams got down on Ted because he was involved in that. And there were some other things . . . something about Ted being in business outside of hockey. Adams didn't like that!"

As Red assumed the captaincy at the start of the season, he saw no ill effects or changes from either Lindsay or the rest of his teammates. They all respected him.

Management told the press the promotion meant $500 more to Kelly. "I don't remember getting any more money," Red recalled. "I had no interest in being the captain, and I told them that. Whoever is captain gets my support 100 per cent, and that was the way I was. I was interested in playing and in winning."

Joining Red on defence this season was a youngster named Al Arbour, and Red had to adjust to his new partner. "Al was a tall, lanky guy, wore glasses," Red recalled. "He was a great shot-blocker. We were always told to have one defenceman in front of the net at all times. So this one time we're both behind the net, and I think, 'Holy moley, I gotta get back in front!' I go to take off to get back in front of our net, and Al has a hold of my stick! I'm trying to get back, and he won't let me go, and I yell, 'Al let go of my stick!' He did, and I got back there, but that was funny. Al had very heavy glasses. He thought he had an opponent's stick, but it was my stick."

The Red Wings resumed their place atop the league by recapturing their eighth regular season championship in nine years. Howe and Lindsay finished one-two in league scoring, and Glenn Hall had a marvellous sophomore season, missing out on the Vezina by only two goals. All seemed well in the Detroit hockey world as they prepared to face the third-place Bruins in the first round.

But someone forgot to tell Boston they were supposed to roll over and die. From the outset of Game 1, it was evident this was no ordinary series. "This is the strangest playoffs I can recall," observed Adams. "Boston has more hungry players. They're aggressive and they're always digging."

The Bruins disposed of the Red Wings in five games in one of the most startling upsets in hockey history. Adams even declared, "This is Boston's year!"

It wasn't. The Canadiens repeated as Stanley Cup champions in five games.

After the playoffs ended, Adams criticized goalie Hall's play and let it be known that only Howe and Kelly were untouchable on his team.

When asked about the trade rumours, Lindsay was ready. "I've been around hockey too long to worry about trade talks at this date," he answered. "However, I don't think Hall rated the criticism he received after we lost to Boston. He's still the best goalie in the league in my books."

Red was again selected to the First All-Star Team, for the sixth time in seven seasons. He was joined by teammates Hall, Lindsay and Howe but was far behind Montreal's Norris Trophy winner, Doug Harvey, in balloting, a situation he put into perspective.

"Hockey reporters really covered hockey in Montreal," Red recalled. "How many guys covered hockey in Montreal? A lot! They'd see the other teams like us seven times a year. They would see Montreal 35 times. New York might have one writer or two covering the games or something. Boston covered it pretty good. But some of the teams never got covered the same, but the Canadiens really got coverage.

"Not taking anything away from Doug Harvey, but he also had some pretty good players up front to pass the puck to. He was a good puck-handler, and he could make great passes for sure, but I'll tell you, he never scored lots of goals, because he had more offensive forwards to pass the puck to: Geoffrion, the two Richards, Dickie Moore, Béliveau. That made a big difference and it got him a lot of assists and points. I didn't have that at this point in Detroit."

Once again, Adams was looking for scapegoats, and his gaze focused on his former captain and goalie. At the league's annual meetings in Montreal in June, Adams approached the Bruins, who had let it be known that they would entertain offers for Terry Sawchuk, who had dramatically retired halfway through the previous season when stricken with mononucleosis. Chicago's Tommy Ivan had already voiced interest in Sawchuk, but he let it be known that he coveted Glenn Hall even more. Trader Jack was all smiles as his plan fell into place. The Wings made a deal with the Bruins that brought Sawchuk back to Detroit in exchange for young left wing Johnny Bucyk and cash. Bucyk, who had netted only 10 goals in the past season, was considered by Skinner and Adams to be an underachiever, lazy and a poor two-way player; he would end up in the Hockey Hall of Fame.

In July, Adams initiated the second phase of his plan by shipping Lindsay and Hall west to Chicago for goalie Hank Bassen, William Preston, Forbes Kennedy and former Wing Johnny Wilson.

When team vice-president Marguerite Norris read about the Lindsay/Hall trade in the Detroit papers, she was furious. Grabbing the phone she got her brother Bruce on the line: "What are you doing? You can't do that!"

"Well, I've done it."

"You just can't do that!"

"Look, Marguerite, do you want to have a fight about this in the papers?" Bruce asked her from a position of strength, namely the support of their mother. He knew Marguerite's deep pride in the Norris family name and gambled that she wouldn't want a public squabble. He was right.

Though he might have smiled like a Cheshire cat after the call, history would show that it was Marguerite who had led the team to two back-to-back Stanley Cups while she was president. During her tenure, she had kept the ranting notions of Adams in check. Now, Bruce Norris, in the midst of listening to the advice of the irrational GM, was dismantling a championship team. Though she would be officially listed as vice-president for many years to come, the trading of one of her favourite star players, Lindsay, was too much for Marguerite to stomach, and she faded into the background of the Red Wings family.

"I liked Ted Lindsay," Hall recalled. "Adams had told me not to talk to Ted because of the union thing, and I told Adams I would talk to whomever I wanted. He didn't like that. Jack Adams was everything I disliked in a person. I enjoyed my time in Detroit, but I certainly didn't abide by the rule, which was to never say certain things to the general manager. I think I told him where to go on a few occasions, which I knew didn't help my cause. I'd talk to whomever I wanted to talk to."

Red concurred — Hall never held his tongue. "Glenn voiced his opinion when Adams came into the room. Glenn was right there in the seat where the door opened up, and he came to Hall pigeon-toed, he was always pigeon-toed, and he gave it to Hall for something he'd done that wasn't to his satisfaction, and Glenn would say, 'Take a hike.' He traded him because he answered back, not because of his play."

At issue was Adams, not Hall or Lindsay.

"Jack began to change even in the few years before he traded me," recalled Lindsay. "Personality clashes with Jack began to override his hockey judgement. In the Canadiens organization, if you had talent and performed on the ice, you stayed there, no matter what. In Detroit, if you ticked Jack off, you were gone. To me, that's not the sign of a good hockey man. I was the NHL's second leading scorer behind Howe when he traded me and Hall to Chicago. And it was mostly because of my trying to form the Players' Association, which was badly needed at that time."

There was a league-wide breakdown in trust between the players and team owners. Lindsay and Doug Harvey of the Canadiens spearheaded a movement to form a players' union, or "association," which was fiercely opposed by the team owners. As the most vocal, temperamental opponent of the movement, Adams got rid of one union leader and was prepared to take on the other ringleader.

"We had a deal worked out with Montreal to get Doug Harvey," Jimmy Skinner recalled years later. "He had been a troublemaker to the Canadiens brass, and Jack was going to take him. I happened to be in Jack's office when Frank Selke phoned to say the deal was off."

"Jack," Selke said. "I know we had a deal, but I have to call it off. If I trade Harvey away, they'll crucify me here in Montreal."

Adams could understand Selke's predicament. The Wings front office had been deluged with irate phone calls and letters protesting the Lindsay/Hall trade. If the Wings had been able to land Harvey, they would have had the two best defencemen in the NHL.

Under Harvey and Lindsay's direction, the Players' Association was suing for bigger pensions and a share of TV rights fees, and filed an antitrust suit. Support for the fledgling union was shaky in Detroit. "We were the last in the association to hear any of the details," Marcel Pronovost recalled. "We were not totally convinced of all of the facts, so Red got us, the Red Wings players, our own lawyer. When our lawyer contacted the association's lawyer, he wouldn't give us the information we wanted to know. This delay created a window of opportunity for the owners to try to squash it. Gordie Howe was not to blame, nor was Red Kelly. We as a team wanted more information, but it was too late in coming. There was nobody to blame except the lawyers for the Players' Association, from our point of view here in Detroit."

"I hired a labour lawyer," Red recalled. "His name was John Hird. We wanted him to advise us in Detroit whether these union reps were taking us in the right direction. We Detroit players paid him. We didn't have him too long, because everything went haywire. But he wrote to the league and to the players' union lawyers, but they never replied. They never responded to his query."

In a further effort to squash the insubordinates, 32 per cent of the NHL's players were moved. Many players were sent to the minors, and a large number of rookies made their debut in 1957–58. Only the Canadiens refused to tamper with their roster, and Selke likely smelled another Stanley Cup when he surveyed the confusion around the league.

As the Wings began the season, it soon became painfully clear that they weren't what they used to be. They still had a talented core of veterans — Howe, Delvecchio, Sawchuk, Pronovost, Wilson and Kelly — but, as Pronovost explained it, "the supporting cast couldn't always remember their lines. You could tell that things weren't going to be the same."

After the first 11 games, the Wings were mired in fifth place, a measly point ahead of Toronto. The situation took its toll on coach Skinner. "I began to get these awful migraine headaches, had trouble driving, sleeping," he explained. "Jack Adams made me have an eye exam, but my eyes were fine. I stepped aside and recommended Sid Abel, who was around town doing TV telecasts, and I stayed on in the Wings organization handling the farm system. It was all just getting to me."

On the union front, it went south quickly in November. After attending a union meeting in Toronto on October 4, Red and the other Detroit reps — Pronovost, Howe and Delvecchio — came back to discuss the options with their teammates. When the Red Wings went public with their withdrawal from the lawsuit, the news did not go down well with their ex-captain.

"Lindsay, who was now with Chicago, and I never had any meetings, with him or anybody," Red recalled. "I assumed that he was still in contact with Gordie. One day I came to the Olympia and there's a whole bunch of writers there, and they cornered me and they said, 'Toronto just went on strike, and so what are you guys doing?' I said, 'We're behind the union one hundred per cent, but we're not going on strike.' Well, bedlam! Everybody left just like that! They ran.

"Then Ted came to the Olympia after that meeting in Toronto, but everybody was gone. I never talked to Ted at any time. I was a farmer and I didn't really condone going out on strike. Everything the union was fighting for I agreed with, but we weren't going to go out on strike. Then I found out later that they had gone on strike in Toronto, but they never talked to us! That's what happened."

Angry and unsatisfied, Lindsay accused the Red Wings players of capitulating under pressure from Jack Adams, a suggestion that

Red scoffed at. "Adams did come around the dressing room and point fingers at us, but he didn't scare me or anybody," he said. "He never scared me one iota at any time! No way!"

In the end, the players' union and lawsuit crumbled, but not before a court settlement on February 5, 1958, promised the players a $7,000 minimum wage, increase in pension benefits, hospitalization coverage, a limit to the number of exhibition games to be played and assurance that a player would be the sole judge of his physical fitness to play after an injury. Though deemed something of a failure, the settlement was a first step in the right direction for players' rights.

In Detroit, under Abel's tutelage, the Wings rebounded, finishing in third place, a point ahead of Boston but 26 points behind their first-round opponents, the league-leading Canadiens.

Before the first playoff game was three minutes old, Rocket Richard — back from a career-threatening Achilles tendon injury that had forced him to miss December, January and most of February — scored the first goal in an 8–1 Canadiens rout. Game 2 was all Montreal again, 5–1. The Wings forced overtime in Game 3 before losing 2–1, and the Habs completed the sweep by a 4–3 score. The Rocket scored more goals, seven, than the entire Detroit team in the series.

"The Rocket was at the tail end of his career," Pronovost recalled, "but I have always said there is not one hockey player today, yesterday, nor perhaps tomorrow, who could electrify a crowd the way the Rocket could. When he grabbed the puck, the crowd came alive, whether he was in Montreal or anywhere else in the league. And it seemed that he always saved his best for Detroit."

As Red headed back to the farm for the summer, it was now anybody's guess upon whom the cantankerous Jack Adams's scapegoating gaze would fall next. It got him to thinking about his future. *What else could I do with my life, besides farming and hockey?* he wondered.

And then there was Andra . . .

• • • • • •

CHAPTER NINE

LOVE *and*
BETRAYAL
in DETROIT

The spring of 1958 was a very unsettled time for Red Kelly and Andra McLaughlin. Their courtship, on and off so many times over the years, was coming to a crossroads.

Andra found herself more and more torn about her skating future. Her desire to be with Red increased, but she was uncertain of what her new life would be. Her mother continued to strongly object to her choosing to be a hockey wife over being a performer. Her father, Charles, was more concerned over her moving away to Canada.

"My contract with the Hollywood Ice Revue had ended," Andra recalled. "When they asked me if I would come back to skate, I said no. I didn't want it anymore. I didn't know what I wanted."

To make his intentions official, and to apply pressure, Red sent her an engagement ring and waited and waited. Andra was clearly torn. Sensing her dilemma, her father took her aside.

"Andra, look, all you've ever known was skating rinks, performing and hotel rooms," Charles McLaughlin said to his daughter. "Why don't you just get away from all of us for a while? Really get away.

Clear your head. Enjoy life. See the world a little bit. You'll be away from skating, away from Red, away from us. Clear your head and then decide what you want to do with your life."

Andra reluctantly agreed, and a 14-month trip was planned to Europe and Africa.

"I gave the ring to my father to send back to Red," recalled Andra. "I said to my father, 'I've been terrible to Red, because every time we decide to get married, we're pulled here and there.' My father always knew that I was in love with Red, that I really loved him."

Red got the message that the ring would be returned. "I waited, but it never came back," he recalled.

With a heavy heart, Andra left on the whirlwind tour overseas while Red slowly got on with the rest of his life.

As his 31st birthday approached in early July, he saw that the Red Wings' future did not seem as bright as it had once been. He needed a backup plan, and the farm was . . . well, just not what he had in mind. Though he loved the hard work, the wide-open spaces and being around his family, he was starting to think outside that box. He bought himself a summer cottage.

"My cottage was up at Cedar Island, just south of Windsor," recalled Red. "It had a big beach. I bought it near a friend of mine, Bill Pew, who had come from Port Dover. He had a big tool company in Detroit. He got me to buy the big cottage next to him because he wanted a good neighbour."

Then Red started to explore using his fame more. "I took a summer position as a representative for Re-Nu Tools, a Detroit company that re-salvaged tools for the automobile industry," he said. "I would visit GM, Chevrolet, and of course all they wanted to do was talk hockey."

Red also participated in a sports tour throughout western and northern Michigan for the Stroh Brewery. It was a paid trip for a couple of weeks. "We would go to banquets, get into games, tug-of-war in the mining districts," recalled Red. "We had some good workouts. There would be a whole bunch of guys on that rope and you're on the ground!"

Next, he started building a bowling alley just outside of Simcoe. "We had always gone bowling in Detroit, a ten-pin league," Red recalled. "I thought they could use a good bowling alley in Simcoe, and so I built one. We had drapes and we could change from five-pin to ten-pin bowling in six of the twelve lanes.

"My big concern when it started was to have someone running it that I could trust. I knew I could trust my brother, Joe, and brother-in-law Mike Monague. It was new to them, but they were real people. They would share in the operation three days a week. They were both farmers, and in the winter bowling was quite popular and they had time to run it and earn extra money. It ran summer and winter.

"My mother used to bake pies, great pies, and we sold them at the bowling alley. So, it was a family thing."

It was evident that Red was doing a lot to get his mind off Andra. He went to North Dakota to work for two weeks at a hockey school and also fit in time to help on the farm. When he got the chance, he went dancing in Port Dover, which he still loved to do. He met a local girl.

"She was a nice girl, a local doctor's daughter," recalled Red. "I thought she might be the one, so I asked her to marry me. She accepted, but as soon as I had left her, I'm driving home and I felt sick, awful, because I realized I wasn't in love with her. I called her right away and I told her I wasn't in love with her, that I couldn't marry her. It had nothing to do with her, that it wasn't her fault; that she was a wonderful girl and everything, but it was just me. She broke down and cried. Better I tell her immediately than end up being split later on."

For the first time in a long time, the Red Wings had their training camp at the Olympia. Prior to the season, coach Sid Abel told Jim Proudfoot of the *Toronto Star* that he was trying to figure out whom to play with Gordie Howe to increase his production. And he took a shot at his best defenceman. "I look for our defence to be much better," he said on October 11. "Red Kelly can't have another year as bad as he did last season."

The criticism harkened to a few incidents in the previous season. "In one game, I had been on the ice for a long shift and came off and was no sooner sitting when Skinner yelled for me to get back out there," Red recalled. "I said, 'Give me a second.' I was going to take my time to get back out there, to catch my breath. What does he do? He didn't wait but threw out a young rookie, and we got scored on. After the game, when Adams questioned him on the move, he blamed me for not going back out there. I had just said, 'Give me a second.'

"At another game, my two uncles were attending: Father Leo Kelly from Wallaceburg and my uncle Bill Kelly. They sat in Jack Adams's box, right behind the visitor's bench. After the game, I saw my uncles in the parking lot. They were visibly upset. My uncles said, 'They were really on you, criticizing you. Mrs. Adams was yelling at you for this and that. It was all we could do to stay there.' I couldn't hear her on the ice. You don't hear the crowd, but you just know that if she's on you there, then who knows what is being said at home? Adams was blind, often accusing players of not being in front of the net or whatever when in fact they weren't even on the ice. I thanked them, but there was nothing I could do. I could only go out and play the best I could. But my uncles had to tell me about Mrs. Adams. It really bothered them."

Through the first part of that 1958–59 season, the Red Wings, now with Howe as their captain, played slightly less than .500 hockey. On January 14, the team had gone six games without a victory when Red was hurt during a practice at the Olympia. "I was at the blue line, away from the play, when a puck was shot towards me," Red recalled. "I wasn't expecting the shot at all. It was a fluke thing. The puck hit me just under the ankle bone on the outside of my left ankle. Oh, it hurt! I went down and knew right away that something was not good."

X-rays revealed a fracture. He was placed in a plaster cast that went up to his left knee and given a set of crutches. He was possibly done for the rest of the season. The injury was kept quiet. With Red out of the lineup for what was officially described as a "bone bruise," the Red Wings lost their next three games, sinking their record to 16 wins, 21 losses and six ties.

As the team prepared for a January 21 contest in Chicago, Adams asked Red if he could possibly play the next game. He was banking on Red's loyalty to the team. "The team doctor said playing on it wouldn't do any permanent damage, if I could stand the pain," Red recalled.

Before the Wings headed to the Windy City, Red's cast was removed by the team doctor. The ankle was taped tightly from the instep up to the knee prior to the start of the game. He could stand little pressure on the left leg and had real difficulty turning to the opposite side, or pushing off with that foot, but he suited up.

"The first game I go in against Chicago and now I've got Bobby Hull coming down against me," Red recalled. "Strong as a bull, fast, hardest shot in hockey. Bobby Hull! Holy, man! I can't take a chance on him going to my left, because that's the direction I can't turn — towards the boards. So I have to play closer to the boards and leave a big hole in the middle of the ice, so that when he comes down, I'm able to turn and go with him. I didn't have a very good night against him."

The Wings snapped their three-game losing skid with a 3–2 win. Again with Red in the lineup, they beat the same Hawks back at Olympia by a 2–0 score on January 29. Red's return was heralded in the press as the reason for the Detroit wins.

"The days of Leonard Red Kelly's greatest glory are behind him but the highest scoring defenceman in National Hockey League history is one of the reasons the Detroit Red Wings expect to make the playoffs," wrote Lewis Walter. "It was more than a coincidence that the Wings about-face at Chicago came as Kelly returned from a three-game absence. Still playing with a painful bone bruise Kelly has steadied the Detroit defence."

"They would tape me up before every game," Red recalled. "Whenever they took the tape off after a game, it would start to bleed. It became quite raw. Eventually the doctor had to devise a new type of binding that just covered the ankle. I played, but I couldn't turn to that side at all. If I was into a shoving match along the boards, I always had to give way. There was no doubt that my effectiveness was compromised, and I even started getting more penalties, too, because I had to use my stick more to catch and hook guys up because of the ankle."

Dutifully, Red played the rest of the remaining 36 games in the season on a broken ankle and never publicly complained. Even when Abel fined each Red Wings player $100 for "indifferent play," Red didn't object.

"Our trouble is that our veterans aren't producing," lamented Abel. "Our stars are letting us down." With Howe and Sawchuk both having banner years, the press assumed Abel was pointing at Kelly. Management never disclosed his ailment as Detroit missed the playoffs for the first time in 21 seasons, finishing dead last.

"The summer after I broke my foot, I worked in Detroit and I had seen in the paper where I was criticized, but I didn't pay attention to them," he recalled. "What are you going to do? They reported in the Detroit papers that I had a bad year; I was slowing down; I was finished. I'm thinking, 'Well, the brass knows what's happened. What the hang? Why aren't they telling the reporters what really happened to me?' Adams planted some of those stories. Nobody ever defended me, or mentioned my playing with a broken foot. Sometimes it was hard to take."

There was a positive change in the offing, though.

In New York, Andra McLaughlin had just returned from her trip across Africa and Europe. Arriving at her father's office, she had the determined look he knew so well.

"Well, is it still Red Kelly that you're in love with?" he asked his daughter.

"Yes," she answered. "But he's probably engaged or married to somebody else by now."

"How do you know?"

"Well, how do you know he isn't?"

"Go over there and open that drawer," he directed her. She opened the drawer and got the shock of her life: Red's engagement ring was still in its box, ready to be sent back to him. Her father hadn't returned it.

She was still uncertain. "So what?" she said. "He could have bought somebody else a ring by now!"

Her father smiled. He knew. He always knew. The next move was hers to make. She nervously called Red.

"Hello, Red? This is Andra."

"I know," he answered.

"Red . . . is it too late?"

"Too late for what?" he asked, toying with her.

"To get married. Does the offer still stand, or is it too late?"

"No, it's not too late," he replied, smiling for the first time in a long time. "How soon can you get here?"

"I'll fly up tonight!"

"Great! I'll meet you at the airport!"

When she got off the phone, she was all tears and smiles as her father hugged her.

"Don't tell your mother about this, but go ahead. If it comes out, I'll deny knowing anything!" He was truly happy for her.

"When she flew in that night, I hid behind a pillar in the terminal," Red recalled. "Andra comes up the runway into the terminal and she stops and is looking around and there's nobody there. I thought, *Well, I'll just give her a little taste of her own medicine,* you know, after everything I had been through. Then I stepped out, and . . . well, everything went well."

The reunion was blissful.

"Red had everything arranged in that short period of time,"

Andra recalled. "We were getting married that Saturday, four days later, on the Fourth of July."

"When we got the marriage licence on the Friday, it was the eve of a busy holiday weekend," recalled Red. "They stayed open later so we could get it. We left from there to go to get Andra's dress on West Grand Boulevard in Detroit. It was past closing time, but there was the saleslady out on the street, holding her dress and shoes!"

"She was a hockey fan," said Andra, "and she never told anybody until after we were married, so that the news wouldn't get out. My father knew [about the engagement], but [my parents] truly didn't know about the wedding until after, when they read it in the *New York Times*."

Red personally had a problem — he knew he couldn't get married without telling his family. Andra agreed, so Red called the farm the evening before the wedding.

"Hi Dad, this is Red."

"Yeah."

"I'm calling to tell you that I'm getting married tomorrow!"

"You are? To who?" his father asked, with that sardonic Kelly wit.

"To Andra!"

"Oh, is that a fact? Well, I guess we'll have to change our plans tomorrow then!"

His parents hastily packed up the car and drove through the night to get to Detroit for the 9 a.m. wedding at St. Brigid Roman Catholic Church.

"The priest, a Father Moran who was a friend of Red's, was really wonderful," Andra recalled. "The church had been decorated for another wedding at 10 o'clock. So we got married much earlier than that, and at the end of the ceremony we had to practically race out of the church!"

Jack Adams filled in for Andra's father and walked her down the aisle to give her away. Budd Lynch was Red's best man, and Budd's wife, Fran, was the maid of honour. Red owed the broadcaster a lot.

"Budd Lynch handled everything," Red recalled. "He arranged the whole darn thing, did it in three days! In those days, you had to have public banns read in a church three times before the wedding could occur. Somehow that happened in three different parishes, and we were able to get married."

Right after the wedding, the couple scooted away for a quick visit to see Andra's aunt, Sister Cora McLaughlin, who was a nun at the Sacred Heart Convent in nearby Bloomfield Hills, north of Detroit. All the nuns were happily waiting to see and congratulate them, and Andra placed her wedding bouquet on the chapel's altar as a blessing of their marriage.

"Then we went to the reception at the Western Golf and Country Club," continued Red. "We had a big brunch out there, a wedding cake and all, but none of it would have happened if it hadn't been for Budd."

There had been no time to arrange for a proper honeymoon, so the happy couple whisked up Woodward Avenue to the home of their friend Morton Nells, who was away for the Fourth of July weekend and had offered his empty house for their first couple of nights together. "Red also had a cottage nearby, which I didn't know at the time," Andra remembered. "But we couldn't go there because he had it rented out to a group of nurses."

For Andra, the joy of finally marrying the love of her life was tinged with sadness because not only had her parents missed the most important day in her life, but her mother was deeply hurt by the circumstances of her daughter's wedding. "My mother saw the story in the paper, and she was shocked," Andra recalled. "That was pretty tough. She was so angry she didn't want anything to do with us. It hurt me that I had hurt her. I loved her and I didn't want to hurt her, but I loved Red! My mother turned her back on us. I missed her terribly."

Later, Red and Andra travelled to the hockey clinics where Red was an instructor in Grand Forks, North Dakota; Moose Jaw,

Saskatchewan; and St. Thomas, Ontario. He was learning the mechanics of teaching and analyzing the game, which fuelled a hidden passion for coaching. Red also worked on his slowly healing ankle.

"We also spent a lot of time at Red's cottage that summer, which had a great sandy beach in front of it," Andra recalled. "Red would run barefoot on the beach to strengthen the ankle, and he also rolled his foot on a tennis ball quite a bit as well. I had told Red that Sonja Henie had broken her foot once and had used the same tennis ball technique to strengthen it. He worked really diligently to heal and strengthen that ankle before training camp."

The Kellys headed to Detroit and rented a small house from a couple that had moved to England for two years. The city was already familiar to Andra because she had skated there quite a few times, so she settled in nicely. She began to teach young figure skaters, including a blind student.

After opening the season with a tie, the Red Wings won five in a row. Things were looking up, and Red's ankle was feeling much better with each game. He was back to his old self — almost. The Wings won only 4 of their next 12 games, and the grumbles around the dressing room started. Then, in a November 18 game at Maple Leaf Gardens in Toronto, Red got into a fierce altercation with Gerry Ehman, eventually swinging his stick at him.

"Ehman took a two-handed cut at my sore ankle," Red told the press. "Hang it all! That's my livelihood! I respect the other guy's right to work. I expect him to respect mine. You must have noticed, though, I didn't even come close to hitting him."

On the home front, after spending their first Christmas together as husband and wife, Andra's alienation from her parents continued; she had never known a Christmas season without them. "They were a tough few months," Andra recalled. "But then after Christmas I discovered that I was pregnant. Red knew how sad I was and approached my mother and told her we were expecting and said, 'We need you. Andra needs you!' Well, my mother was there in a shot! That changed everything — her first grandchild. I was so happy to have her and my father back in my life, in our life."

Halfway through the season, Toronto reporter Trent Frayne approached Red to do a piece for the *Toronto Star Weekly* magazine about the resurgent Red Wings' improved play in general and his play in particular. Frayne came up to Red's room at the Royal York.

"Your team's going better this year and you're playing a little better. How come?" Frayne asked.

"Well thanks. I'm glad to hear that," Red answered hesitatingly, with a little chuckle. "The team's just playing better that's all." He knew that one had to be careful what one said to the press. A bad or ill-timed comment could come back to bite you.

"Aw, come on. There's more to it than that," Frayne pressed, sensing immediately that Red was holding something back. He leaned closer. "All the reports coming out of Detroit; they said your legs were gone — that you were over the hill . . ."

Frayne purposely threw the comment at him and watched him closely for a reaction. He knew that Red was a proud man. Red attempted to hold back a smirk and didn't answer right away, thinking, unsure. Frayne sensed he was onto something and waited. Red looked at him pensively.

"Well, maybe it had something to do with my ankle . . ."

Frayne's ears perked up.

"Your ankle?"

"Yeah, well, it was . . . broken."

"Broken?"

"Yeah, last January, in practice. The club announced that I had a sprain. I guess they didn't want other teams to know it was broken and maybe start taking whacks at it. I didn't figure it was up to me to say anything, although I must admit now that I was surprised when I got fined the $100."

"Let me get this straight . . . you played the last half of the season on a broken ankle?"

Red explained at length about being asked to play on the broken ankle, the ankle and leg painfully taped each game. He talked about how his playing ability was compromised, the constant pain. He was frustrated with the rumours that he was washed up and had lost his confidence, only to have it restored by marrying Andra.

"But now it doesn't matter," he said. "It's over. My ankle isn't broken anymore. So, what's the difference?"

Red discussed his career and life, his recent teaching stints at hockey schools. The two men shook hands, and the interview concluded.

Red and Andra's life was going along nicely — tranquilly, actually — until the morning of February 4, 1960. Frayne's story, in the upcoming *Weekend Magazine*, was leaked to the press days before. When reporters contacted Jack Adams for comment about Red having played with a broken ankle, the Wings GM was caught off guard. "Kelly's ankle was not broken at all," he said. "All our players have in their contracts that when they are hurt, they are the sole judges of when they shall play."

"Kelly Claims Broken Ankle Caused Poor Play Last Year," went the headlines. All the major Canadian papers carried the story. In Detroit, the headline was even wilder: "Was Red Kelly Forced to Play on Broken Foot?"

"I read the Detroit paper that day and thought the headline was more sensational than the story," recalled Red. "So I thought, *Oh well, no big deal.*"

When the phone rang at the Kelly household that morning, Andra answered it. It was Ted Lindsay's wife, Pat, calling from Detroit.

"Andra, are your bags packed?" Pat Lindsay asked.

"Are our bags packed? What do you mean?"

"Well, Red's going to be traded real soon! Like maybe today!"

"What!" Andra exclaimed. "I can't believe it!"

She was quite shook up as she and Red headed to the game against the Rangers that night. Red told her to forget all about it.

"There was whispering going on all through the Olympia," recalled Andra. "I was about four months pregnant at that time, and my obstetrician, Dr. Jack Ronayne, saw me and he came down to where I was sitting and said, 'Andra, I want to talk to you outside.' I didn't want to miss Red playing, but I went, and he told me, 'Red's been traded to New York.'

"He wanted to brace me for the shock, I guess, with my condition. So I had to go back and watch Red play the rest of the night, knowing that he wasn't going to be there anymore. I felt just awful."

The Rangers won 4–1, and afterwards Red was informed that Adams wanted to see him in his office.

"I showered, got dressed and as I'm going down that long corridor along the side of Olympia Stadium, all the way to the front of the building to where the offices are, I can hear some people saying, 'You're gone, Kelly! You're gone,'" Red recalled. "I didn't mind them. So I went up the stairs to Adams's office."

Adams was behind his desk, and Bruce Norris was standing beside him.

"Kelly," Adams started, using Red's last name for the first time in 13 years. "We've traded you to New York."

"Oh, is that a fact? Well, I'll think about it."

"Think about it? Think about it? What do you mean, you'll think about it?" Adams yelled at him, his plump face turning red as he shoved his finger near Red's face. "You be there at eight thirty tomorrow morning to meet Muzz Patrick at the Leland Hotel! What do you mean, you'll think about it?"

"Just what I said, I'll think about it!" Red said defiantly, turning and walking out of the office, slamming the door behind him.

Once home, he and Andra were devastated. He was seething. To think of everything he had given to the Red Wings organization — missing only 24 games in 13 years; playing almost half a season on a broken ankle; giving it his all, every night; ignoring the fact that management didn't defend him when the whispers started about his being washed up, over the hill, when they knew he was injured; playing forward and losing a First All-Star Team berth because of it; everything he had given to them, and this was how he was rewarded. And, to boot, he was being traded to a last-place club, and thus his play would not lift the Rangers enough to pose a threat against the Red Wings. The whole thing stunk!

"When we got home, we put the TV on, and there was Budd Lynch announcing my trade with tears in his eyes. Then of course Andra broke down," Red recalled. "We talked about it all night long. I thought about it and thought about it, hardly slept. Andra and I went to church the next morning; [then] we made up our mind about what I was going to do."

He decided to call Muzz Patrick at the Leland Hotel. "I'm sorry, Mr. Patrick, but I'm not going to New York," Red told him. "I'm retiring. It has nothing to do with you and nothing to do with the Rangers. I've thought about it and thought about it, and I'm retiring. I'm sorry for the bad news and to be causing you this confusion."

The trade was supposed to be Kelly and centre Billy McNeill in exchange for defenceman Bill Gadsby and forward Eddie Shack. McNeill called Adams to tell him he was also retiring; widowed only a few months previously, he planned to move west with his two-year-old daughter. The deal was dead.

"I'm very disappointed and hurt," Red told the media. "Everything I ever did or tried to do in hockey was for the Red Wings. I don't think I could put my heart and soul into playing for another club. I shouldn't say I'm completely stunned, because it was always in the back of my mind that this could happen to me. It had happened to others — Ted Lindsay for example. So, while I was hurt when it happened, and still am, I was always kind of prepared."

A few days later, Clarence Campbell called. "Red, think this through. If you don't report to New York, you'll be blacklisted," the NHL president warned him. "You'll never be able to play hockey again. You'll never be able to referee. You'll never be able to coach.

You'll never be able to be a stick boy. You'll be right out of hockey, and you'll be out forever! Adams wants to suspend you, but I want you to think about this. I'm trying to hold him off."

Red didn't hesitate in answering. "Well, that's fine Mr. Campbell. Thank you very much for your offer. I've given everything I have to hockey since I've been knee-high to a grasshopper. If that's what you want to do, you go ahead and do it. I've thought about it long and hard. I'm not reporting to New York. That's final."

With the click of a phone handle, one of the most storied hockey careers in the history of the NHL was over.

......

CHAPTER TEN

TORONTO
METAMORPHOSIS

Retirement is supposed to be stress free, but it was not for Red Kelly. The press hounded him for his version of the story, and he obliged. He had nothing to lose.

"My feelings were hurt," Red said. "I hope I'm not out of hockey completely. I'd be interested in coaching, and I've been talking to some people about it. A fellow has to retire sometime, and now looks like a good time to me."

Was he traded as a result of the *Weekend Magazine* story? "I'd say it didn't help matters, but the way the Detroit papers handled it seemed to change it around and make it worse," Red said.

With a media frenzy over players refusing to accept a trade, NHL president Clarence Campbell had no choice but to jump into the fray. It was a first for everyone. "My concern is for the welfare of the players," Campbell told the media. "This is a big decision and it must be given very thorough consideration. There is nothing urgent that it must be done now. I am giving both players a chance to get over the initial disappointment. The league will take no action until Saturday."

On Saturday, the NHL Board of Governors was meeting in Florida and the Kelly situation was front and centre, which created a confusing situation. Was Kelly suspended by Adams or not? Red had supposedly been placed on waivers, which gave him five days to decide if he really wanted to retire or not. It was felt that no deal could be made with Kelly while he was on waivers, so the governors voted to waive the "period of grace." It was reported that Red had been directed by Campbell to call Adams and accept an expected deal to Toronto.

"I never called Adams," Red recalled. "I was never ordered back to Detroit. Those things never happened. I don't know where the press got that one, but I never called or spoke to Jack Adams ever again."

It was a hectic weekend for Red and Andra. "On Sunday, I called Sam at Re-Nu Tool Company, where I worked during the summer, to see if I could start work tomorrow, Monday morning, full-time. He said to come in the next day, so I had that taken care of."

Red didn't know that Re-Nu had received over 45 calls from customers who wanted him to contact them. He also wasn't aware that Toronto coach and GM Punch Imlach and his assistant, King Clancy, had been talking about the Kelly situation as they flew into Boston for a Sunday game. Imlach said years later that his one aim had been to build a team to beat the Canadiens; to do that, he needed someone to handle their big centre, Jean Béliveau. "I knew Kelly could help us," Imlach wrote. "I knew how well he skated, checked, made plays. I figured he could play centre and that he was the one guy I could put out against Béliveau."

Clancy called and got the okay from a surly Adams to talk with Red, but Adams said he didn't have Red's phone number, which they found odd. They spent the rest of the day tracking Red's number down through Joe Primeau, who got it through a priest at St. Michael's who kept in regular touch with Red.

The next day, a Monday, Red went to work at Re-Nu Tools while Andra taught figure skating. When she got home that evening, the phone rang just as she was coming in the door. It was King Clancy. "King asked me if Red would like to come to Toronto to play for the Leafs," she recalled. "I told him to call back and ask him. In my heart I knew he would love to go back home to Canada. When Red arrived home later that night and I told him who had called, I saw his face light up."

Clancy called back to talk to Red. While Red said he was retiring, his fellow Irishman knew how to play the situation.

"Hey, wait a minute!" King urged in his raspy but enthusiastic tone of voice. "Punch wants you on his hockey club!"

The phone line was silent.

"Well, I don't know . . ."

"Look, would you come up to Toronto for a day? We'll pay your transportation and expenses, and I'll meet you at the airport. Then we can pick up Punch, have dinner and talk."

"Well I'm still not sure . . . I'll have to think about it. Call me tomorrow when you get back from Boston."

Red got off the phone and felt more optimistic than he had in a long time. It was almost like he was back in Father Regan's St. Michael's office signing with Shovel Shot Cooper.

"I don't know what King Clancy said to Red when he first telephoned, but he sure rejuvenated him in a hurry," Andra later related to writer Margaret Scott. Red and Andra spent the rest of that night talking things over. On Tuesday morning, he still went to work at Re-Nu Tools.

"After one day at work, Andra mentioned that I didn't have the glint in my eye which I used to have when I would leave to play hockey," he later told writer Milt Dunnell. "The same thing had been going through my mind — that I didn't tackle business with the same enthusiasm I had for hockey. That's when we both began to wonder whether we had made the right decision."

King and Red talked a few more times, and Red agreed to come to Toronto that evening to chat. Though the conversations were supposed to be kept under wraps, writer Red Burnett got wind of the talks and called Red on Tuesday morning for comment. Surprisingly, Red was in the mood to talk.

"This is a big decision for me to make," Burnett quoted him in the Tuesday afternoon edition of the *Toronto Star*.

> It means pulling up stakes after 13 years in Detroit and perhaps turning my back on an excellent business opportunity. I may fly to Toronto to talk with King and Imlach. Mr. Campbell advised me to take my time and I mean to do just that. Leafs would like me to play against Canadiens Wednesday night. I feel flattered by King's offer but it is not that simple. The way I feel now, it will be the end of the week before I have threshed this thing out to my own satisfaction.
>
> In addition to my problems, my wife has a skating school and her pupils are all upset over the latest developments. Several of them are preparing for competitions and they were in tears for fear of losing her. She informed them she would finish the year with them regardless of my situation. As a kid, I always wanted to be a Maple Leaf but that was before I became a Red Wing.

"Kelly is just like me," Imlach told Burnett. "He likes to sleep on important matters instead of jumping to conclusions. I want him to be sure he wants to continue in hockey as a Maple Leaf before he gives us an answer."

For his trip into Toronto, Red had told Andra, "Oh, I'll just go talk to them. I'll be back tonight." She knew better.

"I knew he would be playing for them even though he hadn't played in almost a week," she recalled. "I thought, *You're not going to be coming back tonight! You're going to be there!* So, without him knowing, I packed his bag so tight, squeezing in everything I could."

Late on Tuesday afternoon, Red flew in to meet with Clancy and Imlach. "I made reservations to fly out of Windsor," recalled Red. "I used a different name, P. Kelly, so nobody would know I was going to Toronto. I wore a homburg hat, carried a bumbershoot umbrella and wore a white shirt and silk tie. I was in disguise. Clancy met me at Malton Airport around 6 p.m., though he didn't recognize me at first. I walked around his back and tapped him on the shoulder. He was still looking out the window. He jumped a little and said, 'Whoa! For a moment there, I thought you weren't coming!' Then he took me down to the Westbury Hotel and checked me into a room that was usually reserved for their publicity guy, and they registered me as Miss Fay Bainter!"

It was cold, with wet snow, and Clancy took Red over to the Gardens where they entered a back door near the corner of Carlton Street, away from the prying eyes of the press and ticket-purchasers. Upstairs in the executive offices, Imlach was waiting.

"King brought Red up and we sat down and talked," Punch wrote in his book *Hockey Is a Battle*. "He agreed to play for us. We settled the money side of it. Then we phoned Jack Adams and said, 'The deal is made.' 'That's fine' Adams said. 'Send Reaume.' Then he hung up the phone. No good luck to Red, good luck to you, or anything. It was around seven o'clock at night by then. We wired the league's registry, the place where all deals have to be recorded."

"We weren't completely done, but we stopped and went to dinner," Red recalled. "We went to Winston's, a big restaurant downtown, near the *Globe and Mail* newspaper offices. I was in the back seat. We get to this one stop and Clancy suddenly yells, 'Duck!' I said, 'What?' And he yelled again, 'Duck!' So I did, and they said they had waved at the sports editor of the *Globe and Mail* newspaper, Jim Vipond, who was crossing the street in front of us. They didn't want anyone to know. But we get to the restaurant and all the Montreal Canadiens were there eating."

"The Canadiens had come in early for their game against us the next night. Rocket Richard looked up at Kelly and said, 'Hi Red,'" wrote Imlach. "He then looked at King and me, a little surprised. He knew what was up right away. But he wasn't the kind of guy who ran to tell a newspaperman."

"We were going to continue talking, but we couldn't do that very well as the tables were too close, so we went back to the Gardens," recalled Red. "We finished up about midnight, I signed and went to bed."

The next morning, Red called Andra to tell her they were going to Toronto. She wasn't surprised, but she was when the phone rang again; it was King Clancy.

"What can we do for you, honey?" Clancy asked her.

"What can you do for me?" she replied, shocked at his congeniality.

"Yeah," Clancy said. "We want to do something special for you because Red has agreed to play for us here in Toronto. So, what can we do for *you*?"

"Put No. 4 on his back. I'm used to looking at No. 4, and he won four Cups in Detroit."

"Done!"

"Then all hell broke loose," wrote Punch in his book. "The next morning the papers had stories from Miami quoting Clarence Campbell, the league president, as saying we couldn't make a deal for Red or any other player who was under suspension. I said to hell with that! We've already made the deal. Adams had agreed to it, Red had signed, and that was that. Which it was."

"So at the Leafs' players meeting, 11 a.m. Wednesday, Kelly was there," wrote *Globe and Mail* hockey writer Scott Young. Red "exchanged a few words with each player who entered. Shook hands with some. Listened to the cool notes of Mr. Imlach's variations on the old theme of how to stop the Canadiens, donned a Leaf sweater for pictures."

"They wanted me to play that night against the Canadiens," Red recalled. "Problem was, I didn't have any equipment, and, especially, I didn't have my skates."

Red went down to Tommy Naylor's equipment room and picked out some sticks. Clancy had relayed Andra's number request to Imlach, who went to see Naylor.

"We got a No. 4 open?" Imlach asked.

"We do," was the answer. Imlach breathed a sigh of relief. It had been a number made famous by Leafs legends Hap Day and Harry Watson.

Trainer Bob Haggert, trying to figure out how to get Red's skates from Detroit on time for that night's game, called his Red Wings counterpart Lefty Wilson.

"I wanted to see Red's first Toronto game that night, so my boss was a real hockey fan and he said, 'You go!'" Andra recalled. "Lefty Wilson had dropped Red's skates off at the airport that morning. I was flying to Toronto, so I brought his skates with me."

Naylor turned from the receiver to those around him and announced, "They're in the air!" Andra delivered the skates to the Gardens that afternoon.

Ticket demand for the game that night was "of playoff proportion," observed Gardens manager Henry Bolton. The Red Wings reported the same scenario for the Toronto rematch at the Olympia a few nights later.

"I couldn't believe what was happening," Andra recalled. "There seemed to be so much joy in the city to be getting Red Kelly that it made me cry. Red was coming out of his retirement to return to what he loved best in the world, to a team and city that really, really wanted him!"

The scene was set for Red's Maple Leafs debut, and he was "as nervous as the dickens." The crowd of 14,651 gave Red a prolonged standing ovation when he stepped onto the ice in blue and white for the first time, to take the faceoff against Jean Béliveau.

"The hair on the back of my head stood up. It made me feel great," Red recalled. "I was like a violin when you've tightened the strings and then you flick them and, snap! That was me when they dropped the puck."

The Habs spoiled his debut by beating the Leafs 3–2 on two goals by Rocket Richard. Red, playing centre for Frank Mahovlich and Gerry Ehman, confessed that the week-long layoff hadn't helped him.

The Leafs hosted his old team the next Saturday night. As he came onto the ice, he saw Marc Reaume wearing No. 4 for Detroit.

"I was in high gear going in. No question," he recalled. "There was no way I was going to lose. I was going to do anything to win that game. If I had to go through that brick wall, I'd go through that brick wall!" The Leafs broke out in the third period and scored seven goals to paste the Red Wings 7–1. It was one goal short of a record for a team in a single period.

Toronto scribe Jim Proudfoot found proud papa Pete Kelly in the stands. "After twelve-and-a-half years of rooting for the Red Wings, I found it kind of strange," Pete said of cheering for Toronto. "But I sure enjoyed the clobbering we gave Detroit tonight!"

Pete Kelly did not rest easy at the games, said Red. "Andra would sit beside him. It was quite an experience for her, because he'd give her an elbow once in a while. He really followed the game, never said too much, but, boy, he'd make every move I made!"

The Leafs won the return match in Detroit the next afternoon, this time 3–1.

With Red in the lineup, the Leafs won six of their next seven games. The team was humming along, and Red was contributing, scoring the winning goal against Chicago on February 20. He attributed it to a new attitude. "We're a happy team," he told

Proudfoot. "It doesn't matter how much you pay a fellow . . . you take a team like this one where there's excellent feeling all around, we're bound to give more than we even realize we're capable of. Why this outfit even has a good time practicing . . . I'm enjoying myself!"

In New York on February 28, some Rangers fans threw eggs and garbage at Red because he had refused to be traded there. He could understand their feelings. Years later, he recalled, he went to see his daughter skate in an ice show there. "We were going in by the stage door, and the guy there almost wasn't going to let me in. 'You refused to come here, you know!' Yeah, they remembered."

On March 6 in Boston, Red broke a 1–1 tie when he stole the puck at centre ice, passed it to Ehman, took Ehman's return pass and fired a 30-footer past Harry Lumley. He also got an empty-netter to seal the deal and clinch a playoff berth for his second-place Leafs.

It would be Toronto and Detroit in the first round. Prior to Game 1, Imlach had $1,250 in dollar bills stacked in the centre of the dressing room floor. On the blackboard he wrote: "This represents the difference between winning and losing!"

With the series tied at a game apiece, Red scored two second-period goals in Game 3, his 94th career playoff game, and set Mahovlich up for the winner in the third overtime as his Leafs defeated Detroit 5–4.

Reporters in the dressing room attempted to prod him into needling his former team. Red didn't bite. "No, there's no extra pleasure scoring against my former teammates," he said. "The only pleasure I get is scoring goals. I'm happy where I am now. That's all I have to say. If someone else wants to start a controversy, that's okay with me. I'll let my playing do my talking for me."

Detroit took Game 4, but in the following game at the Gardens on Saturday night, the Leafs poured it on, winning 4–2, to take the series lead. Red poured it on, too, notching a goal and two assists. Attending the game that night was the Canadian Liberal leader, Lester B. Pearson, who wrote a piece for the *Toronto Star*. "For the

Leafs, I thought that — from a team in which everyone gave everything he had," Pearson wrote, "Red Kelly and Mahovlich stood out. Kelly has certainly shown that you can gain by free trading." Pearson would directly affect Red's life in years to come.

The next afternoon, the Maple Leafs beat Detroit 5–4 to head into the finals against the Canadiens.

"There was no way Detroit was ever going to beat us," recalled Red, who ended up with three goals and six assists in the series. "It was great to win and go on. I had nothing against the players in Detroit. A lot of them were my teammates for many years. I had no bad feelings against them, but I certainly had some feelings against the management there."

The Canadiens were heavily favoured to win the Stanley Cup Final — though Habs boss Frank Selke said Toronto had made many improvements, specifically the addition of Kelly. "Kelly is an intelligent player. He is the type of player whose work improves that of his mates," said Selke.

The Canadiens took the first two games at the Forum, 4–2 and 2–1.

"I'll tell you something," said Imlach after Game 2. "We'll win the next two at home if that's the best the Canadiens can play!"

It was not to be. Montreal won their fifth straight Stanley Cup on 5–2 and 4–0 victories. Red did not score in the series but got three assists.

In the Leafs dressing room after the loss, Imlach was understandably grumpy. "I'm not satisfied with that try," he said. "What we did just wasn't good enough. Obviously, we have to be stronger. I've got from now until next September to make the changes I decide are necessary."

As Red left Maple Leaf Gardens that night with Andra, he felt the weight of the slogan that was inscribed on the wall in the dressing room: Defeat Does Not Rest Lightly on Their Shoulders.

He had come through the most tumultuous period in his life: he had played half a season on a broken ankle; got married; been traded to a new team and permanently moved from defence to forward. It had been a whirlwind of controversy and confusion, and he had not only survived it all but had thrived in his new environment.

He looked forward to a quieter summer with Andra. But change was coming in their life together: they were expecting their first-born.

CHAPTER ELEVEN

CASEY, STANLEY
and MIKE

Keenly aware that parenthood was just a labour pain away, Red decided to join a foursome for a quick round of golf at the Kingsville Golf and Country Club, only 10 minutes from the cottage, on Labour Day weekend.

"I was in the middle of the absolute best golf game I had ever played," Red recalled. "Everything was going perfect, I was hot ... then the yell came from the clubhouse — Andra was having labour pains. Holy, man! I dropped the clubs right then, right out of my hands, and rushed to the car and sped back to the cottage!"

"Red came right away and loaded me and my carry bags into the car," Andra recalled. "We raced towards the Ambassador Bridge, and when we got to customs Red was frantic."

"Quick, quick, let us through! Let us through!" Red yelled excitedly to the border guard. "She's going to have a baby!" They were waved through quickly.

"I had to get Andra over to New Grace Hospital in Detroit," Red remembered. "It was about an hour away. I didn't know how close her delivery had progressed. I thought the baby might be coming right there and then. Little did I know that sometimes these things take time."

It was a long labour, a situation Andra attributed to being fit and athletic. Dr. Jack Ronayne kept a careful eye on her. "He was the obstetrician for several of the Red Wings' wives. He had 12 children of his own," Andra recalled. "He was an elderly man but wonderful, with a wonderful family. I had taught some of his children skating, so we knew each other well. That's why I had the baby in Detroit with him. I trusted him."

Two full nights later, on September 5, 1960, Andra Catherine "Casey" Kelly came into the world, weighing seven pounds, two ounces. As avid baseball fans, Red and Andra had given her the unisex nickname even before the birth, a tribute to the famous baseball man, Casey Stengel.

"Andra got through the long ordeal and birth without any problems," Red recalled. "We were very fortunate that everything went all right. Casey and Andra were healthy, and I was ecstatic!"

Casey allowed Andra to reconnect with her parents.

"The birth of Casey was a joyous time," recalled Andra. "It was the first grandchild in my family, my parents' very first. Casey was named after my mother, Andra Catherine, so that was nice too. They drove up from the farm in Connecticut after Casey was born. My mother was just so happy to see Casey and us. It was a very emotional reunion, for sure."

Things became even more hectic a few days later, when Red left the cottage for the Maple Leafs training camp in Peterborough, Ontario. "It was a race to see whether I got to camp or not," Red joked to *Toronto Star* reporter Gordon Campbell. He wasn't there very long before Punch Imlach had him in for the annual contract negotiation. They quickly came to an amicable agreement.

"He is a big guy, and it's great to have him signed," Imlach said of Red's inking. "We may have trouble with a lot of lesser guys."

Imlach eventually got everybody signed, and the Leafs started the season with only three losses in their first 14 games. A big part of their success was that Kelly and Mahovlich started where they had left off the previous season. While "the Big M" was being feted for his scoring achievements — he had scored four goals against the Rangers on November 5, bringing his season total to 11 — *Toronto Star* sports writer Milt Dunnell sought out the person he felt was responsible for Mahovlich's prolific production. "Red Kelly isn't claiming the credit as suggested by some," wrote Dunnell. "All the redhead knows is that when Mahovlich cranks up in his own end of the rink, and throws in the clutch, it's time for Kelly to take off for the far net."

"I block out a man or two to sort of clear the way for Frank," Kelly told Dunnell. "Then I drop into a hole and wait for the puck to come out. If he can't get through, the chances are I may get a shot. I don't think Frank is much faster than he always has been but he didn't always take off as frequently as he does now."

For Red, starting the season with the Leafs was an absolute pleasure. "It was like a new life," he recalled. "I thought I was out of hockey, and it ended up that I wasn't. It was like pulling on a light switch, from darkness to light."

Andra, Red and Casey moved into a small two-story house in Leaside, northeast of downtown Toronto. They had decided to rent for this season, until they could scout out a nicer, more permanent home to purchase. The area was an instant fit, and the proximity to the local Leaside Arena allowed Andra to resume teaching skating.

"Dr. Sidney Soanes, a respected person in figure skating circles, lived in Toronto," Andra recalled. "I remembered him and my mother corresponding for many years. I gave him a call, saying I was moving up the street from him. He got me a job right away."

Despite the Leafs' early success, Imlach was not satisfied with the team's production and moved young right winger Bob Nevin onto Kelly and Mahovlich's line. "We fit together like a glove," Red recalled. "Nevin was a great player on the right wing, and we just

THE RED KELLY STORY

worked together. The three of us just clicked as a line. I knew where
Frank would be, and if I could get the puck to him, I knew the puck
would be in the net. The same with Bob."

In early December, Imlach was asked to rate NHL players. "I used
to think that Jean Béliveau was the greatest," Imlach told Red Burnett:

> But Kelly has convinced me with his work since joining
> Leafs. I have the evidence to back my opinion that Kelly
> is the most valuable player in this league and should be
> the leading candidate for the Hart Trophy. He has played
> centre, defence and left wing like an all-star. Howe is a
> great forward but he can't play defence. Doug Harvey is a
> great defenceman but he couldn't play forward. He [Red]
> rates as top contender for the Lady Byng as well.
>   "He has amazed us with his all-around ability. I
> never realized what a complete performer he was. Kelly
> does everything well both on attack and on defence. He has
> been a major factor in the success of our club from the day

*he joined us and besides his abundance of natural ability
and competitive fire, he is a great team man. When we got
Kelly from the Red Wings was the luckiest day of my life
and hockey's best deal.*

Though the Leafs started December with a humiliating 6–3 loss
in Montreal, they went on a tear, winning 14 of the 20 subsequent
games against only four losses, which vaulted them to second place.

By January 26, Red was seventh in league scoring with 48 points
and had accumulated a mere 10 minutes in penalties. The Big M was
in third place with 56 points, only six back of league-leader Boom
Boom Geoffrion of Montreal. When Red finished January with
a flourish, getting three goals and four assists in four games, the
Hockey News selected him as player of the week. In a 6–3 home win
against Boston on February 11, Red moved into the Maple Leafs
record book when his 44th assist surpassed the team record set by
Teeder Kennedy 10 years earlier.

But Toronto was much more than Red and his linemates. Imlach
had assembled quite an array of hockey talent that was just blos-
soming. In goal was Johnny Bower, protected by defencemen Tim
Horton, Carl Brewer, Allan Stanley, Bob Baun and Kent Douglas.
Up front, besides Red, Mahovlich and Nevin, were captain George
Armstrong, Dave Keon, Bob Pulford, Dick Duff, Billy Harris, Ron
Stewart, Eddie Litzenberger and Eddie Shack. They would be a
force to be reckoned with.

By March 4, the Leafs had pulled ahead of the Canadiens and
were in first place. That night, against the Rangers, Red garnered an
amazing 50th assist. But then, in the final minutes, he tore a groin
muscle. He went to hospital, where doctors confirmed the muscle
tear and prescribed rest with daily treatments. They were hoping he
could return in a week, but there was really no rushing a groin tear.
The best treatment was rest and time.

With the Habs breathing down the Leafs' necks and only six

games left in the season, the absence of Kelly had Imlach in a tizzy about his team's chances of finishing first. "I think first place will be decided on either the 69th or 70th game," he predicted, "and we always win the squeakers."

Red Burnett noted a key missing figure. "The length of Red Kelly's absence due to a groin injury may have a large bearing on the race and also presents a problem for Imlach," wrote Burnett. "He can rush Kelly back in an effort to clinch first place and risk having him on the limp for the playoffs or keep him out at the risk of losing first place in order to ensure a healthy Kelly for the Stanley Cup battles."

Red's injury was very slow to heal, and during his absence the Leafs sputtered, losing first place to the Canadiens and winning only twice in their final six games. Mahovlich's goal-scoring stalled at 48, two shy of the magic 50. Red found it very frustrating to watch. "I remember going down to the dressing room to talk to Frank," he recalled. "He was so close to 50, and I thought if I could only encourage him. I went down and told him, 'Frank you never know . . . you may never get another chance to get 50. Get out there and get it! You can do it!' I tried to pump him up, but . . ."

With the Leafs in freefall, Red was desperately needed back on the team. On Sunday, March 12, with the team away in Boston, he went for a light skate. For an hour he took it easy, skating around gently, testing out the injury.

"After a while, I decided to push it a little bit more and give it a stronger go around, a little harder, to see how it would respond, but as soon as I cranked it up, the muscle gave out on me," Red recalled. "I fell on the ice, and the Gardens maintenance staff came out to help get me off the ice. I had hurt it again. I had tried too fast. The playoffs were coming and I wanted to be there."

With Red out of the lineup, the Leafs met the fourth-place Red Wings in the semifinal. Toronto won the opener but dropped their next two. The pressure was on for Red to return — and he did for Game 4, another loss.

"I hated to lose, but there was not much I could do," Red recalled. "That groin was still affecting me. My stride was only two-thirds of what it should have been. My play was compromised, no question. I couldn't give that extra push."

Detroit eliminated the Leafs, winning the series in five games. In the Stanley Cup Final, the Wings were outclassed by a young, powerful Black Hawks squad that won Chicago's first Stanley Cup in 23 years.

In a year-end interview, Canadiens top man Frank Selke had a chat with the *Detroit News*. He discussed a variety of topics, but when he was asked which player had had the best season in the league, he was quick and unequivocal in his answer: "Red Kelly, until he was hurt late in the year. He made a scoring star out of Frank Mahovlich. If Kelly hadn't been hurt, Mahovlich would have scored 60 goals. But when Red wasn't there to pass to him, he became just an average hockey player."

There was no denying Red's influence on the Big M's play. The year before Red's arrival, Mahovlich had registered only 39 points, but with Red as his centreman, his points more than doubled to 84, with 48 goals and 36 assists, good for second in league scoring.

If there were any balm to soothe Red's playoff disappointment and still-tender thigh, it came in the form of winning his fourth Lady Byng Trophy.

A month later, he was advised of a special award via a letter dated June 28, 1961:

Dear Red,

As President of Maple Leaf Gardens, I congratulate you on winning the J.P. Bickell Memorial Trophy . . . I can't tell you how happy we are to have you on our club. This award is named after a past Maple Leaf president and one of the finest citizens we have ever had in Canada. It is

*nice to know that it has been won by someone very worthy
of the honour.*

*Sincerely yours,
Conn Smythe*

The J.P. Bickell Memorial Cup was not an annual award; it was presented only when the Maple Leaf Gardens directors believed a player deserved the special recognition.

The first order of domestic business for Red and Andra was to find a more permanent home. "We purchased a lovely house on Airdrie Road in Leaside and we moved there," recalled Andra. "Quite a few hockey players lived in the area. I was so excited; we had bought our first house."

Another person had come into their lives that would have a very direct influence on Red and Andra's future — Keith Davey. "When I first came to Toronto in the winter of 1960, I was staying at the Westbury Hotel," Red recalled. "Keith Davey worked at Foster Hewitt's radio station, CKFH, which was right across the road, and he used to come into the restaurant for breakfast and would see me there. He was a big hockey fan, and so he introduced himself to me, and we often ate breakfast together and got to know each other quite well. In 1961, he became the Liberal Party national campaign director. We kept in touch. We often talked politics, the Liberal Party, and about Canada, a subject I felt strongly about."

Red's patriotic interest was so piqued that he accompanied Davey to a few Liberal events, where his presence created a stir. Davey told Red that he would make an excellent Liberal candidate for the federal election in June 1962. But every time Davey broached the subject, Red humbly balked.

The Progressive Conservative Party, under prime minister John Diefenbaker, had run the country for four years, and the Liberals were led by Lester B. Pearson, a Toronto-born statesman who had been a key diplomat on the international scene for years. Pearson had won the Nobel Peace Prize, and many felt the time was right for a new federal government.

Davey kept at Red. "No doubt you are aware of the not inconsiderable press publicity you are receiving as a 'potential' Liberal candidate," wrote Davey to Red on September 27, 1961. "I trust that this publicity neither embarrasses you nor gives you cause for consternation. This is one of the penalties you must pay for being my friend. Everyone in the party, including Mr. Pearson, would be delighted to have you as a candidate. 'Mike' himself has expressed the desire to talk to you about this possibility at your earliest convenience." A meeting with Pearson was arranged for Friday, October 13, in Toronto.

"Keith Davey took me over, and I met Mr. Pearson at a hotel at Bloor Street and Avenue Road," Red recalled. "Lester Pearson, they called him Mike, was very friendly and congenial, and I had great respect for him. I told him honestly that I had been pondering the offer to run, but that I didn't think I could do both effectively — play hockey and be a Member of Parliament. I expected him to really twist my arm, you know, but instead he understood and agreed with me totally. I thought Keith Davey was going to fall off his chair. Pearson's respect for me and my situation had just the opposite effect on me, and the more we talked that day, the more I found myself really entertaining the idea of wanting to run for him and the party. I respected him so much, and the fact that he didn't push me."

The Leafs' 1961–62 season started as it always did, with the 48th Highlanders Pipes and Drums performing on the ice at Maple Leaf Gardens. Former Liberal prime minister Louis St. Laurent came to ice level and presented the J.P. Bickell Memorial Cup to Red, who received a huge round of applause.

Through October and November, Toronto did not lose a single game at home, while on the road they played slightly less than .500 hockey. On November 23, Red scored two goals during the second period and notched another in the third against Glenn Hall in Chicago Stadium to get his second career hat-trick in a 5–2 win.

Andra's skating lessons started to gain traction when she was featured in a story by the *Toronto Star*'s Joe Taylor. As she put a few of her students through their paces at the Leaside Arena, she talked of her joy in teaching and the inspiration of her old coach Edi Scholdan, who had been killed in a plane crash in Prague nine months prior, along with the entire U.S. figure skating team.

"I hope that I would be able to continue with his teaching methods," Andra said of Scholdan's tutoring. "He was able to develop within a person a great joy for skating which is so important. He made it fun, rather than a grind — you couldn't help loving it. I hope I can do the same."

Her priorities were clear when asked about teaching full time. "Red and Casey come first," she said. "The rink is only a couple of blocks from our home, so I can slip home for supper and it requires only three days a week. If I had three or four pupils with the talent and the desire to work — and I think maybe I have — then perhaps I might, but right now the family comes first."

For Red, talk of an approaching milestone started to pop up after he scored goal number 199 on December 9 against Boston. He would have to wait five more games before getting his Christmas Day present in Chicago Stadium, when he scored at 4:39 of the first period to hit the 200-goal milestone. The puck was retrieved from behind Hall as a souvenir of the accomplishment.

Knee, shoulder and leg injuries forced Red to miss a total of 12 games in January, but that didn't stop him from garnering the First All-Star Team centreman slot at the season's halfway point, with Henri Richard, Stan Mikita, Dave Keon and Ralph Backstrom right behind him in the voting. Teammates Brewer and Mahovlich joined him on the First Team, and Bower as the goalie on the Second Team.

In the January edition of *Liberty Magazine*, Red was featured in an article titled "Hockey's Gentle Destroyer." It not only summarized his career but also delved into his home life with Andra and 16-month-old Casey.

"Red's a great reader and . . . can play the piano and sings a fine tenor — songs like 'Peg O' My Heart'," Andra told writer Tom Alderman. "He doesn't like me to mention it. He thinks people will think he's cutting in on Boom Boom Geoffrion's territory."

Red detailed his game day regimen: he awoke at 8:30 a.m. and exercised before having a breakfast of pineapple juice, coffee, toast with honey from a Simcoe farm and a bowl of Corn Flakes. After reading the paper and doing the crossword, he headed to the Gardens for a team meeting, then returned home at 1:30, laden with fan mail — approximately 400 letters a week. "I sign all those who ask for autographs. Why Not? Kelly's a short name. I sympathize with Mahovlich though," Red told Alderman. Red's lunch was a T-bone steak, baked potato and fruit salad, along with more pineapple juice, and was followed by a three-hour nap. Andra's "Hockey Whip" concoction was described: orange juice, a raw egg, three teaspoons of sugar and part of a squeezed lemon.

"Sure I'm a little slower than I used to be," Red told Alderman. "I was at my peak at 28 and 29 — but I'll quit the day I can't keep up with Nevin and Mahovlich!"

The article also described Red as he watched Casey playing in the living room playpen. "I can't understand it," he told the reporter. "Five months ago she could say Mommy and Daddy, but she hasn't picked up a single new word since!"

In early March, the Leafs went on a winning streak, and Red scored his 20th goal for the second time in his career as the Leafs beat the Bruins 5–1 in Boston on March 4.

Amid the Leafs' short winning streak, and after much cajoling, Red finally threw his hat into the political ring on March 14, when he announced he would seek the Liberal nomination in York West.

*Red as a young
Red Wing. He had
developed into a
force of his own and
was widely considered
the best all-around
player in the NHL
and key to the Red
Wings' success.*
© LOUIS JACQUES /
HOCKEY HALL OF FAME

*1952–53 NHL First
Team All-Stars —
Gordie Howe, Elmer
Lach, Doug Harvey,
Terry Sawchuk, Red
and Ted Lindsay.*

Charles and Andra McLaughlin, Andra's parents. Initially reluctant to allow their daughter to give up her successful skating career to marry a Canadian hockey player, they were soon won over by Red's humbleness, sunny disposition and love of their daughter.

Red with coach Jimmy Skinner, Ted Lindsay and Gordie Howe.

(OPPOSITE) *Red as a Red Wings star circa 1957. He was often referred to as the sparkplug of the Red Wings attack.*
© O-PEE-CHEE/HOCKEY
HALL OF FAME

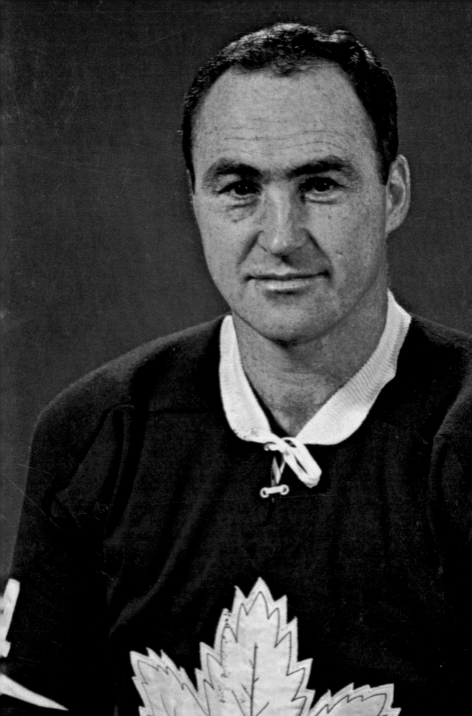

(TOP) *Red scores on Boston goalie Bobby Perrault as Ted Green (6) and Leo Boivin (20) watch helplessly during the 1962–63 season.*
© HOCKEY HALL OF FAME / HAROLD BARKLEY COLLECTION

(RIGHT) *Red and Andra at home in Pittsburgh with their four children: Casey, Patrick, Conn and Kitty.*

(OPPOSITE) *Red as a Maple Leaf on a CHEX cereal box used between 1963 and 1965.*

LOS ANGELES

HOME OF THE KINGS

KINGS
ILLUSTRATED

50¢
INC. TAX

The many moods of Los Angeles coach Red Kelly gracing the cover of one of the Kings programs. The two years coaching the expansion Kings had its own set of challenges.

When he wasn't playing hockey Red spent a great deal of time behind a desk, whether it was as a member of parliament for York West or managing his CAMP aircraft maintenance system company out of Malton Airport. Here he is in his office at the airport.

(TOP) *Andra and Red in their Dunvegan home with his old teammate and Mr. Hockey, Gordie Howe.* (BOTTOM LEFT) *A later photo of Red's parents, Pete and Frances Kelly.* (BOTTOM RIGHT) *Red and Andra Kelly.*

(TOP) *Red and Andra posing in Vancouver when Red was inducted into the Order of Canada by Governor General Adrienne Clarkson in January 2002.* (BOTTOM) *Canada Post Original Six defencemen stamp unveiling on October 2, 2014, with Harry Howell, Pierre Pilote, Red and Bobby Orr.*

His local candidacy would be unopposed within the party and much heralded.

"The Liberals offered me five ridings to run in, to take my pick: York West, York Centre, Parkdale and two others. I looked at them all and I thought York West had been Conservative for most of its existence. It didn't have much of a local team in place, and so I selected it because I thought that if I lost the election, I haven't hurt them any, given a Liberal had not been elected in the riding for quite a while. It was the largest riding population-wise in Canada at the time."

While Red went off to play for the Leafs, his Liberal team, led by Clem Nieman, went to work putting his campaign together, knowing that an election call was imminent. The normally small York West organization grew — excited at the prospect of having a star candidate, new members came out of the woodwork.

Back on the ice, injuries hampered Imlach's squad in the last half as they limped towards the playoffs, going winless in their final five games. They finished second, 13 points behind Montreal but 21 points ahead of their first-round opponents, the fourth-place Rangers.

It started as a homer series, with each team winning two games on home ice before the series switched back to Maple Leaf Gardens. Red was the hero in Game 5, with assists on the first two goals. The game went into a second overtime; goalies Bower and Gump Worsley were sensational. Finally, at the four-minute mark, a scramble developed around the New York net, and the puck lay on the ice just behind Worsley's outstretched body. Red saw the loose puck, reached in from the side and tapped it in for the winner to send the Gardens crowd into a frenzy. New York argued vehemently that Worsley had smothered the puck, but referee Eddie Powers disagreed, having been right on top of the play.

"I knew Frank [Mahovlich] had the puck inside the blue line," Red explained to reporters after the game. "I was just hustling to get back into the play when the puck came loose from under Gump and

I shoved it in. Gump had the puck under his arm above the elbow with about one third of it showing. He moved a little and it squirted loose. He thought he had it smothered."

"Red could probably win an election tomorrow running in the Communist party ticket after that goal," joked Harold Ballard, chairman of the Leafs board of directors. During the celebration on the ice, Bower skated two-thirds the length of the ice to shake hands with the dejected Worsley. "I told him he was great," explained Bower afterwards. "He grabbed my hand, looked at that wildly cheering crowd and said, 'John, you were as good or we would have won. We sure as heck gave them their money's worth!'"

The Leafs eliminated the pesky Rangers in the next game with a 7–1 rout. Red finished the series with seven points. Their next opponents would be the defending champion Black Hawks, who had defeated the Canadiens.

The 1962 final opened in Toronto on April 10. Red assisted on the second goal as the Leafs won the first game 4–1. They took the second 3–1. The Hawks won the next two back at Chicago Stadium, 3–0 and 4–1. In Game 4, Bower injured his left leg and backup Don Simmons was summoned out of the stands and pressed into action. The Hawks thought they'd caught a break, but Simmons was more than up to the task as he and the Leafs won Game 5, 8–4.

From the puck drop of Game 6 back in Chicago Stadium, the Leafs were on their game, outhitting and outshooting the Hawks 13–4 in a scoreless first period. Toronto again outshot Chicago, 14–8, in the second, but the goalies were again flawless. The Hawks tallied first thanks to Bobby Hull, but the Leafs stormed back two minutes later on a goal by Bob Nevin. When Dick Duff scored the go-ahead goal at the 14:14 mark, the coveted hockey prize was within sight.

As time wound down, Chicago came at Toronto full bore, but Simmons held his ground, and the Cup was Toronto's. The team poured onto the ice to celebrate. Despite the hour, more than 2,000 cheering fans, including an exuberant Andra and Casey, greeted the returning champions at Toronto International Airport at 3:30 in the morning.

"It wouldn't have been nearly the same if we'd have won it at the Gardens Tuesday," Red told *Toronto Star* reporter Jim Proudfoot after disembarking from the plane. "By taking it on the road in Chicago's rink, we proved we deserved to be champions." Proudfoot wrote that the series was won by all of Toronto's centremen, who outplayed Chicago's. It was Red's fifth Stanley Cup.

The next day, April 24, the champions were feted with a tickertape parade through the downtown core. More than 60,000 fans crushed in on the line of convertibles carrying the Leafs and the Stanley Cup to City Hall, where Mayor Nathan Phillips declared, "You've had the greatest reception in Toronto's history!"

"It was fantastic," recalled Red. "It was my second [championship parade] in Toronto, as it happened to us at St. Mike's when we won the Memorial Cup, but for the Leafs organization it was the first in a while. It was such a sharp contrast to Detroit, which didn't ever really have anything. It was so exciting to be part of such a thrilling, happy moment."

A week later, Red formally accepted the federal Liberal nomination in the riding of York West. To add weight to his candidacy, Red greeted Lester Pearson as he landed at Malton Airport on May 1. Pearson had just attended a dinner at the White House in Washington for Nobel Prize–winners given by U.S. president John F. Kennedy. He and Red went to Red's nomination meeting that evening at Etobicoke Collegiate.

Liberals packed the auditorium. They were standing three deep on all sides, cheering and stomping. Pearson fired up the crowd with an attack on Prime Minister Diefenbaker and his government's cancellation of the Avro Arrow fighter plane that had been built in the riding, resulting in the loss of 14,000 local jobs. Miles ahead in speed and technology of any other fighter, the Arrow had put Canada at the front of the aerospace class. Its cancellation not only put thousands out of work and killed a national dream; it also ensured a mass exodus of scientists and technicians to the United States to work at NASA and its space program.

The crowd reserved its loudest cheers for their new candidate, chanting, "Go Kelly go! Go Kelly go!" As Red made his way to the platform, "The Irish Washerwoman" was played by a guitarist and accordionist. "The Leafs have asked me to play another year," Red told them. "And I think I can do it and represent you in Ottawa too."

"Go Kelly go! Go Kelly go!"

"I figure a political party is like a hockey team, it needs legs as well as brains!"

"Go Kelly go! Go Kelly go!"

"I can help do the legwork while men with experience such as Mr. Pearson can help restore Canada's prestige overseas."

"Go Kelly go! Go Kelly go!"

"I've gotta work for you and you gotta work for me," Red declared. "I have a lot to learn, but I'll give you all I have!"

"Go Kelly go! Go Kelly go!"

Pearson said it was a much more exciting gathering than the dinner he'd just attended with Kennedy. "I am delighted with my new teammate!" he yelled to the crowd. "Red is typical of the men and women of all kinds of backgrounds, experience and qualifications who are flocking to the Liberal Party."

The event gave Red a huge emotional boost, but he knew it was going to take a strong team effort to oust his Progressive Conservative opponent. "We were running against John Hamilton," Red recalled. "He had been one of the top guys in Diefenbaker's cabinet at one point, but he had run afoul with Dief for some reason or other and was out of cabinet. But he was a class guy. He had won the riding by 19,000 votes in the last election. He was very well liked. Even I liked him!"

Attempting to counter his opponent's popularity in the sports world, Hamilton circulated a photo of himself with former Leaf Sid Smith and current Leaf Allan Stanley.

"I told my campaign team I was a rookie but that I would do whatever they wanted me to do, go wherever they wanted me to go," Red said. "At my first all-candidates meeting we drew lots to decide speaking order, and John Hamilton spoke last. The other candidates had papers in their hands and were waving them around — though I never saw anything on the papers, they looked important. So I'm sitting there and thinking, *Holy, man.*

"I made a very low-key speech, and when it was over I thought I had done poorly and even apologized to my campaign manager, Clem Nieman, for letting him down. Then Hamilton, an experienced and eloquent speaker, got up, and with his cue cards, political knowledge and practised sense of timing, he gave a very impressive performance. But there was no time for post-mortems, because we had to get to another candidate's meeting that same night. I made a better impression at that one, as I stepped it up a bit."

Red was coached into becoming a better speaker.

"I got a little help in practices, standing behind a podium at a local church," he said. "My [political] team made notes, suggestions and comments and gave me some good pointers. I just tried to be myself, and I went to every event that my team wanted me to go to. I was on street corners, shaking hands at factories and knocking on doors — well, kind of.

"One time my campaign team had me up in Rexdale, and I'm driving back and I think, *Gosh, I've never knocked on a door!* So I stopped, got out and knocked on a door. A woman came to the door, and I introduced myself that I was the Liberal candidate here, and she says, 'I've just moved here from Saskatchewan. You must know Metro Prystai?' I said, 'Well, yes! We were teammates in Detroit!' And she says, 'Well, then I'm gonna vote for you!' I said, 'Well, that's great!'

"So I knock on the next door, and a lady came to the door and she said she was going to vote for me too. So I decided, *That's it! I'm not knocking on another door.* I was two for two. And I didn't knock on any more doors!"

Red found himself in high demand to help other Liberal campaigns in other ridings, and it was sometimes troublesome as voters flocked to him to talk hockey and get his autograph while sometimes forgetting the local Liberal candidate he was supposed to be promoting.

"The big election wind-up event was at Maple Leaf Gardens," Red recalled. "Pearson and everyone were there and we Liberal candidates were to come in from ridings all over Toronto, 17 or 18 of us. My organization had me meeting with a local group that night, which I attended. Now I'm late getting to the Gardens. I go to the Wood Street entrance and they stopped me. 'It's too late to go in,' they said, 'Mr. Pearson has just started his entrance to the stage. You would disrupt everything if you went in now.'

"So the overflow crowd was down at Massey Hall. 'We'll take you down there,' they said. Massey Hall was jammed; they're hanging from the rafters there. They brought me to the front and shoved me onto the stage. Then they say to me, 'Say something!' I don't know what I said, but they were hollering and stomping, gung-ho! No matter what I said, they cheered."

He credited his campaign team. "They were just unbelievable! I couldn't have asked for a more dedicated team — campaign workers and volunteers, leadership. I worked hard for them because they worked so darn hard for me. And I believed in Mr. Pearson so much. I really ran because I wanted to get him elected prime minister. I knew he would be good for the country."

Election day was June 18, 1962. It had been a long, gruelling campaign for both the Liberal candidate in York West and his pregnant wife, who was due any day. Andra made as many appearances as she could, but she ended up hospitalized for a week as a precaution. Everything was fine, they were assured, but the baby had decided to wait — maybe until after election day.

"I was completely exhausted at the end of the day," recalled Andra. "I was just bushed. I remember lying on the bed, catching a breath, lying there looking at the ceiling, kind of in a tired daze. We were going down to Red's headquarters later to watch the election results. Red walked into the bedroom and I looked up at him. He had just come in from last-minute campaigning, but he had a kind of funny, disbelieving, concerned look on his face. I looked at him."

"Red? What's wrong?"

"Oh nothing, except . . . I think we're going to win!"

. . . . . .

CHAPTER TWELVE

PLAY IT AGAIN, RED!

The campaign ended on June 18.

It was an early roller coaster ride for the crowd at Red's election headquarters on Dundas Street West, as returns swung back and forth, with Kelly and Progressive Conservative incumbent John Hamilton alternating in the lead.

By the time Red and Andra arrived at 9:45 p.m., he was in front by 2,000 votes. The crowd roared when it was announced that "the new member for York West and his wife have just entered the hall!"

"I got down to my campaign headquarters, and the televisions were set up," Red recalled. "We had 20 polls and we had 20 TVs rolling, and poll captains for each one. A big cheer would go up here, then a groan there, as the results came on the screens." When the final results came in late from the Alderwood polling station, a great cheer resounded. Red had won the riding by a strong margin.

"Teamwork pays off in election campaigns the same as in hockey," Red told the press.

His rival, Hamilton, was quoted as saying, "I'm too old to cry, but it hurts too much to laugh."

"We beat Hamilton by about 4,000 votes," recalled Red. "When he called to concede, I thanked him for calling, told him that it had been a hard-fought campaign, that he had been a great representative of the riding and that he was a class gentleman. I had always been struck by his dignity."

Red's victory was bittersweet in that the Liberals, under Pearson, had increased their seats dramatically but still lost the election, 116 to 98. The silver lining was that the ruling Conservatives had been reduced to a tight minority government. To survive, the Diefenbaker PCs would have to be propped up by the Social Credit Party, which held the balance of power with 26 seats.

Now the work began. Red had made a promise to his prospective constituents. "When Red got elected, he said to me, 'Andra, we have to move! I know it's a great place and all, you have a great job here, but I have to live in the riding where I was elected. I had promised. It's my duty,'" Andra recalled. "So, the house went up for sale. Swoosh! Gone! I was so sad, so upset. I loved that house!"

Red found a house he liked in Etobicoke, in Metro Toronto's west end. "When he first took me to see it I thought, *Oh, no! I'm going there, but I'm not going to like it! I'm not,*" said Andra. "But as soon as we arrived, well, it was a beautiful place. It had a beautiful tree outside. And that's where we lived, on King George's Road in Etobicoke."

Then there was the impending birth, too, a situation that could have been complicated. "I had been having morning sickness, and so the doctor had prescribed me a new medication, thalidomide," Andra recalled. "Unknown at the time, but it would cause babies to be born with deformities, sometimes without arms or legs. I took it briefly, but I was never good at taking medication. I took only a few pills, felt much better, and so I stopped taking them. I didn't tell the doctor, but I stopped taking them. They had taken an X-ray of me when I was expecting, and the baby's elbows were close to each other and it looked like he might be a victim like other babies that had been born at that time.

"The afternoon of the evening that I finally had the baby, Davey Keon's wife, Lola, had called and wondered what we were doing for dinner. I had been packing all day for our move to the new house, and I said I was too tired to even think about dinner, and so she said, 'Never mind. Davey and I will come over and we'll bring dinner.' They brought over fish and chips, and we were sitting there eating, and then Lola said to me, 'Are you going to have the baby soon? I think you are.' I asked why and she said, 'Oh, I just think you are.' Suddenly I had a pain and I said, 'Uh oh!' Red drove me right down to the hospital.

"It was a tough birth, and I worried, but Patrick arrived just perfectly normal on June twenty-third, weighing over eight pounds. I thought of those other babies and that medication with the side effects, and I was so relieved that he was perfectly normal."

Through the spring and summer of 1962, Red prepared to be the Member of Parliament for York West. On top of all the briefing notes and voluminous amounts of documents he received to digest, his first big decision was to set up a constituency office to meet people with local issues. With the crazy schedule he anticipated, the decision was easy: he would have a home office, with Andra as his secretary.

Toronto Star reporter Milt Dunnell caught up with Red in early September and asked him how he could possibly balance 70 NHL games and 140 Leafs practices without missing any House of Commons sessions, which were set to begin on September 27. "It never hurts anybody to be active," Red told him. "I expect to play all the Leafs games, take in most of the practices and spend a lot of time in the House of Commons."

Dunnell asked him if he was working on a debut speech for Parliament. "The way I see it myself, when you're playing on strange ice against a strange team, you're a little bit cautious until you feel out the other side's strengths. I don't think I'll be in a hurry to make my maiden speech," Red replied.

On the hockey front, Dunnell wanted to know about contract negotiations with Imlach, and whether the dual duties would complicate things. "I don't expect trouble with Punch," answered Red. "He'll be cooperative, as long as he knows I intend to do my job. I always enjoy our contract talks. I like the way he deals."

Red didn't experience any bad negotiations with Imlach, but others did. When the Rangers signed veteran Doug Harvey to a reputed $30,000 contract, the bar had seemingly been raised for everyone around the league. Mahovlich left the Peterborough camp when he felt Toronto wasn't offering enough, but returned after further negotiations were handled by league president Clarence Campbell, who was deemed the final arbiter in all cases.

"I know what every player in the league earns," Campbell told Dunnell. "I give a player the chance to tell me his story in confidence. I also give him a chance to say how he rates himself with respect to other players at his position. I also get the club's version. If a man complains to me that he has been treated unfairly, I am able to judge whether he is being paid the equal rate for people of equal skills at his particular job. The records show what a player has done over a period of time."

A few weeks later, after the 1962 All-Star Game in Toronto, Chicago Black Hawks owner Jim Norris offered the Leafs a million dollars for Mahovlich's services, which was agreed upon at a cocktail party by Leafs board member Harold Ballard but then hastily scrubbed. It intensified the debate as to the true worth of star hockey players.

For Red, training camp did not go smoothly, as he was fighting the flu throughout, but he still mustered enough strength to go after Chicago's Stan Mikita, who had creamed rookie Jim Pappin in an exhibition game in Peterborough.

In the second game of the season, Red clearly was still in a weakened state when he himself was hit by Johnny Bucyk of the Bruins; in the next game, hits by the Rangers Harry Howell and Al Langlois had him wobbly. Red complained to team doctors of feeling woozy, but after a thorough examination they attributed it to his still fighting off the flu.

He was sworn in as a Member of Parliament and took his place in the House of Commons in Ottawa on September 27, when the 25th session of Parliament convened with a Speech from the Throne read by governor general Georges Vanier. For Red, the experience of being in the hallowed halls of the nation's Parliament was humbling.

"My first impression was one of awe," he recalled. "I was in awe of the atmosphere, of the rules and of the political personalities present. Eventually I came to look on it more as a kind of sport, not unlike hockey. You had several teams; you had a speaker who was the referee. The sergeant-at-arms, like a linesman, was sometimes called upon to break up the fights. You even had the press gallery to give the thumbs up or down sign, and in those days the fans in the public gallery occasionally broke into applause during some of the heated debates."

Because they held a minority government, the Progressive Conservatives' survival hinged on every vote; losing a vote on a bill in the House of Commons would result in a failed vote of confidence, forcing an election call. Therefore, as a member of the official opposition, Red was expected — and needed — at every vote, without fail.

It was a challenge making it all work. "I came home to Toronto to practise in the morning," Red recalled. "Then I'd catch a plane and go to Ottawa for the afternoon and evening sessions and come home on the last flight, the midnight flight, and get home at one or one-thirty in the morning. I'd go down and practise in the morning and do the same thing all over again. We played Saturdays, Sundays and Wednesday nights. The House didn't sit on Wednesday night and it didn't sit on Saturday and Sunday. The only time I had a real problem is when we played in Montreal on a Thursday night."

On January 2, Red helped out on a historic play. Andy Bathgate of the Rangers scored his ninth goal in as many games to tie an NHL record — but he didn't actually score it. Bathgate, in front of the Toronto net during a mad scramble at Madison Square Garden, attempted to pass it across to a teammate. The pass was intercepted by Red, but his attempt to clear the puck ended up in his own net. "It's better that way! They'll remember it and so will I," Bathgate crowed to the press after the 3–1 Rangers win. "I thanked Kelly after the goal. It's the best thing he's done since he joined parliament."

As his play helped propel linemate Mahovlich to the top of the All-Star balloting at the season's halfway point, Red was making marks of his own. Against Montreal on January 23, he outduelled Jean Béliveau for the puck at the opening faceoff, split the Habs defence and then flipped a backhander past Jacques Plante at the 49-second mark of the game, a 5–1 Toronto win.

A week later back at the Forum, Red was faced with one of those schedule-conflicting Thursday-night games.

"Canadiens are wishing that Red Kelly, member for York West, had remained in Ottawa with Lester Pearson and his Liberal team for the nuclear arms debate," wrote Red Burnett. "The redhead who passed up yesterday's House of Commons show, exploded in nuclear fashion himself last night as he fired three goals and assisted on another as Toronto Maple Leafs shot down the Canadiens 6–3 before 15,334, the largest crowd of the season at the Forum. With the Leafs trailing 2–0, he netted his first goal in the opening session and the tying counter in the second. His third goal came on a penalty shot in the third. Kelly now has 14 goals."

"On that penalty shot, I picked up the puck and went in on Plante," recalled Red. "Just as I crossed the blue line, I let the shot go because Plante was standing over by the one post and he wasn't expecting me to shoot that soon from so far out. I was on the wrong foot, too, but I saw where he was standing, not quite set, so I shot high immediately where he wasn't standing. It was in the net and he wasn't even expecting it."

Red's political world exploded on February 5, when Diefenbaker's Conservative government was defeated on a vote of confidence. At issue was the prospect of American nuclear missiles on Canadian soil, protection from a possible Soviet attack. A general election was slated for April 8.

"Red Kelly stands at a crossroads today," wrote Burnett on February 7. "One sign points to politics, the other to hockey and a normal home life. He'll decide in a few days which street to take." There were three factors at play, said Red:

> *God, family and country.*
>
> *I don't feel the third duty should be allowed to interfere with the first two. That is the reason I haven't said that I will or won't run for re-election. I am wondering if I can afford the time away from my family to do a good job in Ottawa. I haven't said I won't play hockey next season. That is something else I have to decide. I've got my family growing up and it is pretty important for them to have a father around the house. I will discuss the situation with Clem Nieman and then make a definite announcement. Right now I've got a lot of serious thinking to do.*
>
> *I have talked to many young members of parliament during the past six months and they all agree the salary is not sufficient for a man with a young family. A lot of them have to hold two jobs to make ends meet. This puts a terrific physical strain on the individual and just about excludes a normal home life.*

In the same interview, Andra told Burnett she wouldn't be disappointed if Red decided against re-election. "I can count the hours we've been together since last September 26 and we spent most of the time talking about the children," she said. "It has been a terrific grind for Red both physically and mentally."

Teammates offered their opinions. "Kelly is a highly intelligent person," said George Armstrong. "I'm sure he wouldn't do anything that would hurt his play and in so doing hurt the team's chances of finishing first and winning the Stanley Cup."

"I think Kelly should run again," added Dick Duff. "I think he'd be a shoo-in without having to campaign too vigorously. And I don't think it would cut down on his effectiveness as a hockey player."

In a February 13 game at the Gardens, Red notched two assists and scored his 16th goal of the season with 58 seconds left in the 6–2 Leafs victory. On the very next play, a frustrated Howie Young took exception and grabbed his nearest target, Red.

"I came down the ice outside of our blue line, and I gave Howie the 'howdie-do' fake and went around him," Red recalled. "He was caught flat-footed and reached out with his hand and caught me under the chin. My feet went out from under me, and I fell back and my head hit the ice. I went out for a couple of seconds. I know Eddie Shack came over and sort of cradled my head."

Red was diagnosed with a concussion. After missing the next game at home against the Rangers, he donned a white helmet for the return match at Madison Square Garden on February 17. "I wasn't particularly happy with wearing the helmet, but the doctor advised me to wear it, and I listened to the doctor," Red recalled. "With the helmet, I didn't always sense the opposition players coming up behind me, especially where they could drive me into the boards. When I put the helmet on, I lost that feeling, that loss of that 'sixth sense.' But I wore it. I had no choice. I never did get used to it."

As February rolled into March, with the federal election on and the Stanley Cup playoffs fast approaching, it was decision time for Red — to run or not to run in the election. After talking it over with Andra, Red opted to throw his hat back into the political ring. He had a few things in his favour this time around. First, he was the incumbent. Second, the Liberals had formed a formidable campaign team in York West, and they worked hard for him. Third, Dick Duff

might have been right when he implied Red's incumbency and fame
might make it possible for him to not have to campaign all that hard.

The most compelling reason for Red, though, was Pearson. "I
had so much respect for Mr. Pearson," recalled Red. "He had so
much class. A Nobel Peace Prize winner, a respected diplomat, a
great leader. I just thought that his election as prime minister would
be good for the country. He was such a great man and it was time
for change. I wanted to do whatever I could to make that happen."

It didn't take long for the Conservatives to take the gloves off and attack Red at a local riding nomination meeting in York West. "The riding needs a member who actually lives and works among us, not some imported name figure," blared a young lawyer named Alan Eagleson, who would win the Conservative nomination on March 5.

Eagleson had started to make friends in hockey circles, representing a few players during contract negotiations, but was not the power in hockey he would later become. Some Leafs chose to support their lawyer over their teammate.

"Yeah, there was a small group siding with him, meeting with him, which was slightly upsetting," recalled Red. "Whatever Eagleson said about me was like water falling off a duck as far as I was concerned. He'd be in a room and be telling you the sun was shining, and when you opened the blinds it would be pitch black. It didn't matter to him, he'd say anything to sway voters."

As Kelly's political campaign was rolling out, the Leafs finished on top of the NHL for the first time since 1948. In 62 games, Red scored 20 goals to go with a team-high 40 assists.

The Leafs faced the third-place Canadiens in the first round, winning the first two games on home ice, 3–1 and 3–2.

Red, Tim Horton, Punch Imlach and King Clancy all missed the flight to Montreal and were threatened with a $100 fine by Leaf executive vice-president Harold Ballard, a rising power in the organization. All four arrived in time for Game 3, though, and the Leafs subdued the Habs 2–0, backed by the shutout goaltending of Bower.

Though Montreal won the fourth game, the Leafs eliminated the Habs with a lopsided 5–0 Bower shutout win, despite being outshot 35–33.

A downcast Montreal coach Toe Blake went through the Toronto dressing room to offer his congratulations, and told the press the Leafs would beat Chicago or Detroit. "They're simply too strong."

When Red wasn't present at the start of an all-candidate's meeting one evening, Eagleson went into full attack mode. "Red

Kelly won't be appearing," Eagleson boasted to the assembly. "He's been gagged by the Liberals' brain trust and won't be saying another word on the political platform with the other candidates."

But when Red did finally appear, Eagleson seemed embarrassed, especially when Red apologized for having run late at his last engagement, a coffee party. "Gee, I'm told I was getting hit pretty hard!" Kelly said to laughter as he looked at Eagleson.

"It's okay, Red, you can take it!" someone shouted. The debate went well, and Red found himself in greater demand, including by veteran politicians. "Paul Martin called and asked me to come down to Windsor to campaign with him and attend his nomination meeting," recalled Red. Martin first was elected to the House of Commons in 1935; his son, Paul Martin Jr., would serve as Canada's prime minister from 2003 to 2006.

Red tried to beg off, busy with campaigning and hockey. Andra called to excuse her husband, but was told that a Liberal politician could not say no to Martin's invitation, and that Martin would return the favour by campaigning in York West for Red.

"Reluctantly, I flew to Windsor, but it turned out to be the best thing that happened to me during the campaign," recalled Red. "Martin was a real professional politician. In one day I saw how a campaign was run. Everything was timed to the last minute as we went around to factories, nursing homes and shopping centres, meeting hundreds of people. He knew how to work a crowd. I had a little problem in that we were engaged in a playoff series with the Detroit Red Wings, and everywhere we went people would say hello to Mr. Martin and then try to talk hockey with me. He would get way ahead of me and then come back to rescue me from a crowd and move on.

"That night, I was to address his nomination meeting. The place was packed. There were people hanging from the rafters. I sat on the stage waiting for him to finish his speech, but he went on and on; 30 minutes, 40, 50, an hour, as the crowd grew noisier and noisier.

I wondered what I could possibly say when he finally did finish. To tell the truth, I do not even remember what I said, but that trip was a great experience. My wife says it turned me into a politician. As promised, Martin came to campaign in my riding, as did Judy LaMarsh and others."

Even his leader fell under the Kelly spell. "I once spent an afternoon during the 1963 election with Red Kelly, a great hockey star, who was seeking election, at my urging, in York West," wrote Pearson in his memoirs. "While motoring from one meeting to another we noticed some youngsters playing ball in a vacant lot. We both thought it would be fun, and might interest our press entourage, if we stopped for a few minutes to watch. We also stopped the game because Red was soon recognized and was surrounded by excited youngsters clamouring for his autograph.

"He was somewhat embarrassed that no one took notice of me, and asked one small boy, happily contemplating Red's signature: 'Don't you want Mr. Pearson's too?' The reply put me in my place: 'Mr. Pearson? Who's he?' Even as Prime Minister, I had to accept that in the autograph market it would take five 'L.B. Pearsons' to get one 'Red Kelly.' My sporting experience helped me to accept this."

Monday, April 8, was election day. It was also the eve of the Stanley Cup Final.

Red received 41,103 votes, which easily defeated Eagleson, his nearest rival, by 16,542 votes. Red told the Canadian Press that night that he "would wait until after the NHL hockey playoffs before deciding whether or not to hang up his skates — permanently."

There was no word from the future hockey czar. "I heard years later that Eagleson purposely sought the Conservative nomination in York West just to beat me! I never heard a peep from Eagleson that night, not a word," Red recalled. "He never called, conceded, said congratulations, nothing. He was not in the same class as John Hamilton had been the election before, that's for sure. I respected Hamilton.

"Again, I was so proud of my team. They had worked their butts off. I couldn't say enough about them, but I couldn't join the celebrations that night, because we opened the Stanley Cup Final against Detroit the next night. I had to get home to bed!"

Red woke up the following morning to the news that his Liberals had defeated the Conservatives, 128 seats to 95 and, though still a minority, would be forming the next government, with Pearson as the new prime minister.

The Leafs opened the final at home. Duff beat Terry Sawchuk twice in the first 68 seconds to set an NHL record for the two fastest goals from the start of a game. The Leafs never looked back and took Game 1 by a score of 4–2. Game 2 was also a 4–2 victory. In Detroit, Sawchuk stopped 32 shots to pace the Wings to a 3–2 win. In Game 4, Red's two goals propelled the Leafs to yet another 4–2 win. He benefited from his familiarity with his former teammates.

"As a Wing, I had been taught to shoot low, about a foot off the ice and just off the post of the net, and Terry knew this," Red recalled. "I remember having a close-in chance on Terry and thinking two things. One: *What would Rocket Richard do on Terry?* And, two: *What would Terry expect me to do?* So when my chances came, I put my shots upstairs, and I was able to beat Terry."

Excitement was in the air back in Toronto, with Lord Stanley's mug in the building. "If my players don't clinch this thing in the next game, they're a bunch of donkey heads," snarled Imlach.

The temperature in the Gardens rose quickly when Keon scored a short-handed goal to finish out the first period. Detroit's Alex Delvecchio evened things up in the second. The game was a tight-checking affair; the goaltending duel between Sawchuk and Bower stretched into the third period before Eddie Shack got the go-ahead marker with just under seven minutes to go.

Near the two-minute mark, Bob Pulford took a holding penalty and the Wings pulled Sawchuk for a two-man advantage. Play was frantic, and Bower held his ground until Keon got a hold of the puck and fired it into the empty Detroit goal to seal the deal with five seconds to go.

At the final buzzer, pandemonium erupted as the players poured onto the ice to mob Bower and then shake hands with the Wings. "We tried, but it was like growling against thunder," said a defeated Gordie Howe.

Red had two goals and two assists in the series, but the main number was six — six Stanley Cups. A picture of Red and Mahovlich was taken with the Cup, showing the Big M holding up two fingers and Red holding up six on two hands.

Up in the stands, his father, Pete Kelly, had a special moment. Detroit owner Bruce Norris and former GM Jack Adams, the two men who had traded his son, got out of their seats and walked down the aisle where Pete Kelly was puffing on a cigar. Pete saw the two men coming and planted himself in front of them, grinning from ear to ear.

"Gee, isn't it funny how that Stanley Cup seems to follow my boy around?" Pete Kelly said. The two men huffed, turned and walked in the opposite direction.

In the jubilant dressing room, many Leafs veterans openly stated their desire to return in the fall to defend this Cup, but Red was wary of making that prediction.

"I'm not certain," Red told *Toronto Star* reporter Jim Proudfoot with a heavy sigh. "I'll give it some serious thought, but right now I'm just looking forward to a vacation."

• • • • • •

CHAPTER THIRTEEN

STANLEY, CONN *and the* MAPLE LEAF

Though Red and Andra slipped away to Cedar Island after the playoffs, he didn't have much chance to rest. The first session of the 26th Canadian Parliament opened on May 16, and he was there for the Speech from the Throne, which laid out the Liberals' plans for the life of their government. In an effort to see each other as much as Red's hectic dual life would allow, he and Andra altered their living arrangements.

"We got an apartment in Ottawa so that we could all be together, and Andra would come up with Patrick and Casey," Red recalled. "They would go and listen to the bands on Parliament Hill. Patrick would be on Andra's shoulders, where he would first hear the bagpipes, something he would take up later in his life. The problem was I was being called to go all over the dang place. I was never here. Andra saw me more when she was back in Toronto, so our little experiment didn't work out very well. She eventually moved back to Toronto."

Andra served again as her husband's secretary in the family home.

"People would be lined up outside to see him," Andra recalled. "It was a very hectic time."

It finally came time for the Honourable Red Kelly's maiden speech in Parliament. "I was scheduled to speak in the evening and my wife told me she would prepare a typical pre-game meal to get me ready for the big event," Red recalled in the *Canadian Parliamentary Review*. "Things moved faster than expected in the House and I got the floor in the afternoon. The rules say you must not read your speech and I wanted to deliver my maiden speech on a topic on which I could speak freely and genuinely without notes." He had been kidded a lot for not having spoken yet in Parliament; some said, "Kelly can skate but cannot speak." He had a lot to say when he stood up that day, and all eyes were on him.

"Mr. Speaker, first let me say that I must admit that I had been a little slow in getting up to make my first speech, but I received so much publicity in the last Parliament by not speaking, that I could not hope to achieve that much again," he joked. He then looked at the speaker. "A speaker's job is a little bit like the referee in a hockey game. Sometimes they have to hand out a misconduct penalty." After the laughter subsided, he got serious.

"Mr. Speaker, Canadians have become lax about their physical condition. The only exercise some members get is rising to speak often, but that is not a well-balanced program."

He urged his government to look at adopting an all-out physical fitness program for all Canadians. Then he turned his attention to issues of national unity, namely a new flag and national anthem.

"I was raised by my parents to honour both our flag and anthem. I have travelled a lot. At the start of a game in a foreign country, the band would play 'God Save the Queen.' We stood to attention and we were proud to do so. But during the last few years, they started to play 'O Canada' the odd time. You felt great pride and your chest stood out a little more. They were singing about our land, our home."

When he urged the adoption of a new national flag representative of all of Canada, a heckler from the opposition benches yelled out, "The Maple Leaf?"

"Yes," Red answered. "The Red Ensign has been borrowed from Britain and now it is time to give it back and have our own distinctive flag. It is time to cut the apron strings from Britain." There were a few boos from the opposition. When Red sat down to applause from his Liberal colleagues after speaking for 20 minutes, fellow Ontario MP Russell Honey leaned over and said to him, "Red, I couldn't have said that. I would never get re-elected!" Many Liberal members commented it was one of the best speeches they had ever heard in the House.

The debate over a new Canadian flag was just beginning and would drag on for many months. When Red got home for supper that evening and told Andra that she had missed his debut speech, she was disappointed that she hadn't been there to witness it.

If there were any questions concerning Red's future career in hockey, they were summarily answered in the fall of 1963, when he showed up in Peterborough for his 17th NHL training camp and signed his contract on September 11.

Imlach said he didn't mind Red's dual obligations. "We are just as interested in Kelly's welfare as a Member of Parliament as we are in him as a member of the Toronto hockey club," Imlach told Red Burnett. "We are confident he can fill both positions more than adequately."

Burnett asked if Red had been given any special exemptions in regards to attending practices. "We've decided to play it by ear, fully realizing that Kelly has a duty to perform for the people of York West," said Imlach.

Unlike his counterpart, Jack Adams in Detroit, who never stood pat, Imlach wouldn't tinker too much with success. His squad had just won him two straight Stanley Cups, and he was looking forward to winning a third.

During the pre-season exhibition tour, an incident occurred

that has lived on in lore. "It was in Quebec, after a game against the Quebec Aces," Red recalled. "We were staying over before heading to Montreal for our next game. It's after the game, and we're walking down the street in Quebec City, and they were fixing the roadways. There were these big hunks of cement barrels along the roadway. The guys got monkeying around a little bit, and they were daring Tim Horton that he couldn't move one of those large cement things. Pulford was kidding him along, really egging him on. Tim was as strong as an ox and picked up one of those barrels and let it go. It started rolling down the hill and was bouncing down the hill! We were lucky it didn't hurt anybody.

"The police came and arrested Tim and wanted to put him in the back seat of the police car but Tim's got a grip on each side of the open door. Of course, with his strength, they can't budge him. One of the cops took his billy club and whacked him on the hand. He let go, and then they shoved him in. He spent that night in jail. Imlach found out and went down the next morning and cleared it up and got him out because we had to fly to Montreal. It was some hijinks!"

At the opening game of the 1963–64 season, Prime Minister Pearson dropped the ceremonial first puck at centre ice at Maple Leaf Gardens. In the presence of both his bosses, Red fittingly scored a goal in the 5–1 Toronto win over Boston.

The Leafs sputtered out of the starting gate with a win record slightly above .500. In his book *Hockey is a Battle*, Imlach wrote that he started to question his thinking at not having changed his lineup. "We had the same team that had finished first the previous spring and had manhandled Montreal and Detroit in the playoffs," Imlach wrote. "Red Kelly was having his worst scoring year in a long time, maybe because mixing parliament and hockey was too much. Frank Mahovlich was dropping off into being just an average player, except on rare nights. But two of the most serious declines involved two of our best young players. Dick Duff didn't score a goal until November and Bob Nevin was the same."

Games in Montreal were still a scheduling challenge for the MP/Leaf. "This one time I couldn't leave the House because we had votes that started at noon and went one vote after another. We were a minority government, so I stayed there right to the last vote at six o'clock," recalled Red. "The deputy speaker of the House, Lucien Lamoureux, had his chauffeur waiting outside for me, and I hurried out to his car, and they shot me to the airport, and I flew to Montreal. A limousine whisked me right to the Forum. When I got there, the team was just going onto the ice for pre-game warm-up. I was able to get dressed just on time for the opening faceoff.

"I didn't get a chance to eat properly, and so I was not as sharp as I would have normally been. In this particular game, the puck was shot up along the left boards. I got the puck, and a Montreal defenceman was coming at me. I was going to deke him and go to the inside. Well, Jean Béliveau was right behind me, and I pulled up for a second to deke the defenceman in front of me when Béliveau gave me a cross-check from behind, and I went headfirst into the boards. I was knocked out cold.

"I just remember coming out of Dr. Bill Head's room after they had checked me out, I guess, and Imlach's got me by the arm. He asked me, 'Red, do you know what day it is?' That's the first thing I remember. I said, 'It can't be Saturday night, because we're in Montreal.' He sat me on the bench for the third period, but he didn't play me. I sat on the bench because you don't want the other team to know they've hurt you. You don't want to give them the satisfaction."

Watching the game at home, Andra, pregnant with their third child, was concerned. "I was hysterical. I called to see how Red was," Andra recalled. She knew Bill Head, Montreal's team therapist, from her days in the ice show, when he had helped her with a back injury. Head told her not to worry, that Red would not return to the ice that night.

Following a game in New York, the Leafs were delayed at LaGuardia Airport due to inclement weather. While they were waiting for the weather to clear, Red and a few of the Leafs noticed a familiar American politician who was also grounded. Red urged Eddie Shack to introduce himself, knowing "the Entertainer" would entertain.

"How do you do — I'm Eddie Shack. I play for the Toronto Maple Leafs."

"Yes, I know who you are," answered Richard Milhous Nixon, shaking his hand. "And I know you won the Stanley Cup last year, and I recognize some of the other guys."

After a few moments, Shack returned to Red.

"Hey Red, who the heck did you say that guy was, anyways?"

Guffaws of laughter filled the air.

Red and some of his teammates went over to the former American vice-president and future president to chat for a few minutes.

Another example of how politics was never far from Red's life occurred when he received a letter from Conn Smythe on January 14, 1964:

Dear Red,

I note in the Gardens program that you made a speech in parliament on a new flag. Enclosed is a very good article by the Gardens' Secretary, Brigadier Ian S. Johnston, one of the finest soldiers in the last war. This might give you a new slant on what the old flag means to millions of Canadians. I had a nice letter from the Prime Minister, in which he says there is to be a free vote on this subject, and I would like to have a talk with you sometime about that.

Sincerely,
Conn Smythe

It was a volatile time in the country. The Front de libération du Québec, or FLQ, seeking Quebec's independence from Canada, had begun a bombing campaign. There would be many incidents and deaths in the years to come. All threats were taken seriously by the police.

After a game in Montreal, the Leafs were going back to Toronto and Red was off to Ottawa. "When I got to the train station, the FLQ had threatened to blow up the trestles, and [the authorities] wouldn't let the train go through until they had checked all the trestles, and so I didn't get back until five or six in the morning," recalled Red. "I was sharing an apartment with Eugene Whelan and Larry Pennell then. They were just getting up as I was getting in. They said, 'Red, where've you been? We have to get to caucus!' That was a long day.

"There was another time when we were sitting in the House and there was a bomb. Above us was the visitors' gallery and the press gallery. This one fellow who had been in the visitors' gallery had gone into the washroom to light a bomb and made a mistake and blew himself up."

On the ice, January began positively for the Leafs as they won three of four games, but things began to go wrong when Bower was out with an injury and Don Simmons subbed in relief. The worst was an 11–0 loss at home to Boston. "It was one of those games when nothing went right," Red recalled. "We kept trying like heck to get back in the game, and then they would shoot the puck and, boom, it's in the net again. Whenever they shot it, it went in the net."

Imlach was in panic mode. Yet when reporters cornered Leafs president Stafford Smythe for a comment on his team's performance, he was adamant that there would "be no trades this season." Behind the scenes, Imlach had a different take on things, and rumours started that the Leafs were after Andy Bathgate of New York. "Sure, we may talk to them," Imlach was quoted as saying. "But I'd say it's a thousand to one against a deal."

Between home dates, Red was in town when Andra went into labour on January 24. "We had a boy, and he was a big baby, over 10 pounds," Andra recalled. "We named him Conn Lawrence. Conn,

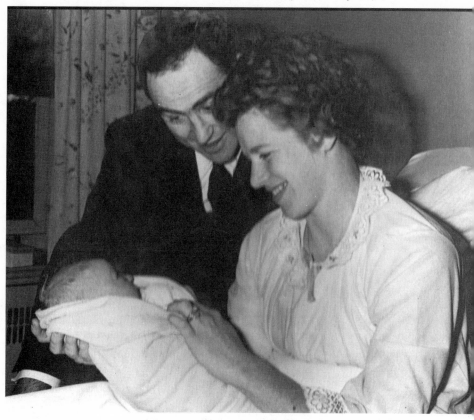

after the king of Ireland, though Conn Smythe always thought we had named him after him. Then I was later reading in the paper that Conn Smythe was also named after the king of Ireland. Red and I both liked the name. It seemed to suit him."

Conn Smythe, who had ceded power to his son, Stafford, but still owned the team, continued to have the national flag on his mind. A new design dubbed the Pearson Pennant was leaked to the press; it showed a red three-leafed branch on a white centre, with blue stripes on each side. A new flag had been a part of the Liberal Party election platform since 1961; the plan was to replace the Canadian Red Ensign, which featured the British flag top left and the coat of arms of Canada on the right.

"Conn Smythe had written to every member in the House of

Commons, both sides," recalled Red. "He was for the Ensign. I went up to see him, and he explained that he and many soldiers had fought for that flag, had been wounded for it and had died for it. To him it was a great source of pride.

"At that first talk, I listened to him and didn't really have anything to counter his argument about the old Ensign. I said I would take his point of view to Ottawa. I went back to the House, back to our Liberal caucus, and then I heard all sides of the debate and learned that Canadian soldiers were not recognized by the Ensign but rather the Maple Leaf on their collars, arms and so on.

"Back in Toronto, I got another request to see Mr. Smythe, and I had all these new arguments, and what surprised me was that he listened and didn't really have a comeback. A week later, I'd get another note to see him, and he's got a new set of arguments, and I would respectfully listen to him and he would listen to me. That was the beginning of my flag debate with Mr. Smythe. It went on for quite a while, and he wouldn't let it go."

Heading into a February 22 encounter at home against the Rangers, the Leafs had won only two of 12 games, and Imlach acted. After a team meeting which both Bob Nevin and Dick Duff had attended, it was announced that they had been traded to New York, along with Arnie Brown, Rod Seiling and Bill Collins, in exchange for Andy Bathgate and Don McKenney. When they all showed up at the Gardens for that night's encounter, two players turned left instead of right as they usually did, and two turned right instead of left. It made for an angry and awkward situation within the dressing room.

"When McKenney and Bathgate arrived, they were met with a stony silence," Bob Baun wrote years later. "Andy came on quite gregariously and Tim Horton took it upon himself to welcome him to the Leafs."

"Dick Duff had been there a long time. He was a great guy who had scored some important goals," Red recalled of that trade. "Bob Nevin had been great to play with, and you hated to see them go.

I didn't know what Punch was thinking, but I guess he thought Bathgate would help. But they gave away a couple of young guys. You play with someone for so long, but it happens — casualties of war!"

Though some of the Leafs were disgruntled by the deal, they beat the Rangers 5–2 that night and 4–3 the next day back in New York. With the Leafs on a roll, the Habs were clearly worried by the trade. "Before that deal, Toronto hadn't beaten New York in five games, then they win two in a row from Rangers," lamented coach Toe Blake. "What a steal. Leafs bought the Stanley Cup. It looks like it."

"I don't think it is right for deals so late in the season," chimed in Jean Béliveau. "It does not seem right to push players off a playoff team with 13 games or less to play."

While Red was put on a line with Bathgate and Mahovlich, he seemed to have trouble adjusting in the first few practices. "It's too early to say the line won't jell. Kelly can make it work," observed King Clancy from the side boards.

The *Toronto Star Weekly* magazine had a feature on "The Other Red Kellys" in the March 21, 1964, edition. "Gang way for the Kelly clan," started the story by Thelma Dickman. "That's what the neighbours say when they see Andra Kelly's red head bobbing brightly down the street. She's usually towing red-haired, three-year-old Andra Catherine by one hand, red-haired, not quite two Leonard Patrick Jr. by the other, and somehow hauling a wagon holding a red-haired infant named Conn Lawrence. The entourage is often escorted by a Siamese cat named Wing."

The story covered Andra's time as a skating star. "I adored the audiences, the excitement, costumes . . . even the hours of practice," Andra said. "But you can't be a top figure skater and a wife as well, not if you want children."

She also addressed her multiple roles — wife, mother, teacher, secretary — and defended her husband's many roles. "When parliament is in session Red leaves for Ottawa right after the Monday practice, stays down all week and is back Friday night or Saturday morning. If there's a Wednesday night game he comes back for that and then returns to Ottawa," explained Andra. "People who criticize Red for missing time from parliament are barking up the wrong MP. Red hasn't missed more than six votes out of 37 that have been taken — and he's never missed a major one. His attendance record is better than a lot of the other MPs."

Keeping the team together was not unique to this generation of Kellys, said Andra. "Whatever happens to the Kelly clan, I'll always remember Grandfather Kelly's answer when I asked him how they managed to keep their family so close and loving through all the years. 'Well,' he said and gave me a hug when he said it, 'we've never gone anywhere in the world where we couldn't take the children.' I think that about sums up Andra and Red Kelly and all the little Kellys — a family that doesn't go anywhere unless we can go together."

In a March 21 game against Detroit, Red scored the winning goal in a 5–3 victory at the Gardens. But more noteworthy was his "Gordie Howe hat trick": a goal, an assist and a fight. Red was still wearing the helmet, but that did not protect him as Al Langlois rode him hard into the glass, cutting him. Blood gushing from his face, Red went after Langlois, a rare Kelly fight. Afterwards, Red was sewn up with four stitches.

The doomsayers who complained about the earlier trade with New York were silenced when the Leafs finished the season on fire, losing only once in their final nine games to wind up third with 78 points, seven more than Detroit. The Canadiens and Black Hawks finished slightly ahead of them. Kelly had switched places with Mahovlich, from centre to left wing, and the move seemed to ignite the line. Red told Red Burnett:

> I rather like the wing. I played there as a Jr. B with St. Michael's College and several times as a Red Wing. I find I don't have to skate as far or as much on the wing. All you have to do is patrol your own side of the rink and take

care of the opposing right winger. The switch has not ham-
pered me and helped Frank. He has more room to navigate
the centre. Now he cuts in off both wings as well as down
the centre. I think the club is as strong as last season's club.
Bathgate and McKenney have helped our power play a
great deal.

When Burnett asked him if he would favour hockey over politics for the duration of the playoffs, he wasn't committing. "I'm not
saying, but the House will recess Thursday for 10 days which will
allow me to think only of the playoff games at hand."

The opening game at the Forum was a brawl-filled affair that set
an NHL playoff record with 31 penalties as the Habs won 2–0. In
Game 2, the Leafs went ahead 1–0 when Mahovlich worked hard to
regain the puck in his end and fed Red a perfect pass at the Montreal
blue line. Using the defenceman as a screen, he zipped a foot-high
shot between goalie Charlie Hodge's legs.

"That was a typical Kelly goal," observed New York goalie Jacques
Plante, who was rinkside. "He fakes you with a shoulder and then
sends a wrist shot home as you move. There's no defence against it."

Red fed Mahovlich to put the Leafs ahead for good. "Red was
going just as fast out there, and we were clicking," Mahovlich said
after the game. "He made a fine play for his goal on my pass and
then set me up beautifully for the winner."

"The performance of the Big M and Mr. K Saturday night is likely
to cause confusion," wrote Milt Dunnell in the *Toronto Star*. "Nobody
knows for sure now which is the firecracker and which is the fuse."

In Toronto, the Canadiens took the third game 3–2, but the Leafs
evened it up with 5–2 win in Game 4 on the strength of big Frank's
two goals and three assists. Montreal won the crucial fifth game to
move within one win of taking the series.

As Red stepped onto the ice for Game 6, he surpassed Rocket
Richard as the all-time leader in playoff games played, with 134. It

was a good omen, as the Leafs rebounded to win the game 3–0 to force a Game 7.

In Montreal, the intense play see-sawed back and forth in the deciding game. Keon was the hero, scoring all three Leaf goals, the last into an empty net to make it 3–1. Imlach was pleased that both McKenney and Bathgate played instrumental roles.

The Leafs were into the Stanley Cup Final against Detroit. It was the third Cup Final in four years for the Red Wings, and bookies had them as 3–1 underdogs to the two-time champion Maple Leafs.

In Game 1 in Toronto, the Red Wings were up 2–1 and Toronto was on a power play when Wings defenceman Bill Gadsby gave the puck away to George Armstrong, who beat Terry Sawchuk for the tying goal. With overtime imminent, Wing Norm Ullman fired a dangerous cross-ice pass that Bob Pulford intercepted, breaking in alone on Sawchuk. With two seconds left on the clock, Pulford rifled it into the Detroit net to steal a 3–2 victory.

Detroit played a strong second game, taking a 3–1 lead into the third period, but Red brought the Leafs closer with a tally at the 12-minute mark. The Leafs tied it up with just under a minute remaining to send the game into overtime. The Leafs had been outshot 41–28, and in the overtime session, play remained mostly in Leaf territory. Finally Larry Jeffrey gave the Wings the series-tying goal.

The third game, two nights later at the Olympia, had the Wings build up a 3–0 first-period lead. But the Leafs fought back to tie the game with 1:13 left on the clock. Alex Delvecchio notched the winner with 17 seconds left, neatly tucking a Howe pass from across the goalmouth past Bower.

In the fourth contest, the Leafs came out flying, outshooting the Wings, with Keon giving Toronto a 1–0 lead. Detroit turned on the heat in the second period, notching two goals. Then, with four minutes left in the period and two Wings in the penalty box, Keon got his second goal of the game, which tied things up heading into the second intermission.

The Leafs appeared to be sagging in the third until a long bullet off the stick of Bathgate sailed over Sawchuk's right shoulder, finding the top corner and giving the Leafs the lead. Detroit coach Sid Abel threw caution to the wind in the game's final two minutes, putting five forwards and no defencemen on the ice. The strategy seemed to work; the Wings applied pressure on Bower. Then Pulford stole the puck and broke away. Sawchuk made a fabulous save on Pulford, but was in no position to react to Mahovlich, who backhanded the rebound past the sprawling goalie for the insurance goal that tied the series.

When the Leafs rolled into Toronto that night, their train car stayed parked near Union Station as the players slept. When they woke up, Imlach ordered them to the Gardens for a 9:30 a.m. practice. "We went right to practice after arriving the next morning," Red recalled. "Some of the guys were a little peeved at Punch. There were certainly some grumblings."

Sawchuk starred for the Wings in the fifth game, keeping the Leafs off the board until late in the third, for a 2–1 Detroit win.

Before the series shifted to Detroit for Game 6, the Maple Leafs indulged in a bit of brinksmanship, placing the Stanley Cup, packed neatly in its case from Toronto, in the Wings dressing room, among the Wings' baggage. Abel would have none of it. "It belongs to them right now," he said. "Let them carry it as long as they're supposed to. We'll be happy to take care of it after we win it."

As the sixth game began, the Leafs showed no intention of handing over the Cup for keeps. Pulford scored a short-handed goal with just under three minutes left in the first period to put Toronto up by one. The second period was wide open: five goals were scored as the teams emerged tied at three.

At 13:13 of the third period, Leafs defenceman Bob Baun stopped a Red Wing slapshot with his ankle, sustaining what would become one of the most celebrated injuries in hockey history. His ankle buckled under him, and he was carried from the ice on a stretcher.

The Wings, who had been coming on strong, were cooled off in the final frame by the delay in the game.

With 16 seconds remaining in the third period, Red was hurt while carrying the puck towards Red Wings rearguard Gadsby. "Gadsby was just inside the blue line, and I tried to stickhandle around him," recalled Red. "He stuck that big knee out and hit me in the knee, and Howe hit me from behind with a cross-check, boom, at the same time. I remember limping off. I hurt the knee, and I didn't finish the game."

The score remained 3–3 as regulation ended. Baun's ankle, believed to be cracked or fractured, was frozen and taped up by Leafs doctors. Baun returned to participate in the overtime period.

Marcel Pronovost recalled the next sequence of events clearly: "Baun ends up with the puck at our blue line and he takes a shot at our net. Baun's shot hits Bill Gadsby in the butt and deflected into the net behind Sawchuk, and the Leafs win it. And the big story is 'Baun wins it on a broken ankle!' He's the hero!"

When the train carrying the Maple Leafs rolled into Union Station at 4 a.m., Red went straight to Toronto East General Hospital for assessment, and it was grim: torn left knee ligaments. His participation in Game 7 was doubtful.

"Kelly has been treated with cortisone to deaden the pain," wrote Burnett. "But the club does not freeze knees as a matter of policy and [Red] will likely join another left winger, Don McKenney, on the sidelines. Club officials refuse to discuss the extent of either injury and said they wouldn't decide until 6:30 tonight whether Kelly will play."

The night before Game 7, Red was in such great pain that he didn't get any sleep. His parents were staying at the house, and he told them that he wouldn't be playing. "It took me five minutes just to get into the car to go down to the Gardens," he recalled. "I told Andra that unless the doctor could perform a miracle, I couldn't go on."

In the dressing room, Dr. Jim Murray, in consultation with Dr. Hugh Smythe (son of Leafs owner Conn), looked at Red's knee and injected it with pain-killing novocaine before taping it from mid-thigh to mid-calf. Other miracles were performed on Baun's cracked ankle, Carl Brewer's torn rib cartilage and George Armstrong's shoulder, processes repeated each intermission. As the team headed out for the warm-up to a huge ovation, Imlach, ever the showman and a master of psychology, kept Kelly and Baun back in the dressing room. When the cheering had subsided, he sent out Kelly and then Baun, which brought an even louder ovation. Andra was as shocked as anyone to see her husband on the ice.

The Leafs struck first, four minutes in, when Bathgate broke in alone on Sawchuk and picked the top corner. The 1–0 Toronto lead carried to the four-minute mark of the third, when Keon let go a blast that dropped on Sawchuk. Next, Mahovlich got the puck just inside the Detroit blue line and fed Red a pass in the slot. Red slipped the puck to his backhand, and his shot got past Sawchuk to make it 3–0 with 14 minutes to go. As Red got to the bench, he could feel the freezing starting to wear off. The pain increased with each passing minute. The Leafs, sensing blood, added a fourth goal to seal the deal.

At the final buzzer, the Leafs jumped onto the ice, Kelly very carefully, to mob Bower and shake hands with Detroit. As the Stanley Cup was presented by Clarence Campbell, Red was in agony. "I knew I was in trouble, and I shot off the ice as the pain-killer really started to wear off," Red recalled. "I ripped the tape off my leg quickly and got into the shower, under cold water, because I could feel myself getting faint with the increasing pain. I thought the ice-cold water would revive me."

In the shower, the excruciating pain in Red's knee grew more intense. He crumpled to the ground, unconscious, the water still running. As the team came bounding into the dressing room after the on-ice festivities, Tim Horton, Allan Stanley and Ron Stewart were the first to see an unconscious Red and rushed to pick him up.

Anxiety ripped through the room as Red was carried to the

rubbing table in the medical room. Dr. Smythe helped them place him on the table. Concern was written all over the doctor's face as the players and Imlach watched his reaction after a quick examination.

"Is he gonna be all right, doc?" someone asked. The doctor looked at Imlach. "Clear the room for a few minutes," he barked. "And get an ambulance!"

• • • • • •

CHAPTER FOURTEEN

O CANADA!

As Red lay on the trainers' table in the Leafs dressing room, an ambulance pulled up to a nearby door. Police and Gardens personnel momentarily cleared the dressing room and the surrounding area, where the press and photographers were located. They didn't want any pictures taken of Red being loaded into the ambulance.

Dr. Smythe explained that the freezing was wearing off and the pain must have been overwhelming, enough to send Red into shock and make him pass out. Groaning and semi-conscious, Red was whisked away to Wellesley Hospital.

Assured that their teammate was going to be okay, the Leafs started their Stanley Cup celebration in earnest. When Prime Minister Pearson entered the dressing room, he was informed of Red's trip to the hospital. Relieved to hear that he would be okay, Pearson was nonetheless disappointed not to be congratulating him in person. When Red scored his third-period goal, the prime minister had reportedly jumped to his feet yelling, waving his program wildly in the air. "Kelly deserves a cabinet post after that game!" Pearson told reporters.

"I missed the party! Prime Minster Pearson came into the dressing room to congratulate us, and I wasn't there," Red recalled. "Andra and Dad were also waiting for me, and they didn't know until I was gone that I had been taken to the hospital."

"Kelly really gave a gutsy performance," said a Leafs trainer to reporters. "I wouldn't have been at all surprised if after his first turn he'd quit for the night. To think he could not only go all the way, but to play so well is amazing."

After a night at the hospital with painkillers and his leg in a cast, Red was discharged home by ambulance the next morning. After another day of painkillers, rest and treatment, he was feeling somewhat better, enough to answer the call of duty.

"On Monday morning, Andra drove me to the airport and I went to Ottawa on crutches," Red recalled. "She didn't want to take me, but I had to be in the House for two o'clock that afternoon. We were in a minority government. I sat at my desk with my leg sticking out into the aisle."

While his Maple Leafs teammates were enjoying a rainy Stanley Cup parade through the city amidst the smallest crowds in their three years of championships, Red was seated dutifully at his desk in the House of Commons. During a debate over finance minister Walter Gordon's amendments to the Income Tax Act, Social Credit MP Gilles Grégoire of Lapointe, Quebec, stood to offer "congratulations to the member from York West for his Stanley Cup win." The applause indicated that the politicians could agree on something. Red smiled shyly.

Then Conservative MP Paul Martineau (Pontiac–Témiscamingue) added: "Mr. Speaker, the subject of hockey is not off topic (of our income tax discussions), because the member from York West has just been assured of an extra $4,000 from the win, and I wonder if it is taxable!" To laughter, he continued: "Mr. Speaker, he's earned

Leafs' then board member Harold Ballard brought the Stanley Cup by the Kelly household after the Leafs Cup win in May of 1964. Red was away in Ottawa, but Casey, four-month-old Conn, Andra and Patrick pose with the storied trophy. Little did anyone know that Conn was "doing a load" in the Cup at the moment the photo was taken.

O CANADA!

all he got and a lot more too! And I think that is the sentiment of this whole House!"

"Hear! Hear!" went cheers, and members pounded their desks as all sides stood and joined in a hearty round of applause.

"Well that was one reason we wanted to win so badly," Red later told the United Press, with tongue planted firmly in cheek. "We wanted to keep that income tax here in Canada and not let it go south with Detroit in a foreign country."

He was asked about his leg and next season. "There will be no permanent damage," he said. "I guess it will just take a long time to clear up. When I was going through that pain in the shower, I felt as though I never wanted to see another hockey skate. But that thought only lasted a minute. This is no time to think of next season. None of us is in the mental or physical shape to worry about that now."

The Leafs showed their appreciation. "Harold Ballard did a very thoughtful thing. He brought the Stanley Cup, a couple bottles of champagne and a photographer out to the house," Andra recalled. "Red wasn't here, he was in Ottawa. I sat little Conn in the Stanley Cup with Casey and Patrick standing alongside it. The look on Conn's face while the picture was being taken was priceless. Nobody knew he did a whole load right there in the Cup! Our family always chuckles when they see guys today drinking champagne out of the Cup."

Red does not regret the decision to play in that winning game.

"Years later, after I had retired, I'm at the head table at a dinner, and Dr. Smythe, our old team doctor, was sitting at a table nearby," recalled Red. "He came up to me and apologized for having frozen my leg in that seventh game in 1964 and causing me so much pain. I said to him, 'No apologies needed! No way, Doc! I wanted to play! I wouldn't have been able to play if you hadn't done it.'"

Red was not immune to the rancour and occasional public swipes of Canadian politics. The *Toronto Star* ran a letter to the editor from Thomas Murphy of Ottawa on May 1: "Now that the National Hockey League season has drawn to a close, I hope that a certain Member of

Parliament will be able to devote his full-time attention to the more important responsibilities involved in the management of the affairs of the nation . . . I do not question his hockey playing ability, but I do think that in the interests of his constituents, and as a moral obligation to the Canadian public, Red Kelly should have requested his release from his part-time employment upon his election to parliament."

The Liberals continued to press for a new flag, and no one was more passionate about it than Prime Minister Pearson. He championed its need across the country. On June 15, 1964, the prime minister stood in the House of Commons and made the opening motion in the official flag debate, which would last six months. Pearson proposed "to establish officially as the flag of Canada, a flag embodying the emblem proclaimed by His Majesty King George V on November 21, 1921, three maple leaves conjoined on one stem, in the colours red and white then designated for Canada, the red leaves occupying a field of white between vertical sections of blue on the edges of the flag." The debate raged on as the opposition, led by Conservative leader John Diefenbaker, railed against the change. Parliament was forced to sit through the summer.

Red talked over his future with Andra and decided to continue playing hockey. He couldn't give it up. It was in his blood. He had to make it work somehow, though the press was rife with stories of his imminent retirement to concentrate on politics.

"I may be at camp sometime late today or maybe tomorrow," Red told Red Burnett on September 4. "It depends on how our Liberal team does with this flag debate, but I intend on reporting, giving my legs a whirl and talking things over with Punch. But that doesn't mean I'll play."

When he showed up to Leafs camp in Peterborough a week later, he still wasn't sure. "I had to get away for a few days to get physically well," he told the *Toronto Star*'s Milt Dunnell. "I haven't had a day off in months and I'm not missing a dang thing you know. I've listened to flag speeches until they're running out of my ears.

Why, one guy even read his speech — every word. And while he was reading, somebody opened a door and the breeze blew his speech out of his hands. We had to wait until he collected it off the floor."

Red told Dunnell that he needed to get in shape — he weighed over 200 pounds for the first time in his life. He was not sure how his knee would hold up either.

Toronto boss Stafford Smythe told Dunnell that "even 30% of Red Kelly is better than 100% of anybody with whom we could replace him."

There was another opportunity that Red wanted to discuss with Imlach. He had been asked by the prime minister to go to Osaka, Japan, for the World Recreation Congress, which ran from October 2 to 7, and from there represent Canada at the Olympic Games in Tokyo, which lasted until the 24th. While he wasn't expected to be at the Olympics for their duration, he was expected to be there for the opening ceremonies and a few days afterwards. Problem was, the Maple Leafs had training camp and a set of exhibition games scheduled, and their season opener was in Detroit on October 15.

"I talked it over with Punch," Red recalled. "After I explained Pearson's request and my duty to him, Punch asked me: 'Could you be back on time for the first league game in Detroit on October 15th?' I looked up my schedule and then I said, 'I can do that.' He said, 'Great, see you in Detroit then.'"

As Red prepared to head to Japan, the prime minister gave in to pressure from the opposition over the Pearson Pennant flag and appointed a 15-member Flag Committee representing all parties, tasking it with choosing a design for a new flag within six weeks. The committee received 3,541 suggestions from the Canadian public. During the six weeks, the committee met 35 agonizing times in a room plastered floor to ceiling with these suggestions.

"With our skates in tow, Andra and I flew over to Osaka for four days, where I gave a speech," Red recalled. "While there, we found a rink and went to skate at a public session. There were a lot of Japanese skaters out there, and Andra and I went out on the ice, and I just wanted to skate and get my legs, but Andra started to do spins and twirls. The next thing you knew, the skaters had cleared the ice and everyone was watching her go through her routine. They might have been astonished at me a little bit because of my skating, but I wasn't jumping and spinning."

A few days after the opening ceremonies in Tokyo, Red and Andra flew back home. Red was not expecting to play in Detroit in the season opener, just to watch from the bench.

"I arrived in Detroit, put the equipment on for the first time, and I thought I had a good front-row seat to watch the game," he recalled. "Suddenly we're down 1–0, then 2–0. Punch taps me on the shoulder . . ."

"Kelly, get on the ice!"

"Wait a minute!" Red objected. "You told me I didn't have to play. I would just sit on the bench. This is the first time I've really had equipment on!"

"Get out there!"

"What do you mean?"

"Get out there!"

Red sighed and jumped over the boards.

"I got out there and never missed a shift," Red recalled. "I played the rest of the game and was in better shape than a lot of my teammates, who had been working out twice a day at camp in Peterborough. That taught me something — if you want to get in shape, you'll get in shape. It's mind over matter." The Leafs won 5–3 and went undefeated in their first six games.

It was a different atmosphere in the Leafs dressing room during the fall of 1964, and the biggest change was the arrival of goalie Terry Sawchuk from Detroit in the intra-league draft.

By the middle of November, things were not kosher in Leafland. After a dozen games, the Leafs had won only five and were in third place.

After three more losses in four games, Mahovlich, tired of the constant booing and Imlach's ire and drill-sergeant mentality, checked himself into hospital on November 12. The Big M had kept quiet, bottling up his emotions, and had reached a breaking point. Imlach had never been one to coddle a superstar and often publicly criticized a player in an effort to motivate him. In this case, it had the opposite effect, and Mahovlich was diagnosed with fatigue and depression caused by stress.

Red lost his linemate and roommate and was at a loss to help him. "I was quiet, and so was Frank," Red recalled. "We were roommates, but we weren't all that talkative on the whole. He never expressed anything to me about it. We would talk about the games and stuff, but we never got into his situation with Punch. He kept that bottled up inside. He was sometimes an over-thinker."

Back in Ottawa, a new flag design by historian George Stanley was brought before the all-party committee: a single red maple leaf on a white background flanked by a red bar on each side. The Conservatives in the group supported it, figuring the Liberals would be against it, seeing as it wasn't the Pearson Pennant. They were wrong. The Liberals outmanoeuvred them, and on October 22 the committee's final vote for the new flag was unanimous. Some Conservatives cried foul, but it was a done deal.

Red was all for it. His comments were published in the November 12 edition of the *Advertiser*:

> *Today we are willing to support the flag recommended . . .*
> *which is based on the national colours of red and white*
> *and the emblem which is universally recognized as charac-*
> *teristic of Canada. It has been created with the assistance*
> *of some of Canada's leading artists and is thoroughly dis-*
> *tinguishable from any other flag in the world, by propor-*
> *tions and design. To claim that this flag has no historical*
> *meaning is of course absolute nonsense. Its main feature is*

*the maple leaf — the one symbol that is unquestionably
identified with Canada in every part of the world.*

*I can assure you that we stand firm in our determina-
tion that Canada be given a distinctive national flag and
anthem. The government made that commitment in the
belief that it was what the vast majority of Canadians
wanted and we don't plan to let them down!*

When summoned by Mr. Smythe for one last go-around about
the new flag, Red made his final argument. "I relayed the story that
one of Mr. Smythe's old hockey players had told me once, that at one
particular game, when the Leafs were losing, Mr. Smythe had picked
up a sweater and pointed to the Maple Leaf crest on the front of the
jersey and said, 'A lot of men fought and died for that emblem, and
now a bunch of hockey players are letting them down.' He didn't have
a comeback for that quote — but he still never accepted the flag."

The new flag passed 163 votes to 78 at 2:15 in the morning
on December 15, 1964, and would be raised for the first time on
Parliament Hill on February 15.

For Red — or "Senator," as some of his teammates had taken to
calling him — it was back to hockey. On a line with Bob Pulford
and Ron Stewart, he showed that he could still produce. In a 10–2
victory against Detroit in early December, he notched two goals and
an assist; one of his goals was short-handed.

In a *Toronto Star* article a week later, it was pointed out by writer
Jim Proudfoot that it had been a particularly hectic few weeks for
Red. "A political greenhorn, Kelly is a hockey grey beard at 37. It's
surprising, therefore, to note that 'The Senator' is Leafs' second
highest scorer. Next to Andy Bathgate's 21 points, Kelly is tops with
six goals and 11 assists . . . on a team of amazing athletes, Kelly must
rate as one of the most remarkable. He is still trim and energetic.
Beyond that, he is living proof of that old business proverb, 'If you
want a job done well, get a busy man to look after it.'"

Andra was busy too, with three kids, skating lessons and secretarial work for a Member of Parliament. She received help from a surprising source. "In the years when Red was in Parliament and had the home office, I never had help in the house. I did everything myself," Andra recalled. "One day I was down on my knees scrubbing the kitchen floor, and I heard a knock on the door. I looked and it was Harold Ballard's wife, Dorothy. She said, 'What are you doing?' I said, 'I'm cleaning the floors.' She said, 'Well, where's the cleaning lady?' I said, 'I don't have one.' 'What! You have all these children, and you don't have a cleaning lady! I'll send one over to you.'" Dorothy Ballard arranged for her own cleaning lady to start working for the Kellys.

On January 16, in a 4–2 loss against Detroit at the Gardens, Red notched his 250th goal to become the 14th player to ever do so. It put him four goals behind Dickie Moore and 329 behind his old teammate Gordie Howe for first place. After a few more defeats, the Leafs went on a nine-game undefeated streak.

In the last 15 games of the season, the Leafs were hampered by injuries, but they managed to win four of their final five games to finish in fourth place. Their "old" goaltending tandem of Bower and Sawchuk won the Vezina Trophy for the best goals-against average in the league.

Amazingly, Red was one of only three Leafs to play in all 70 league games, and he garnered 18 goals and 28 assists. He was third in team scoring, five points behind Mahovlich and four behind Keon.

The Leafs' first challenge in defending their championship was Montreal, whom they had beaten only five times in 14 encounters.

The Canadiens squeaked out the first two games at the Forum with 3–2 and 3–1 victories. For Game 3 at the Gardens, Imlach benched rookie Pete Stemkowski and put Red back on the Mahovlich line. "Big Frank has said he plays his best hockey with Red Kelly at centre," explained Punch to the press. "I'm trying to get him on track, so Pete has to sit out. If we can get the Big M rolling, it will give us the lift we need and I think Kelly can get him scoring." Toronto won the game 3–2.

After practice on the morning of April 7, Red had to fly back to Ottawa for a confidence vote in the House of Commons that afternoon. A few opposition members had volunteered "to pair" with him, meaning they would not show up to vote against the government in his absence, but he had declined. "I wanted to be in the House," he later explained.

Bower starred in Game 4, a 4–2 win at MLG. Imlach was a true believer again. "From now on, I don't believe in miracles or ghosts," declared Imlach. "Now I only believe in Santa Claus, and I pronounce his name Johnny Bower."

But the Canadiens shook it off and eliminated the defending champs with wins of 3–1 and 4–3 in overtime.

After the hectic season and the contentious flag debate in Ottawa, Red truly relaxed that summer of 1965 at the cottage on Cedar Island. One escape was a trip to Toronto on August 11 to receive the 1965 Eagles International Sports Award, presented to him by former boxer Jack Dempsey. By the time training camp loomed, he was telling Red Burnett about his summer: "I played a lot of golf, did a lot of swimming and chores at the cottage and I'm really in the pink this year."

When pressed about his future in hockey or politics, he wasn't hedging his bets. A new federal election was expected to be called in the next few months. "I haven't made up my mind yet," Red said. "I won't say anything until after the nomination meeting." But his decision was imminent.

"I came home from Ottawa, and I'm walking up the driveway," Red recalled. "Little Casey sees me and says to her mother, 'Look, Mommy! It's Red Kelly!' Holy moley. When Andra told me what she had said, that's when it then struck me. I was never really home, between hockey and Ottawa. I decided right there and then, that's it." But first he had to tell his friend Keith Davey and then the prime minister.

Red and Andra with Patrick, Conn and Casey during a family skate at Maple Leaf Gardens. © GRAPHIC ARTISTS/HOCKEY HALL OF FAME

Red called Davey that weekend. Davey was naturally disappointed, but understood. Knowing that the prime minister would be in Toronto on September 13 to officially open the new Toronto city hall, Red arranged to meet with him. They talked for an hour privately, and Pearson accepted Red's decision to retire from politics.

"It was like a hundred-pound bag lifted from each shoulder," Red recalled. "I had enjoyed the experience. It was a real learning experience, to be in Ottawa, in the House, Parliament, caucus meetings. On weekends, people would be lined up at the office at the house; [I'd be] hearing some of their problems, trying to help them."

Red feels privileged to have been front and centre for the battles of two notable Canadians, Lester Pearson and John Diefenbaker. "Pearson would get fired up by Diefenbaker, they had quite the exchanges, and his face would get red. It was great to witness the back and forth across the aisle between them. It was historic. I knew Pearson would be great for the country, and I was never disappointed at any time."

Andra had supported her husband as much as she could, which was one of the reasons they had chosen to have his office at home. This enabled them to perhaps have breakfast together, and for Casey, Patrick and Conn to maybe have a few minutes with their father. Andra knew how much Red loved his family and how much he missed them as well. She was not disappointed in his decision to retire from politics.

"Having the office at home had many drawbacks," she told Milt Dunnell. "Red wouldn't even come out of the office for his meals. When I'd take in a tray, he would share the food with a constituent who had come to discuss a problem. So Red wasn't getting enough to eat!"

In September 1965, as Red hugged and kissed his family goodbye to head to training camp, he did so with more relish and emotion than ever before. He would be back with them, and often, no longer torn between Ottawa and Toronto.

He was proud at having served his country and having played a part in the new Canadian flag. But now he would be concentrating again on the one thing he loved to do without distraction — play hockey.

• • • • • •

CHAPTER FIFTEEN

A WALK *through*
the VALLEY

The first order of business for Red Kelly before his 19th NHL season was a new contract. Because he didn't have a final deal, Red sat out the first exhibition game against the Bruins on October 14.

"I want to point out that Kelly was never a holdout," Punch told writer Red Burnett at the Peterborough training camp. "We had to revise a few clauses in the . . . contract Red signed last year. He was combining hockey and a seat in parliament at that time. Now he is sticking strictly to hockey so we had to straighten out a few things in accordance with his changed status."

While Red signed his contract, others, including Bob Baun, Tim Horton and Dave Keon, were contract holdouts. Frustrated with Imlach, Carl Brewer quit outright.

Brewer, who died in 2001, was a cerebral figure, said Red. "I got along with Carl most of the time. Carl was a thinker, smoked a pipe," he recalled. "When I came to Toronto, Punch paired me off against Carl in skating drills. I was the old guy and he was the young guy who could skate. Well, I could skate, and if he thought he was going to outskate me, he had another thought coming. Brewer couldn't beat me down the ice."

Red's daughter, Casey, saw her father's speed. "I remember thinking that Dad was always a 'good' player — meaning that he was rarely in the penalty box. And, if he ever did get a penalty, we were shocked," she recalled. "I also remember him being a very smooth skater — so smooth that it didn't look as if he was skating very fast, unless you saw him gliding by other players who were showing the effort of trying to keep up with him!"

To Red, Brewer was still an elite skater. "He was quick and could really stickhandle. During a fight once, a member of Chicago Black Hawks couldn't catch him while Carl was skating backwards." He also had a secret weapon. "Carl always had a little hole in the palm of his glove to grab you, and you wouldn't know it," recalled Red. "He certainly caused things to happen on the ice."

Brewer sat out the season, going to university, and then played a year with the Canadian national hockey team before eventually returning to the NHL.

Horton did sign for a three-year deal reportedly worth $75,000. "We never knew what the other guys got," Red recalled. "We never discussed it with each other. You signed your own contract and that was that."

To help bolster his Brewer-less defence, Imlach obtained veteran Marcel Pronovost from Detroit. "Marcel was a strong addition to the team," recalled Red. "He was an extremely powerful skater and hitter. He was a strong defenceman. He fit in nicely on a team that had a lot of veterans."

When the Leafs failed to put any pucks in the net in their season-opening game against Detroit, Imlach reacted with a prolonged shooting drill at the next practice. "When a baseball team slumps, the manager orders batting practice," he told Red Burnett. "In hockey, you give them half a ton of pucks, let them fire at the goal-keepers and hope they find the target area."

It didn't help: the Maple Leafs only garnered three wins in their first 11 games. The slump was epitomized by a 9–0 beat-down in Chicago on November 7. By the time they hosted Boston on December 11, Toronto's record was an ugly seven wins, 10 losses and three ties.

Then the team started scoring, and for the rest of the month they went on a 10–game undefeated streak to finish out 1965, a Christmas gift for Leafs fans. By mid-January, Toronto was still holding its own, and Red's new linemates, centre Bob Pulford and winger Eddie Shack, were having great seasons.

One day at the practice rink, Tam O'Shanter Arena, Red walked by just as Pulford was being interviewed. "There's a lot of reasons for the goals," Pulford said pointing to Red. "There's one tremendous playmaker and a great fellow. He never forces an opinion on you, but if he says something, it's usually significant. Eddie (Shack) will listen to Red. So do I."

In February, when Jim Proudfoot asked coach Imlach to explain the resurgence in Red's play, he was quick with an answer: "There's a simple explanation, Kelly is doing nothing but playing hockey this season and that makes all the difference. He looks as though he could go on for several seasons now although I couldn't have said that a year ago. It's amazing to see what giving up the other job has done for him. Kelly is playing left wing with Bob Pulford and Eddie Shack, and that's not an easy job. Pulford goes out against the opposition's best, which means Kelly has to check some of the toughest right wingers in the league. And playing with Shack means he has a lot of covering up to do. He gets it all done properly and still sets up scoring chances every time he's on the ice."

Andra had another explanation for Proudfoot as to what had affected her husband's play while he was in Parliament: "It was a long while before I found out he wasn't eating anything," Andra explained. "There was no food served on the planes he was using and there just wasn't time in Ottawa, so he wouldn't bother at all. So I started packing him a bit of a lunch that he could eat on the way out to the airport. But that was all. So, it's no wonder he was slowing down (last year). I just don't know how he did it at all!"

The Leafs had an assortment of goaltender injuries to cope with. Five goalies played in the Toronto net that season, and at one point both Bower and Sawchuk were out, with a pulled groin and a torn hamstring respectively. Bruce Gamble played so well in relief, recording four shutouts in seven games, that it was rumoured Sawchuk might be shipped to the minors once he returned from the injured list. Then Gamble pulled a hamstring, but his 23 games that season helped immeasurably. (Gary Smith and Al Smith, no relation, were the other two keepers.)

Toronto limped into the playoffs having won only three of 10 games. The Leafs nets were in such disarray that in the last game of the season, in Detroit, Bower started the game, Sawchuk played the second period and Gamble was summoned from the press box to play the third in a 3–3 tie.

Red played 63 games and accumulated eight goals and 24 assists. He helped Shack and Pulford attain career highs in goals and tied Mahovlich in total points.

"Our line had a pretty good year," Red recalled. "Shackie scored a lot of goals and so did Pulford. I would have liked to score a few more goals, but the line was scoring, so that's what matters. Eddie would come from behind and give me a shout and I'd throw it back to him, and he could fire.

"Eddie was 'the Entertainer' even then. Oh, yeah! If he was named one of the three stars, he would come out and do a twirl like a figure skater. He'd entertain the crowd. Shack got bonuses for goals, and years later apologized to me when I was coaching him. He said it bothered him that he hadn't passed to me enough when we played together."

As Toronto began the playoffs, the flu ravaged its ranks — Imlach, Kelly and Bower included — which forced a rusty Sawchuk to play the first two games of the semifinal series against the first-place

Canadiens. The Leafs lost both. With Bower in next in the third game, at the Gardens, the Leafs were ahead 2–0, led by the strong, spirited play of Shack, when two crunching bodychecks and ensuing fights with Habs strongman John Ferguson took the starch out of him. The Canadiens came back to win the game 5–2 and take a 3–0 stranglehold on the series. The Habs swept Toronto aside in Game 4 with a final 4–1 victory and then beat Detroit in the final for their 14th Stanley Cup.

Red was non-committal about another season, hinting a little more strongly at retirement. With Red about to turn 39 years of age, Imlach left Red and Allan Stanley, who had also hinted at hanging up his skates, off Toronto's protected list in that June's intra-league draft. Surprisingly, and to Imlach's relief, neither was touched.

The ability to spend time at home with Andra and the kids during the season was a true tonic for Red. They went to the cottage on Cedar Island, and when Red went north in August to be the head instructor at the Haliburton Hockey Haven, he brought the family with him.

There, he spoke to the local Rotary Club and praised the beauty of the region and of their new arena, built just a few years before. He urged the group to continue supporting the local minor hockey association. He addressed the concerns of the upcoming NHL expansion — the league was scheduled to double to 12 teams for the 1967–68 season. "The calibre of play might be down somewhat but very little," Red predicted. "But expansion will also mean more positions will be open for young players coming up."

Some hockey publications didn't even list Red among the possible returnees to the Leafs; most expected the team to go with a younger lineup. But Imlach went with the veterans, even talking Sawchuk out of retirement, which he'd been considering because of back issues.

"Kelly was a champion when he came to us, and I still regard him as one," Imlach explained to Margaret Scott, who asked about the declining Kelly point totals. He reminded her that Kelly played left wing for Shack and Pulford. "That was no bed of roses," Imlach said. "I feel they're both pretty hard to locate on the ice and since they got 56 goals between them, Kelly must have been slipping some of his smooth passes in their direction."

Imlach also commented on the playoff sweep by the Canadiens. "That was inexcusable. The flu bug floored Johnny Bower and Red Kelly, but I got a very poor performance from the rest of the team," he said. "Where were our prolific scorers? It was the same old story of our big guns suddenly becoming silent and that's a big reason why I'm continually disappointed with the spring showing of Frank Mahovlich. He's simply not a Stanley Cup performer."

Red admitted that Mahovlich was frustrating. "He had so much talent, that big shot, that big stride, that big reach," Red explained. "Sometimes his big stride made it look like he was loafing, and sometimes he was, and we'd yell at him if he could check someone. And then he would. But he could sure set the tempo of a game, if he wanted to."

Training camp in Peterborough marked the start of Red's 20th season. In an exhibition game in Kitchener, Mahovlich suffered a broken rib from the skate of Bruce MacGregor, and Red suffered a cut over an eye. In a later practice, Red went down with a pulled groin muscle and missed a few exhibition games. Baun and Pronovost were also out with injuries.

In the season opener against the Rangers, Kelly, now centering a line with young wingers Ron Ellis and Larry Jeffrey, potted the third goal in a listless game in which reporters remarked that Red seemed to be the only one really skating. The Leafs won just three of their first 12 games.

In a game on November 19 at the Gardens against the visiting Canadiens, Red decided to ditch the helmet that he had been wearing since his concussion a few years before. "It was a spur-of-the-moment thing," Red recalled. "I thought it was cumbersome."

With 15,986 fans in attendance, the largest crowd to see a Gardens game since 1946, the "Quiet Line" — Kelly, Ellis and Jeffrey — potted three of the four Leafs goals, Red earning two assists. With two minutes left, the line was back on, though many fans had started to depart even with Toronto winning handily, 4–1.

Red was forechecking defenceman Jean-Guy Talbot when he nabbed the puck and was in the clear on Montreal goalie Gump Worsley. "The old redhead made it look easy, as he picked the right corner of the net with a low shot from about 35 feet out," wrote the *Globe and Mail*'s Louis Cauz. "The goal meant little to most people as it came when the verdict was clearly decided. Kelly was a proud man when the goal light went on. Why did he covet the 271st goal of his NHL career?" That goal put him ahead of Howie Morenz and Aurèle Joliat on the all-time goal list. "I was tied with them until tonight," explained Red. "I was a tiger on that one!"

"I don't think Red got enough credit for his play last year," said Imlach when asked about the Quiet Line. "Pulford and Shack both had great years. Pully got 28 and Eddie 26. And who did they play with? It's no accident these people had good seasons. That's why I decided to put Red with Ellis and Jeffrey. Here was a chance to develop two hockey players."

The win spurred the Leafs, who lost only twice in their next 10 games. Sawchuk was finally starting to recuperate from his off-season back surgery and was playing like his old self, but then he was hospitalized again and missed months of action.

The *Toronto Star*'s Jim Proudfoot called Red a catalyst in the resurgence of the Leafs.

> *There are many ways to get ahead in big time hockey. You can do it through hard work and clean living or as Ron Ellis and Larry Jeffrey are discovering this season, you can play on the same forward line as Red Kelly. Since Kelly*

joined the Toronto Maple Leafs in 1960, his partners have
prospered so regularly it can't be a coincidence.

Early on, it was Frank Mahovlich and Bob Nevin,
then last season Bob Pulford and Eddie Shack scored more
goals than ever before. Now Ellis and Jeffrey are moving
in that same direction.

In the same December 12 article, Imlach praised his centreman. "Kelly's never received the credit he deserves," said the coach-GM. "In fact, he was almost convinced he should retire last spring. Now look at him! Next to Jean Béliveau, he's the best centre I've ever coached!"

In an article for the *Christian Science Monitor* on December 28, Red talked about his new linemates. "Ronnie and Jeff are two young fellows and we're working well together without having to make too much noise on the ice," Red told Alan Grayson. "Confidence is the big thing and when you've got that, you build up a spirit of pride on your line. When you're able to get an additional point or so, it makes the whole line feel good, no matter who gets it."

After 30 games, Red was tied with Keon for the team scoring lead, with 24 points.

"There's no doubt in my mind that Red has helped this club one heck of a lot," Pulford said. "He's plugging and helping the youngsters to find their range and that means a lot."

"He's passing and skating better than ever," added George Armstrong. "And he has his confidence, a very important thing. And the fans are really cheering him on and that helps too."

With less than three minutes remaining in a January 4 game at the Gardens against the Rangers, Red was duelling Harry Howell and Bob Nevin for the puck when Howell attempted to flip him with his stick and Red fell, twisting and injuring his left knee. He left the ice in pain, and Leafs brass worried that he could be gone for at least a month. It turned out to be strained ligaments, requiring rest, and Red missed nine games.

With Sawchuk and Kelly out of the lineup, the Leafs went on an extended losing streak, prompting Imlach to publicly muse that his other stars weren't providing enough leadership.

The younger players were balking at their handling by a coach who refused to change with the times. "Punch was a pusher no doubt," Red recalled. "He liked to practise, practise and practise. In this respect, he had a real problem with some of the young players on the team who rebelled against him. They stopped working for him, and then Punch would yell even more.

"We veterans understood what he was doing, but the youngsters didn't appreciate his drill-sergeant mentality. Even some of us veterans wondered sometimes. That whole situation hurt the team. But every team has its ups and its downs, its winning and losing streaks, its peaks and valleys."

When the Leafs lost to the Rangers and Red Wings, the losing streak was at 10, and the team was in fifth place, on the verge of sinking lower. No matter what Imlach tried — line combos, sitting or playing players, moving defencemen up to forward, changing defence pairings, working the players harder in practice — nothing worked.

The turning point was February 11, with the league-leading Black Hawks in town. His aching veterans suffering through injury-plagued seasons, Imlach decided to rely more on his younger, healthy bodies, and tinkered with his lineup accordingly. Though the game finished in a 4–4 tie, ending the losing streak, a long-absent chant from the crowd — "Go Leafs go!" — seemed to propel the team forward. Finally. Wins against Boston and New York followed.

The next complication was unforeseen.

On February 18, the Bruins were coming into town for a Saturday night tilt. Imlach and Clancy were huddled together for a pre-game chat and a cup of tea in the Gardens lounge.

"Geez, I feel lousy," said Imlach, looking somewhat greyish of pallor. "I've got a congestion here," he continued, pointing to his chest, "and a pain here," pointing to his left arm.

Clancy was concerned. "Punch, you should see a doctor!"

"Naw. No time for that. We've got a game tonight."

Clancy had team doctor Tate McPhedran look at Imlach where he sat. Punch described his symptoms. After examining him, McPhedran said, "I think you should go to hospital for a proper examination."

"I can't," Punch declared. "I've got a game tonight."

"Now!" insisted the doctor. It was 2:30 in the afternoon.

As the players ambled into the Toronto dressing room area later that afternoon, they saw no sign of Imlach or Clancy. The trainers weren't saying anything, and the routine continued as usual. When the players were nearly dressed to go out for the pre-game warm-up, Clancy walked in, alone. He had a serious look on his face. All heads turned.

"Where's Punch?"

"Punch . . . won't be here tonight," King answered solemnly. "I can't say anything more than that, except that I'll be handling things tonight."

You could hear a pin drop. Clancy looked around the room. "We can beat these guys," Clancy urged. "I'm asking you to go out there and give it one hundred per cent! We're the better team! Can you do that for Punch? . . . For me?"

• • • • • •

CHAPTER SIXTEEN

THE LAST
HURRAH

"Is Punch okay?" someone asked King Clancy.

"Oh, sure," Clancy replied. "He's just gone to hospital for a few tests. I'm sure it's nothing serious. Now let's go out there and beat these guys!"

As the Leafs stormed out of the dressing room that February night to face the Bruins, Red could feel the difference in the air. "King going behind the bench changed things, no question," Red recalled. "Some of the players had been upset with Punch, and although they thought they had been playing their best, they weren't. When Clancy came in, it was like a new day. He would throw out one line after another, boom, boom, boom, without hesitation. Everybody went out and got going.

"So it just kind of shows you what a change in your thoughts, attitude and mental state can do — it has to be right in order for you to give one hundred per cent. It wasn't that they purposely didn't play for Punch; it's just that they were not out there playing with the greatest of effort. When Clancy came along, we got into that, and we all played like there was no tomorrow."

They beat Boston 5–3. After the game, the players were informed that Imlach had been admitted to Toronto General Hospital for tests. In all probability, their coach was just suffering from exhaustion.

The next game, they hosted and beat the Canadiens 5–2 to bring their record to .500, moving them into a tie for third place with the Habs. There was a palpable change in the dressing room, and King Clancy was just what the team needed. Practices became fun.

"King talked your ear off behind the bench, and he was always encouraging everyone back there, giving people a pat on the back. The younger players really liked him and his 'rah-rah' easy-going ways," Red recalled. "King played all the lines equally, just kept rolling them out there. We played hard for him, played up to our potential. We continued to play great hockey and kept on winning."

On February 23, Sawchuk suited up for his first start in 11 weeks, against the Red Wings at the Olympia. He survived a first-period collision with Gordie Howe, and his play was instrumental in the 4–2 Leafs win that stretched their undefeated streak to six games. Two nights later, the Red Wings paid a return visit to Maple Leaf Gardens, and Sawchuk started again. His 4–0 shutout was number 99 of his career, and he hit 100 a week later.

With the schedule winding down, the Leafs fell victim to a first-place-clinching 5–0 smackdown at the hands of the Black Hawks in Chicago. The Hawks looked like they were toying with the Leafs.

On March 15, with Imlach out of hospital and back behind the bench, Toronto lost to Detroit 4–2 but rebounded to beat the Hawks 9–5 and then the Red Wings 6–5. "I hope this shuts up a few people who say we won't play for Punch!" said Armstrong.

Imlach was different after he returned, said Red. "When Punch got back out behind the bench, he rolled all the lines, just like King Clancy had. The younger guys responded and were playing so good and so hard that he had to keep playing everyone. And the more they played, the better they played, giving a real effort, more than they had for Punch before."

For the remainder of March, the Leafs played .500 hockey, and on the final weekend of the season, they beat New York 5–1 and Boston 5–2. As he had the last two years, Bower played the final two games in preparation for the playoffs. He had always been Imlach's goalie.

Toronto ended the season in third place, two points behind Montreal, which had finally recovered from its extensive injuries and rocketed to second place, losing only once in its final 14 games. Toronto finished 19 points behind the powerful Hawks, their first-round opponents.

As Red geared up for his 19th playoff semifinal series, a record, it was amazing to think that he had only ever missed the playoffs once in his career — the year before his trade from Detroit, back in 1959. He had surpassed his buddy Gordie Howe in playoff appearances. Dubbed a "War Horse" by the *Windsor Star*'s Mike Dunnell (son of the *Toronto Star*'s Milt Dunnell), Red explained his philosophy of playoff hockey: "I like to get kind of nervous," he told the writer. "I guess you would say on edge. It's not a matter of physical sickness like some fellows get but getting hungry. During the playoffs I think about what I'm going to do before every game. You think about who you're going to play, rehash their moves and try to get yourself up for the game. This is impossible over the schedule but in the playoffs it's a new league, a few losses and you're sunk."

On the eve of the playoffs, Louis Cauz did an extensive piece for the *Globe and Mail* on Red and his record-breaking playoff appearance. When the reporter asked him the first thing that came to mind when he thought about the Stanley Cup playoffs, Red was quick with an answer: "Pressure. You feel the pressure more than anything. It's the most nerve-wracking, tense period of the season. I get tense. I'm all keyed up, ready to explode. But I don't mind. I like being keyed up, this is the way I play best. This is the difficult thing during the season, to get keyed up for a game." When Cauz asked him if he'd like one more Stanley Cup, Red's eyes twinkled. "Four and four. Four with Detroit and four with Toronto. That'd be real nice, then I could say adios."

The Maple Leafs, holed up in Peterborough away from the distractions of the city, were undisciplined but eager in practices, perhaps too eager to show that they were ready to tackle the younger, more powerful Hawks. Their goalies unfortunately paid the price for their shooters' enthusiasm, as Sawchuk was hit twice on the left shoulder by blistering slapshots that left him badly bruised, and a Stemkowski slapshot broke Bower's little finger, meaning Sawchuk would now have to start in net for the semifinals.

No one gave the Leafs much of a chance. The Hawks had set a league record with 264 goals and had five of the league's top nine point-getters.

"The key for us against Chicago was to not let their big guns get any shots on our net," Red recalled. "We had to stay between them and the net, make them shoot from far out. Mikita's line were fast skaters, but were a little smaller than us, so we would have to hit them to slow them down."

The Hawks offence shelled the Toronto net in Game 1 and took a 4–1 lead into the third. With 12 minutes remaining, the Hawks took a penalty, which led to a frustrated Imlach pulling Sawchuk to give him two extra attackers — an unheard of move with so much time remaining. The experiment lasted only 11 seconds, as Pulford incurred a slashing penalty. The teams exchanged goals to make it 5–2, and in the closing minutes of the game, the crowd began to chant, "Good night, Terry!" The Leafs' hitting game had been effective: as Hull complained afterwards, "Pappin fell on me . . . Pulford gave me a crack across the knee . . . I feel like an 80-year-old man."

The Ice Capades were booked into Chicago Stadium the next day, leaving the Leafs without practice ice. Imlach flew his team back to Toronto, landing at 3 a.m., and then declared practice that morning optional. The whole team showed up for a 90-minute workout. Meanwhile, back in Chicago, the Hawks' optional skate produced only four players. The Leafs practiced hard again the next day, while Chicago coach Billy Reay gave his troops the day off.

As Game 2 started, the Hawks looked rusty, while the Leafs had an extra bounce in their step. Tenacious forechecking and hitting paid off when Toronto's Pappin stole the puck in the Chicago corner and passed to Pulford, whose relay to Stemkowski ended up in the Hawks net to put the Leafs up by one. Sawchuk was strong, misplaying only a Mikita snapshot with 10 minutes to go in the 3–1 Toronto win.

The Hawks came out flying for Game 3 back in Toronto. The Quiet Line made the first noise when Jeffrey sent the puck to Red, who saw Ellis breaking and fed him a perfect pass. Ellis's 20-footer put Toronto up 1–0. "Everybody saw the way Larry rifled that pass from our zone to me in centre in order that I could put Ellis into the clear," Red said, praising his linemates after the game.

The goal sparked the Leafs, and they continued to check and hit the Hawks at every opportunity. Again, it was a 3–1 Leafs victory, Sawchuk unbeatable until a late third-period goal.

Imlach reminded Red Burnett it was a team game: "Don't ask me to single out a man. We had to get a super effort from every man to beat them. And we'll have to be even better in the fourth game Thursday because Hawks are that good — a great team. I've never been prouder of this team than tonight."

Prior to Game 4 two nights later, Reay blasted his team in a pre-game pep talk, and it paid off immediately. Kenny Wharram took only nine seconds to put the puck past Sawchuk. After a wild first 10 minutes, the game was tied 2–2. The Leafs, lacking Chicago's firepower, realized they had to slow the game down. They tried to reassert the physical, punishing game that had worked in Game 3, but it backfired as they took penalties. Sawchuk did all he could but was visibly tired in his fourth game in seven days. It ended up 4–3, with the series tied heading back to Chicago.

Reporters asked Imlach which goalie he was starting. "You guess which one and I'll use the other guy," Imlach quipped. At Sawchuk's insistence, it was Bower.

Pierre Pilote recalled Chicago's strategy in Game 5. "Our goal was to really get at Bower," he said. "If we could get Bower out of there, we'd be all set. We knew we could beat Sawchuk. We all thought Terry couldn't see the puck anymore."

Bower played the first period, was shaky, and was replaced by Sawchuk to start the second. A Bobby Hull high blast from close range levelled Sawchuk and brought a hush over the Stadium crowd. Even Hull seemed concerned, but, after a few minutes, Sawchuk amazingly stood back up to a round of applause and then proceeded to stymie Hawks shooters over the last two periods for a Toronto 4–2 victory. Strong skating, forechecking and defensive work by the Leafs smothered the Chicago attack and allowed Sawchuk some needed space.

"It was a big upset," Red said. "Bower was shaky, Sawchuk came in and was terrific, and he stoned 'em! The crowd in Chicago was all upset and threw stuff on the ice. It was at a critical time in the game, too, and the play had to stop to clean the ice. We were down at the time, and that break gave us the time we needed to come back. We were the old guys, but everything just clicked for us. The 'over-the-hill-gang' was rolling downhill now! We had 'em on the run."

The momentum shift affected the opponents too. "There was a certain point in that fifth game," Red recalled. "I forget how many minutes were left, five or six, and Chicago gave up. They had a last big chance, stopped by Sawchuk, and then they literally gave up. You could see it. My first impression was that these guys aren't champions. Champions don't ever give up until the final play, the final whistle, the final buzzer — champions never lose heart. When we saw that, we knew we had won not only that game but the series. The last game of the series was ours to win."

Pilote agreed. "Going back to Toronto after that fifth-game loss, we were defeated. Sawchuk had taken the wind out of us."

On the flight back from Chicago, Leafs boss Stafford Smythe approached Red and offered him a four-year contract to keep playing with Toronto. Red didn't bite. "I told him no. I was retiring. Four more years! Holy moley! That was a long time, and I was older. A bad injury was always around the corner, and then what?" Red recalled. "But he wanted me to stay and play. I said I was retiring and thinking of going to coach in L.A. Imlach had told me no problem when I had mentioned it to him — so I thought at the time." The offer, and Red's response, was kept hushed.

In Game 6 at Maple Leaf Gardens, the Hawks barely showed up. Sawchuk made 35 saves, but the Leafs played flawless defensive hockey and were full of confidence as they outshot Chicago and won the game easily, 3–1, eliminating the NHL's most powerful team.

"We were never built as a playoff team," recalled Chicago goalie Glenn Hall. "Defensive teams win Stanley Cups, and we were just too offensive minded. We won first place with firepower, yes, but that didn't work in the playoffs. That philosophy in itself explains why, despite our regular season dominance through the 1960s, we only ever won one Stanley Cup."

The Canadiens had disposed of the Rangers in the other semifinal series, setting the stage for an All-Canadian Stanley Cup Final — apropos on so many levels. "In 1967, Canada was celebrating its hundredth birthday," recalled Red. "The country was all excited. There was a centennial emblem, a centennial song, a centennial choir, a centennial everything. Parties and celebrations were slated to happen all over the country throughout the year."

Montreal was hosting Expo 67, the world's fair, that summer, and all the provinces had pavilions for visitors to see. "As the series started, there was a lot of talk about Montreal winning the Stanley Cup and displaying it in the Quebec pavilion at Expo 67 in Montreal," recalled Pronovost. "We heard that they already had a spot where they were going to display it. And we thought, *No way! We're gonna display it in the Ontario pavilion!* That gave us some incentive."

Also on the horizon was NHL expansion, with the league slated to double its size to 12 teams, adding teams in Philadelphia, Pittsburgh, Oakland, St. Louis, Los Angeles and Minnesota. These playoffs would be the last for the old six-team league, and it seemed appropriate that it would be won by one of the two teams that had captured 18 of the past 24 Stanley Cups. The pundits felt that it would be a lopsided final, with the Canadiens too powerful and the Leafs too old and tired.

Reporters liked stirring the pot with both fiery coaches, making it "the Punch and Toe Show." Imlach raged over the comments by Montreal's rookie goalie Rogie Vachon, who said he figured the Leafs would be easier to beat than Chicago.

"You tell that Junior B goalie he won't be playing against a bunch of pea-shooters when he plays against the Leafs," hollered Imlach. "I just hope Blake doesn't disappoint me by putting someone else in besides Vachon. We'll take his head off with our first shot!"

Game 1 at the Forum was an easy 6–2 rout for Montreal. Sawchuk was tired, and when the Habs scored their fifth goal on him with 15 minutes left in the third period, Imlach replaced him with Bower. The Toronto coach also rested some of his star players for the duration of the game.

"Isn't this a thing?" Blake chortled to the press, unable to resist a dig after the Montreal win. "Vachon's got to be the only Junior B goalie in history who has come up and won five straight games in Stanley Cup playoffs."

Many wrote the Leafs obituary after that night. "Even the guys from Toronto talked as if the body was ready for burial," Imlach wrote years later. At the next morning's practice, Bower looked sharp, so he got the start.

After practice, Imlach and Clancy headed to the press room at the Forum, telling anybody who would listen that their Leafs were going to win the Cup. Imlach went down to a tailor on rue Sainte-Catherine and ordered a new suit to wear when they won. The scribes all thought Imlach was crazy, with one writer from Los Angeles asking, "Are you for real?"

From the puck drop, the Leafs showed they had life. A first-period Stemkowski power-play goal gave Toronto a 1–0 lead, which quieted the Forum crowd. In the second period, Red played on a checking line with Ron Ellis and Brian Conacher, the son of the legendary multi-sport star Lionel Conacher, who had been playing for Canada's national hockey team.

"Punch liked to play me with the young guys," Red recalled. "He told me the team played better when I was there, which made sense to me, because I played for the team. I'd help this guy and that guy. If I had a new young winger with me, then I'd help him. Punch knew that. I'd tell him, 'You don't have to worry about our line, Punch. We'll do our bit. We won't get scored on, and we'll score a few too!"

Another power-play goal, by Mike Walton, put the Leafs up 2–0 in the second. The Canadiens regrouped and on two successive power plays came at the Leafs, but Bower was more than up to the task, turning everything aside. Horton put the Leafs up by three going into the final period. Bower put on a steely performance in the 3–0 victory. With seven minutes left, the unsettled Forum crowd started booing their heroes as the Kelly-Ellis-Conacher line kept the Canadiens tied up in their own end. Imlach started to change his lines quickly while the desperate Blake kept his lines out much longer, hoping for some magic. When Red's line pushed the play into the Habs end with time winding down, a frustrated Béliveau took a slashing penalty to muzzle any chance of a Canadiens comeback.

Blake ripped his team before the next game. They hadn't played well in the last game and deserved to lose, he said. The Habs scored just over two minutes into Game 3 and got 20 shots on Bower in the first period alone, but it was 1–1 at the break, and thanks to the heroics of Bower and Vachon, it went to overtime, and then a second OT.

A mid-ice hit by Allan Stanley on young Henri Richard in the second extra stanza had the youngster seeing stars and out for the game. It also brought the Leafs to life. Both goalies were forced to make great saves until the 8:26 mark, when Pulford tipped a wide Pappin shot into the open net behind Vachon. The Canadiens left the ice in disbelief, down 2–1 in the series. Bower had stopped 60 shots over five periods.

But in the warm-up to Game 4, Bower stretched the wrong way and tore a hamstring. Sawchuk was forced into action, and it wasn't his night. One goal went off his skate; another was a floater he should have caught. Though Montreal barely outshot Toronto, 40–37 over 60 minutes, the final score was a Canadiens 6–2 rout. "I've got one thing to say, gentlemen," Sawchuk told reporters. "I just didn't have a good night."

Prior to Game 5, word leaked out that Red was contemplating retirement. "Kelly has denied any arrangement or understanding by which he would become coach of the new Los Angeles Kings," wrote Milt Dunnell. "Still, there is pretty strong evidence he is going there."

"There was no big hullaballoo! Expansion was coming, and things were happening, and I had told the Leafs that they should be aware of what's going to happen," Red recalled. "I had made up my mind that I was going to retire at the end of that season. I thought they should be aware of that for their future plans and scouting."

Back in Montreal, the city and its players were brimming with confidence prior to Game 5. "You could see and feel the overconfidence everywhere," Marcel Pronovost remembered. "Sawchuk had had a bad game, two bad games really, and with him in net the rest of the way, Montreal thought they had us now."

Before heading onto the ice, the Leafs got some inspiration from an added source. "Frank Mahovlich was always as quiet as a mouse in the dressing room," recalled Pronovost. "But before we went on the ice that afternoon, the Big M stood up and yelled, 'We're gonna beat these guys today!' He marched out of the room, and everybody charged out after him."

It was Sawchuk who was the difference-maker, though.

With the game tied 1–1 in the second period, the Leafs seemed to take control. At the three-minute mark, Red took a shot that was stopped by Vachon, but the rebound was stuffed in by Conacher. Then, a seemingly harmless 40-foot shot by Pronovost sailed past Vachon's left foot. Keon got the fourth goal for the Leafs.

To start the third period, Blake replaced Vachon with veteran Gump Worsley in an effort to shake up his team, but it didn't work. At the final buzzer, as the Leafs mobbed Sawchuk, the Forum was three-quarters empty. The underdog Leafs were now in the driver's seat.

After the game, Blake was in a very foul mood with reporters: "I shouldn't let you guys in here," he snapped, his voice hoarse from screaming through the game. "Punch doesn't let you guys into the room when he loses."

He was livid about the refereeing. "There should have been a penalty on the Leafs' second goal!" Blake contended. "Go and tell Punch that! Tell Punch to get the films of the second goal and show them to the referee! Ask them about the Lady Bynger's trip!" He meant Red Kelly.

"Yeah!" John Ferguson piped up nearby. "A Lady Bynger's trip! Yeah! That's what it was! You bet your life if it would have been me, it would have been a penalty!"

A reporter remarked to the coach that home ice hadn't been a factor in the series thus far; Blake agreed but qualified his answer with a prediction: "Home ice won't be a factor until the seventh game. That's right, only in the seventh game (in Montreal) — when we win the Cup."

Imlach was unusually subdued, "I'm all talked out," he sighed at one point. "I'll let my team do the talking tomorrow night."

The Leafs dressing room was calm as the players suited up. Imlach's "old pappies" knew what they had to do, and they also knew that Sawchuk had to be on his game for them to have a chance. As Punch stoically addressed his troops, Red and crew sat quietly listening, focusing on the task at hand.

"We have to win this game tonight. If we go back to Montreal for a seventh game, all bets are off!" Imlach said. "Bill Gadsby played 20 seasons in this league and never won a Stanley Cup. You're 60 minutes away."

He looked directly at the younger players. Then his gaze fell on the veterans. He chose his words carefully. "Some of you have been with me for nine years. It's been said that I stuck with the old ones so long, we couldn't possibly win the Stanley Cup. For some of you, it's a farewell. Go out there and ram that puck down their throats!"

With the Stanley Cup in the building, drama and excitement filled the air. As the Leafs skated onto the ice, there was a thunderous ovation from the Gardens crowd. Worsley took his place in the Montreal net opposite Sawchuk, and both were flawless in the first period.

At the six-minute mark of the second, a Canadiens point shot went off a Leafs defender and bounced the other way. Red saw opportunity and took off with the puck with Ellis by his side on a two-on-one. "Red, he was so smart with the puck, such a smart hockey player. He waited just long enough for me to stay onside, and then I got into position for either a pass or a rebound," Ellis recalled. "Red shot the puck at just the right angle." Worsley made the save, but the rebound went exactly to where Ellis was, and he stuffed it into the open side.

The second Toronto goal was less planned. Pappin made a cross-ice pass that hit Stemkowski's right foot and caromed off the right-hand goal post into the net before a sprawling Worsley could fall on it.

In the third, ex-Leaf Dick Duff stickhandled past Horton, fooled Stanley and beat Sawchuk with a backhander between his legs.

The Canadiens kept pressing and managed to get a faceoff in the Toronto end with 55 seconds left on the clock. Worsley went to the bench in favour of an extra attacker. This was it. The most important faceoff of the year for either team, in the circle to Sawchuk's left.

"Punch sent us old guys out there to close the deal," Red recalled. "Pulford, myself, Stanley, Armstrong and Horton. We knew what we had to do."

The crowd was on its feet as Béliveau settled in opposite Stanley.

Just before the puck was dropped, Montreal forward John Ferguson skated into the faceoff and whispered to Béliveau. Stanley watched them chat carefully, listening as much as he could through the crowd's booing at the delay. After Ferguson positioned himself in front of the Toronto net, it was Stanley's turn to delay the puck drop. He talked to Red, who moved from behind Stanley to the front of the net.

The puck dropped.

Stanley won the faceoff, and drew the puck back to where Red had been, then moved to block Béliveau from getting to it. Red knew exactly what he had to do. He leaped into the void towards the open puck. A Canadien was headed towards him, fast.

"I scooted over, grabbed the puck and flipped the puck up to Pulford," Red recalled. "He took a few strides just over our blue line and passed it over to Armstrong, who was breaking to our right. Armie just skated just over centre ice and fired a wrist shot right into the empty Montreal net."

The Gardens exploded. Fans jumped up and down, cheering, crying. The Leafs players all leaped onto the ice to congratulate their captain. The crowd threw programs and cups on the ice in celebration. The cheering continued as the ice was cleaned. Finally, the teams were able to line up again, and 40 seconds later the crowd started loudly counting down: seven-six-five-four-three-two-one. The final bell sounded, and the Toronto players all jumped on the ice again and mobbed Sawchuk. They had done it! The Maple Leafs

had won their fourth Stanley Cup of the 1960s. They hugged, shook
hands, tousled each other's hair. It was a magical moment.

As the teams lined up for the customary handshakes, the
Canadiens congratulated the victors, and Blake sought out Imlach.
Despite the rivalry, the men did respect each other. Blake would
later say, "This is the toughest series I ever lost."

Red and Horton embraced as the Leafs gathered around at centre
ice. League President Clarence Campbell came to the hanging
microphone. "Ladies and gentlemen, it is now my great pleasure and

responsibility to present the Stanley Cup to the Maple Leaf hockey club for the 11th time," announced Campbell. "Now I ask the captain of the Toronto club to come forward and accept the trophy."

Armstrong came forward, his son Brian running beside him, and Campbell presented the Cup to him as the crowd cheered. Armstrong waved to the players to gather for a group photo around the table on which the Stanley Cup sat. Then he carried the Cup to the dressing room.

In the exuberant crowd, Andra Kelly was overcome with emotion, tears of pride and joy streaming down her face, knowing that this was Red's last game. What a way to go out.

Keon, the tireless Leafs centre who excelled at checking, was awarded the Conn Smythe Trophy as the outstanding player in the playoffs. "Sawchuk probably would have won the Conn Smythe had he not had those two bad games against Montreal," recalled Red. "Keon had a great playoffs."

For Red Kelly, who had gotten an assist on the last insurance goal, his eighth Stanley Cup was as sweet as the first. As he and Frank Mahovlich posed with the cup, they restaged their 1963 photo: this time, Frank flashed four fingers while Red flashed eight on two hands. "We had won the Stanley Cup in my last season, my last game," recalled Red. "And to have won it eight times, you know that's almost one every two and a half years. It's what you dreamed about as a kid. To win one Stanley Cup, that would be a big goal, you know, but gosh, I won it eight times. Each time was great."

This time, Red said, two things were key to the Toronto victory: "the goaltending, obviously, but just as important was the work of our third line. When your third line can more than hold their own but also get a few, that's all the difference in the world."

Pete Kelly's kid from Simcoe, Ontario, was definitely going out on top. Red came ninth in voting for the Hart Memorial Trophy — the only Leaf to earn votes. He was fifth in team scoring with 38 points in 61 games, and his playmaking assisted linemate Ron Ellis to third place on the team with 45 points. Red had only four minutes in penalties.

No other player had ever won eight Stanley Cups without playing for Montreal. Red was only one of 20 players to have scored over 250 goals in his career, finishing with 281 goals and 542 assists for 823 points in 1,316 games — 846 games as a Detroit defenceman and another 470 as a Toronto forward. In that time, he had only amassed 327 minutes in penalties (and 51 in the playoffs) for an average of .025 per game, proving those four Lady Byng Memorial Trophies were well deserved.

Despite Stafford Smythe's lucrative four-year offer to keep Red playing for the Leafs, Red knew that it was time to go, to retire from playing the game he loved so much, to go out on top — and healthy. "I looked back and thought, *Boy, I've been pretty lucky. I've won the Stanley Cup in my very last game!*" Red recalled.

After 20 years, he might have been finished playing hockey — but hockey wasn't quite finished with him yet.

• • • • • •

CHAPTER SEVENTEEN

BRIGHT LIGHTS
of HOLLYWOOD

A funny thing happened to Red on the way to the Forum — the Los Angeles Forum, that is. Well, for starters, there wasn't one yet. It was still being built when Red committed to coaching the Los Angeles Kings.

Red quietly met with his old Toronto teammate Larry Regan regarding the Kings coaching position that winter. The problem was Regan had not yet been named the general manager of the new expansion team by their showboating owner, Jack Kent Cooke, who wanted to announce a GM and coach at the same time. So there was only silence out of L.A. heading into the expansion draft.

In Toronto, after years committed to his work in Ottawa, Red finally got to be in another Stanley Cup parade. There was a celebratory party at Stafford Smythe's mansion in Etobicoke as well. But Red and Andra's minds were on other matters, namely preparing for their move to Los Angeles while still denying that it was going to happen. They had quietly flown to the sunny destination and picked out a new home.

"I was in Los Angeles, looking at houses with this real estate lady," Andra recalled. "It was a hot day, and she said, 'It's so hot, I need to stop at this place to get a glass of water.' We go into this house, and it was really beautiful, had a huge lot, and I remarked so. And the real estate lady says, 'Oh. Would you like to buy it? It's for sale.' And we did."

Red was coy when asked about his Toronto home being up for sale; in fact it had already been sold, so no "for sale" sign had ever gone up.

The NHL's 1967 expansion was the most ambitious growth in the history of any major North American sport. The evening before the Expansion Draft, held in Montreal on June 6, the spotlight-savvy Cooke dropped a bombshell.

"Jack announced that he had bought the Springfield Indians, and so we got Bill White, Brian Kilrea and Dale Rolfe," Red recalled. "Bill White was probably our best defenceman. We would start the season as the only expansion team to have a farm club."

Of all the owners who came aboard during expansion, Jack Kent Cooke was by far the most flamboyant and outspoken. Born in Toronto, he partnered with Roy Thomson in buying up newspapers and radio stations across Ontario and Quebec in the 1940s. As his fortune grew, so did his interest in sports. He bought and ran the minor league baseball team Toronto Maple Leafs of the International League, and tried to bring Major League Baseball to the city. He owned 25 per cent of the NFL's Washington Redskins in 1961, growing his share of the team until full ownership in 1985. In 1959, Cooke began to invest in American media and moved to Los Angeles, becoming a U.S. citizen. In his new home, Cooke took control of the NBA's Los Angeles Lakers in 1965, and set in motion plans for a new stadium — the Forum — which would house the Lakers and a hockey team. Away from the sports arena, he was a shrewd businessman but an unstable family man. He married four different women during his lifetime, and his first divorce resulted in what was then the largest divorce settlement ever.

As draft day began, Punch Imlach and the Leafs, who through a "gentlemen's agreement" had let Kelly go to Los Angeles to coach, dropped their own bombshell. The rules stipulated that the Original Six teams would only be allowed to protect 11 skaters and one goaltender. Imlach chose to protect Bower and listed Sawchuk as one of his 11 players. "Well, he can skate, can't he?" he suggested, unsuccessfully, to chuckles in the room. The new teams were to pick 18 skaters and two goalies. When an established team lost a player, it was allowed to move a player from its unprotected list to its protected list.

NHL President Clarence Campbell drew team names from the Stanley Cup to determine the draft order. The Kings got first pick of netminders, which were the subject of the first two rounds. Cooke stepped up to the microphone and claimed Sawchuk and, by doing so, irritated the Toronto delegation.

As the draft went on, Imlach grew increasingly antsy and could see the quality of available players declining with each round. Looking for some trading leverage after the 10th round, he moved Red Kelly to Toronto's protected list.

Los Angeles cried foul.

"Cooke had nine chances to draft Kelly, who is much better than any man Cooke claimed in the draft," argued Punch. "If I hadn't grabbed him, another club would have. I lost Brit Selby because Cooke wouldn't pick earlier. What did he want to get him for? A peanut butter sandwich?"

Toronto management stood by Imlach. "Who the heck ever heard of a 'gentlemen's agreement'?'" roared Leafs vice-president Harold Ballard. "If they regarded Red so highly, he should have been their first draft choice! Cookie is in this league one day and he wants to run the show. Looking at Los Angeles's draft list, I'd say we're doing Kelly a favour keeping him away from the Kings. With that team, Red is a cinch to wind up with an ulcer."

While five of the new teams chose veteran players in the twilight of their careers, leftovers that the established teams no longer wanted, Los Angeles went with youth. It was a manoeuvre that caused hockey experts to predict the Kings would finish "in last place or worse" among the six new teams in the West Division.

"I wish Terry well, but I'm afraid he'll be like a man walking the Gaza Strip without a rifle when he goes in goal for that team," said Imlach after the draft. "Kelly is better than any player Cooke drafted; 50 per cent better in my opinion. I wouldn't do anything to hurt Kelly. He's done too much for me. My beef is with Cooke, not Kelly."

"I didn't see that coming at all," Red recalled. "I thought Punch had always lived up to everything he'd ever told me. I was thinking that he's just trying to pull a fast one on Cooke, just monkeying around, a head game!"

Nevertheless, the Cooke/Imlach stunt had to be dealt with, so in a post-draft deal the Leafs got Ken Block, an unknown defenceman, for Red. "Now it's settled and Kelly can get down to the job of adjusting himself from a player to coach," said Cooke.

For Red and Andra, settling in was their first order of business. "We had moved into Joe E. Brown's house, the comedian," recalled Red. "The house had been sitting there vacant, some kind of disagreement with the builder. It was on Mulholland Drive in Hollywood. When we moved in, there was a knock on the door, and it was the actress Janet Blair. She lived in the cul-de-sac at the end of the street. She had high riding boots on, and she welcomed us to the neighbourhood and brought us a snakebite kit. It was an eye-opener, but whew, we were in Hollywood!

"We sure found out why the snakebite kit and why she wore boots; we were in rattlesnake country. We quickly learned that when the kids played outside they had to wear boots. They had to learn to watch for snakes."

As a new coach in a new environment, in an area not known as a hotbed of hockey, Red Kelly had a lot to learn himself. "L.A. paid two million dollars to get into the league, and what did we get? Nothing!" Red recalled. "We had our first training camp in Guelph, Ontario. We had to assess all these players, and right off the bat, Jack Kent

Cooke came to our first practice, came out on the ice and wanted me to introduce him to every single player! Holy, man! There were guys I had never seen before, and all of a sudden, boom! I made it, by hook or crook, I made it. But it was a tough spot to be put in right off the bat."

Cooke often wanted the focus on himself. At training camp one day, he put on his skates and ordered everyone off the ice except Sawchuk. The boss was determined to score on the great goalie, but couldn't despite his best efforts. Finally, to distract the goalie, Cooke looked up into the stands to his wife and yelled, "Jeannie, where'd you get that new outfit?" Sawchuk looked up as well, and Cooke deftly put one behind him and left the ice satisfied.

Jiggs McDonald, the first play-by-play announcer for the Kings, tells a story about how Sawchuk was able to add to his earnings at the expense of his rookie teammates. "Larry Regan had a rule that no player was to have a car at training camp, but Terry did," recalled McDonald. "Because I was the advance man, Cooke had wanted me to find food and lodging for $9 a man. I was able to bring it in at $9.25 a man, much to Cooke's disdain, but we had to eat by this golf course out near Kitchener, and Sawchuk, with the only car, charged each player taxi fare. He really made some money. And Regan didn't try to stop him, explaining that Terry had been a pro a long time and was the Kings' number-one man."

As the Kings broke camp and flew to Los Angeles, Sawchuk's backup, Wayne Rutledge, still hadn't signed a contract. "I was holding out for $12,000," he said. Rutledge recalled the first few months of the Kings season as total disarray. "We had no rink. We practised on an ice pad in Burbank, north of L.A., and also played in Long Beach. We were 20 guys in five cars, and nobody knew where we were going. We were lost half the time. The dressing rooms were like large washrooms with no seats. Between practices, the trainers had to dry our equipment on this patio in the sun. We often went out to practise in still-wet equipment. It was not a great start."

Red had his own issues to deal with. "We practised and played at

Long Beach, a good hour's drive," he recalled. "It was like an away game. In that arena, you couldn't hear a sound, your skates into the ice, anything. The acoustics were terrible, just dead. There was a little building beside the new Forum being built, and that's where we had our office. That's how we started in L.A."

"Will He Prove Critics Wrong?" went the headline of a *Hockey World* story.

"I know it won't be easy," Red told writer Bill Libby. "I have much to learn. So does Larry Regan. Even Mr. Cooke is new to the NHL. I have many special problems facing me, building a new team with inexperienced players and succeeding with it in a city that is new to big-time hockey and where we have had some adverse criticism. But I took the job because I felt I could handle it, and I'm not afraid."

Fear was not in Jack Kent Cooke's extensive, growing vocabulary. "His desk was elevated so he could look down on you," recalled Red. "He had a dictionary open. He would look up and use a different word every day through the day. So his diction was really something."

Cooke predicted that Sawchuk would lead his Kings to the Stanley Cup — not all that far-fetched, given that the six new teams were placed in the same division, the winner facing the best of the Original Six teams in the final.

Realistically, Red hoped to get 40 games out of Sawchuk, which his former teammate hadn't done in the last three seasons. Almost on cue, Sawchuk injured his elbow at the last practice in Long Beach before the season opener. With Rutledge finally signed and in the net, the Kings took to the ice in purple and gold uniforms — or "Forum Blue" and "Forum Gold," if you asked Cooke. With a large crown as the logo in the centre of the jersey, the Kings had a regal air.

Los Angeles won its first ever game by a score of 4–2 over the Philadelphia Flyers. Next, the Kings beat the Minnesota North Stars at home then tied both the California Seals and St. Louis Blues on the road.

"After our first four games, when I held my own, I think Sawchuk

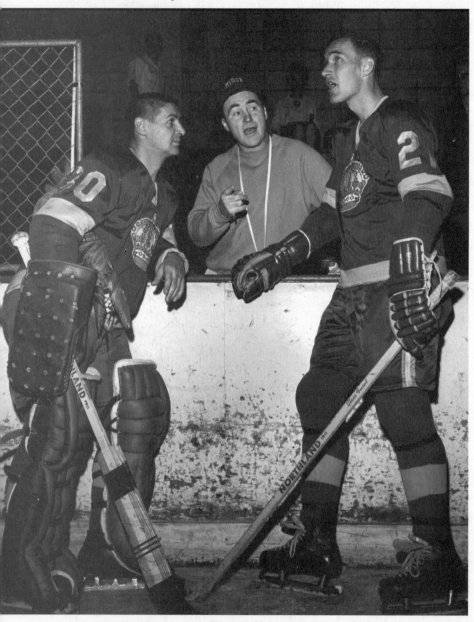

relaxed substantially," Rutledge remembered. "I think until then he felt the weight of the whole organization on his shoulders, with the media hype about him and all."

Sawchuk did finally start the next two games on the road as the Kings beat the struggling Black Hawks 5–3 but then disappointingly lost to the Leafs in Toronto 4–2.

Red had his players buying into his coaching. "I'd go through a brick wall for my coach and the rest of the players feel the same way," remarked winger Lowell MacDonald. "He made me feel great, like I was wanted. This team can skate, is not afraid of work and Kelly has us playing aggressive hockey. That's been the reason for whatever success we've had."

In his home debut, Sawchuk hit a brick wall of his own as he got shelled 6–1 by the Rangers on October 31.

"I don't know what it was," Rutledge recalled, "but the guys seemed to try harder when I was in net. I don't know if they relaxed in games with Terry behind them because they figured, 'Ah, we've got the best in net. If we screw up, he'll stop them,' and the guys figured I needed more protection, but that seemed to be an early pattern."

Early on, coach Kelly noticed a very bad habit among his scorers. He set out to correct it in a way that was innovative for its time. "In Toronto we used to watch game films, which were all right, but in L.A. my biggest thing was standing behind the net and watching my guys shoot," recalled Red. "Every one of them came in looking down at the puck just before shooting. I had to teach them to look at the net, at the goalie before shooting. If you're looking down at the puck, then you don't know where the goaltender is! But it was like water falling off a duck, nobody listened. They kept doing the same thing. No matter what I said, I couldn't get them to change their habits.

"So I rented a movie camera, and put it at the end of the rink behind the goaltender, looking down, facing the players as they came in. I didn't say a thing. So, after practice I said, 'Okay, everybody in the room, and I want you to watch this.' They saw themselves coming in, looking down, and it was effective. It wasn't me telling them — they were actually seeing it for themselves. I got quite a positive reaction from them. It was the first time they had really seen themselves shooting. I had some players . . . like Doug Robinson, a great goal scorer in the minors but had his troubles with us. The next practice, Robinson comes in on net; he's got his head so high he fans on the puck. It was so funny. Well, it wasn't funny, but it was! But he learned, which is all a coach can hope for. They all did."

The Kings held their own, even beating the Leafs and Canadiens on a few occasions. "I thought all those players did wonders for me," Red recalled. "They gave me one hundred and twenty-five per cent, and if the Canadiens only gave seventy-five per cent when we played them, and we gave one hundred and twenty-five per cent, then we had a chance."

Injuries continued to hamper Sawchuk, so Rutledge took on the brunt of the starts, and by the end of November, the Kings had a respectable 10–8–3 record and were in second place, behind Philadelphia, in the expansion West Division. Through December, losing became more frequent as the grand opening of their new arena approached. For Red and his hockey players, adjusting to playing in sunny California was no easy task for Canadian hockey players accustomed to winter.

"It was all different. The guys could go to the beach. Sawchuk had a house right on Hermosa Beach, and then we'd come back east and north to play hockey and suddenly we'd be in winter," chuckled Red. "But we were on the road a lot. We were one of two teams out west; all the other ten teams were in the east. We'd seem to play a good game but lose by one goal. And we didn't even have our own rink until late in December."

The new facility, which would become known as the Fabulous Forum, was outside of L.A. proper, in Inglewood, on a former golf course and across from the Hollywood Park Racetrack. It cost Cooke $16 million to build, but it changed the landscape of sports in the area, especially when the Lakers started winning NBA titles in the early 1970s.

"Cooke built it with architect Charles Luckman, who had offices in New York and Los Angeles," explained Red. "The architect asked me to help him plan the dressing rooms, what kind of cages or cubicles for the players to use, the wire things so they could hang their equipment. The doors were even built higher to accommodate the height of the Lakers basketball team."

On December 30, 1967, the Kings opened the Fabulous Forum, which sat 16,005 for hockey, with all the trappings of a Hollywood premiere. Canadian-born actor Lorne Greene acted as master of ceremonies for the pre-game show. The Flyers spoiled the party by winning 2–0, but hockey had arrived in Hollywood.

"Many television and movie stars began to frequent the games. Donna Douglas of the TV series *The Beverly Hillbillies* dated a couple of my players," Red recalled. "Cooke would introduce them to the players, bring them into the dressing room before or after a game — Peter Falk, Jack Lemmon, Danny Thomas, Glenn Ford, Fred MacMurray, Elvis, to name a few. It was not a distraction, it was neat."

The Fabulous Forum was not so fabulous at first. "In the beginning, the Forum's ice was slow. If you shot the puck down the ice, it wouldn't reach the other end!" recalled Red. "They thought about cooling the ice more, but then the fans at rinkside would be cold. There were a lot of problems in the beginning, things we had to adjust to."

The calibre of play in the new NHL was not what it had been with only six teams. "There were a lot of rookies in the league. When you went from 6 to 12 teams, you really changed things," said Red. "I would see some defencemen's moves and think, *Where did you learn to play hockey?* In those early expansion days, guys made all kinds of mistakes, brutal mistakes. If you made those mistakes in the old six-team league, you'd be sent down to Nevada. But we were in expansion."

Red hadn't counted on the added responsibility of managerial tasks. "After a while I had to look after a lot of things — schedule, flights, food. As a coach I had to examine how close the games had been, how we'd done, did my goalie need a rest, his age, change the goaltender, give him a break or whatever. So I made decisions based on many different things. Travelling from the West Coast, the majority of the other teams were in the east. We had a lot of long road trips the other teams didn't face. Sometimes *I* was tired! And if I was tired, I could just imagine how tired my players were. We had a big disadvantage that way.

"Flights, accommodations, arrangements; I was doing the whole darn thing! Regan was there somewhere, but he seemed busy with other stuff — like punching referees. We had such a hectic schedule. He had discussions with Leafs GM Punch Imlach on how to do it; he was new too. Maybe Larry and I should have been closer."

To help with publicity, the Kings suited up to participate in a figure skating TV special on NBC, starring Peggy Fleming. In their 10-minute segment, the team skated around the Forum ice in full uniform, doing drills and scrimmaging as they would in a full practice, while Fleming did twirls and flips and skated among them. Red was in full uniform and participated like a player while sporting his familiar No. 4. "There was one time in rehearsals where I skated too close to her, and I scared her," Red recalled. At the end of her stint skating with the Kings, Fleming cradled the puck in her skates and kicked it past a cooperative Sawchuk into the net.

Back in the real world, Red was able to share some of his experience as a hockey player with his team, especially as it related to his old teams and teammates. "If we were playing Detroit and Howe was on the ice, he puts the hook on you and the referees aren't calling it because it's Gordie Howe," Red recalled. "I told my guys, 'He's older than you, and you have the legs right now. Don't let him get close to you and take the puck off you. You move the puck before he gets to you, throw the puck by him. Don't wait until he gets to you and ties you up and takes the puck off you. The last thing he wants to do is have to turn around and skate back down the ice. So don't play his game, play your game!' That's how we played, and it worked against the established clubs. Our record was the best against the Original Six, of any of the expansion teams."

As the season wound down, the Kings were holding their own. In a game at Madison Square Garden on March 10, a goal by Cowboy Bill Flett with 20 seconds remaining gave the Kings a 4–3 win. It was the start of a seven-game undefeated streak that vaulted the Kings to the top of the West Division alongside Philadelphia. In the last month of the season, Red played Sawchuk 12 of the final 14 games, preparing his veteran netminder for the playoffs.

Despite the pressures of the team, Red never forgot his family. "On March 17, 1968, I made my First Communion at St. Paul the Apostle Catholic Church in Los Angeles," recalled Casey. "Dad was on a road trip with the team and was unable to be there, so his brother, my Uncle Joe, was standing in for moral support. Imagine my surprise when my dad appeared, suitcase in hand, at the back of the church just before the sacrament of First Communion took place! He managed to catch an earlier flight and had come straight to the church from the airport. This showed how important both church and family are to him."

With a week to go, Louis Cauz wrote an extensive piece on Kelly. "The polls of critics and hockey experts were unanimous — the Kings would finish sixth (out of six)," wrote Cauz. "That was nine months ago. Have you checked the standings? Tied for first place are the Kings . . . So here's a vote for Red Kelly of the Kings — Coach of the Year in the NHL. When the season began Kelly was the only coach in the NHL who had never stood behind a bench and directed a game in civilian clothes. Sometimes, excellent hockey players make excellent coaches."

In the final game of the season, the Kings were tied 2–2 with the league doormats, the Oakland Seals. A win would give them first place. On a go-ahead goal by defenceman Bob Wall, referee Ron Wicks disallowed it, saying Flett was in the crease. "The referee made a bad call, and it cost us a win," said Red. "We would have ended up in first place, a point ahead of Philadelphia. I saw the film and our guy, Cowboy, was not in the goal crease when we scored. Wicks made that call. Well, everyone makes mistakes." Los Angeles ended up second in the West — they were tied with the Flyers in points, but Philadelphia had a better record in head-to-head matchups between the two teams.

"I was so proud of my guys. Unbelievable! My guys worked their butts off. Ed 'Jet' Joyal, 'Cowboy' Bill Flett, Ted Irvine, Lowell MacDonald, 'Frenchie' Lemieux — Cooke had nicknames for all the guys. And when Cooke brought all the Hollywood stars into the room, he'd bring them to meet Ed Joyal. Ed was one of our best forwards. Brian Kilrea was a great guy, a great shot and a great team guy."

Red Kelly was optimistic at the outset of the playoffs, but the Kings' first-round opponent, the Minnesota North Stars, had won six of the 10 regular season meetings with L.A. The Kings were tops in the West with 200 goals, but they had allowed a whopping 45 more goals than they had scored — not a good omen for playoff hockey. Still, they had Sawchuk.

On April 3, Red caused a bit of a stir among the other NHL teams when he donned a full Kings uniform and joined his players for a workout during their pre-playoff two-hour drills, increasing speculation that he might suit up for an actual game. "I'll play only if the emergency is such that I can help the team," Red said at the time.

The assassination of American civil rights leader Dr. Martin Luther King Jr. delayed the start of the Kings-North Stars series. When it did begin at the Forum, both teams were lethargic, and L.A. won 2–1. Sawchuk faced only 18 shots in the second game as he registered his 12th career playoff shutout in a 2–0 win. Minnesota GM and coach Wren Blair said, "I'll bet he's never had such an easy couple of games. We must have helped Sawchuk to another year."

In Minnesota for Game 3, the North Stars put five goals past Sawchuk in the first two periods. Red put Rutledge between the pipes in the hopes of shaking up his troops and resting the veteran, but the Stars tallied twice more for a 7–5 victory. Red came back with the Uke for Game 4; in a hard-fought contest, the Stars prevailed 3–2 and tied the series.

The flu kept Sawchuk from playing in Game 5, but Rutledge stepped in and made 27 saves en route to a 3–2 victory. Back in Minnesota, the Kings had the series all but wrapped up with a 3–2 third period lead, but then a fluke goal got past Rutledge to send the game into overtime. Minnesota won at the 9:11 mark on a goal by the ancient Parker MacDonald.

Red's mind was made up that Sawchuk would be his goalie for the deciding game. "Wayne is a good guy and had played some good goal, but he was no Terry Sawchuk," Kelly said. "I had to go with Ukey. And I figured he'd come up big for this seventh game. If Ukey's on his game at all, Minnesota knew they might just as well stay home."

The North Stars took a 3–1 lead after the first period. Joyal closed the gap with a goal at 6:12 of the second to get it close, but then it all fell apart. Within a span of eight minutes, the Stars poured in five goals en route to a 9–4 pasting.

After the last couple of goals, the Forum fans booed Sawchuk and threw refuse on the ice. On the bench, Rutledge saw some of the players turn around to look at coach Kelly, wondering if he was going to pull Sawchuk. "One thing about Red as a coach, though," Rutledge said. "He very rarely pulled you out of a game. And Terry never pulled himself."

"I was never so disappointed in Terry as I was that night," Red recalled. "I felt that he let me down and the team down. One goal in particular, a dribbler that went in between his legs, hurt. The loss wasn't all his fault, but it was the big game and he missed it, really. That was a game made for Ukey. Seventh game and all, and he disappointed me, disappointed us."

The embarrassing loss left a bitter taste of the mouth of owner Jack Kent Cooke. Despite the better-than-expected inaugural season, Cooke was angry and cancelled the season-ending party.

"The players had been told to stick around after the season, they were going to have quite a party to be hosted by Jack Kent Cooke," recalled Andra. "Some of the players had actually paid another month's rent to stay for this supposed great party. Everybody was upset when they had arrived at the Forum to find out that this supposed party was cancelled. Red felt terrible about this, and I did, too, so we decided, we'll have it at our house! But how?

"I called Gloria and Larry Mann. Larry was an actor and comedian who had appeared on a lot of movies and shows in the 1960s. They lived near us, and, being a Canadian, he was a big hockey fan and became close friends of ours. They were fabulous people. I told them about the cancelled party and that we were going to host it ourselves, but that we didn't know how we were going to do it, entertain the whole team, staff, trainers and their wives — it was so last-minute!

"Larry said, 'Well, we've had that happen before. Don't you worry; we'll take care of everything. We'll get the drinks, and Gloria will give you a list, and you two will go shopping, and we'll do it.' We did pull it together and had the party at our house. It went all night and we had a great time, much better time than anything Cooke would have hosted."

The party fiasco left a bitter taste in the mouths of the Kellys, but they were stuck in L.A. for another season. "I was only going to sign a one-year contract with L.A., but because of what Punch had done at the draft, I signed for two years," recalled Red. "That was fine, we were building something with the Kings, bringing hockey to L.A."

As bad as Cooke may have been, he was not Red's enemy number one in Los Angeles. "On Mulholland Drive, we had coyotes, snakes and other wildlife in the neighbourhood. We had a porch, and I was sitting there one morning, looking at our flowers, when something suddenly caught my eye. I saw something move. I took a closer look, and, lo and behold, it was gopher, eating the flowers. Suddenly the flower just disappeared into the ground. Plop! I didn't know it at that moment, but I was about to have a summer-long battle with the dang gophers. On the farm in Simcoe, groundhogs would stand beside the corn and eat the plant. In L.A., the gophers just pulled the plants into the ground. Swoosh!

"I put traps everywhere, but they would spring the traps, almost laughing at me. This went on for quite some time, and then one day I thought, *I'll get you little rascals.* I got a hose out, turned the water on and put that water hose in the gopher hole, and I said, 'I'm gonna get you yet!' I'm waiting, waiting and waiting, nothing's happening. All of a sudden I heard yelling from the house down below; people started yelling, 'Hey! Hey Red! You're flooding us out!' The gopher tunnel went all the way down there; I was flooding those houses below the hill out. I couldn't believe it!

"I tried all that summer. I never did get the dang gophers. They had won, they were laughing at me. When I left Andra and the kids to go to training camp up in Canada in September, guess what? The darn gophers left as well, just like that. It was me they were battling. I guess they weren't having any fun without me!"

Andra was pregnant with their fourth child and taking care of Casey, Patrick and Conn. As her pregnancy progressed, her general practitioner, an elderly doctor who had served in World War II, realized that with her blood type there could be complications with this delivery. He was right.

Andra had Rh-negative blood, which meant that if her baby's positive blood mixed with her negative blood during pregnancy, her body would automatically produce antibodies to kill the white blood cells in the baby's blood — a dangerous scenario for the unborn child. Today, injections can solve this situation, but in 1968 these advances had not yet been discovered.

Andra loved her L.A. doctor. "He was a wonderful, wonderful doctor. He had been terrific for medications for the children and me. One time, Patrick had cut off the end of his finger on a toy, and the doctor told me what to do over the phone, how to glue it together and it would be fine. It did turn out fine, and Patrick went on to become a beautiful pianist. It didn't hurt his music. [The doctor] was not a specialist, but he had recognized right away that I was going to have a problem with this birth and had told me, 'We need to get you here right away!'"

With Red away at the Kings training camp in Barrie, Ontario, Andra drove herself to hospital, and on September 18, 1968, she gave birth to a seven-pound, two-ounce baby girl they named Christiana Frances McLaughlin Kelly, known as "Kitty." As predicted, there were complications, and the baby came out "blue."

"Because of my blood issue, Kitty needed blood transfusions right away," recalled Andra. "She was touch and go for quite a while, and I didn't get to see her for the first few days. That was tough. Still, after a few days, I was told that I wasn't allowed to see the baby, they hadn't brought her in and I couldn't see her. That upset me.

"Larry and Gloria Mann were visiting me one day, and I told him the situation, and he said, 'Well, I'll just fix that! Don't you worry!' So he went and told them to either bring the baby in or bring me to her, which they did. And I finally got to see my Kitty! The Manns picked Kitty and I up from the hospital and drove us home afterwards while Red was still away at training camp. That was tough. That was really tough because he didn't even get to see Kitty for six weeks. Red sent a lady to help me. She had babysat for us when I was teaching skating in Toronto, and he flew her out to California to look after the other three children while I was in the hospital."

For Andra and Red, the fall of 1968 in Los Angeles was not going to be a pleasant one, for many reasons.

First, at the Kings' training camp in Barrie, the mood was different. "Jack Kent Cooke had certainly soured over Terry," Jiggs McDonald recalled. Regan had been shopping Sawchuk around since the June draft but had not found a satisfactory deal. The Kings had obtained goalie Gerry Desjardins to be the starter. Red told management that whenever a deal was made, he wanted to be the one to break the news to his old friend. "The only thing I wanted was to be the one to tell him," Red recalled. "After all of our years together, I felt I owed him that much."

On October 10, 1968, the team was in Winnipeg for an exhibition game against the Canadian national team. Red called Sawchuk aside to tell him he'd been traded to Detroit. "He cried," Red recalled. "I tried to explain to him that he would be better off, going back to a more established team like the Wings, that he would have a better shot at a Stanley Cup. It was a sad day for the both of us." The great goalie's career was in its last days.

To replace Sawchuk, the Kings acquired Gerry Desjardins. "Desjardins was a first-round draft pick of the Canadiens, and Cooke gave up two draft picks for Desjardins," explained Red. "He was a rookie and he played pretty good through the year. But he got the shakes in the playoffs."

To start the 1968–69 season, the Kings were terrible, with just seven wins after their first 21 games. GM Regan demonstrated his frustration on October 12, when he punched referee Bruce Hood in a hallway in the Oakland Coliseum-Arena. Regan was fined $1,000. "We were being put in the penalty box every time we looked at a guy," recalled Red.

On the home front, the Kellys were robbed. "It was right after I had the baby, my hands were swollen, and I couldn't keep my rings on. I felt pretty safe where we lived, so I left my rings by the bed." Andra recalled. "I took the kids down to the museum to watch little chickens come out of their eggs. When we arrived home and walked in the door, Casey said, 'Mommy, Mommy, look! The movers have been here.' I said, 'What do you mean?' She said, 'Well, we have no furniture anymore.' There was no furniture, not even pictures left on the wall, nothing! So I called the police.

"My engagement and wedding rings were gone. I was so hurt by that invasion; it was terrible. The police said, 'You were lucky!' I said, 'I was?' It was lunch hour, and I had kept the kids home from school. If we had been home when they had come, who knew! I'm there alone with four little kids."

The roads around Los Angeles were also a nightmare. "I once got lost on a highway, and the police showed me an easier route to get to the Forum," recalled Andra. "The new route that the officer showed me was a little longer, but it was easier, and I didn't have to get on that highway, that big freeway, again. I was really nervous about the whole thing, and one day I just thought, *I can't do this anymore*. Boy, I wanted to get out of there!"

With the season not going so well, and his wife not pleased about living in Hollywood any longer, Red approached the Kings owner. "I told Jack Kent Cooke that I was leaving at the end of the season," Red recalled. "He tried to talk me into staying, and then he said, 'Well, don't say anything.'" Their minds made up, Andra hired a realtor, who found two professors from UCLA who bought the house near Christmas with the understanding that the Kellys would be there until the end of the season.

Then another disaster occurred on the home front. "We had a mudslide January 25, on the weekend when the team was playing a game in Minnesota," Red remembered. "The police had to get Andra, the kids and our family dog and her new litter of puppies out of the house. The house was beside the mountains, and a large section of mud came right down off the mountain onto the lawn. What a mess! I thought, *We'll never be able to sell this place.*" But the deal still went through.

There were few highlights in the 1968–69 Kings season. Before L.A. hosted the Leafs for a January 29 match, Red mused out loud about his coaching frustrations. "My guys haven't been playing well of late," Red told his old friend Red Burnett. "We had poor games in New York and Chicago; sandwiched a fair one between those two in Minnesota, but it still left a lot to be desired."

The bright spot throughout the season was the stellar goaltending of rookie Desjardins. On January 29, he almost single-handedly defeated the Leafs for the third time in four games, but his heroics were witnessed by a small crowd of only 9,000. After the game, Cooke went from player to player in the dressing room shaking their hands, stating the win might put an extra 3,000 fans in the seats for the game against Boston the next night. Regan praised his coach: "We played it much tougher tonight. Kelly really has them hopping." The Kings lost to the Bruins 7–5.

Following a March 12 loss to Toronto at the Forum, again with a small crowd, Red fumed about his front office. "They put in a physical fitness program when we got home Monday, after a tough four-game road trip," Red bristled. "And my guys had nothing left, no legs." Cooke wasn't shaking anybody's hands after the game as he headed straight to the nearest exit commenting, "It was awful!"

Red recalled one particular meeting with the Kings owner. "I once sat in his office for two and a half hours. We had just lost ten games on the road, and we come in on a Sunday night. We play Montreal on a Wednesday. We got off the plane, and I told the players to go home, I didn't want to see them until Wednesday at noon. I figured they needed rest; they were handling the puck like manhole covers.

"So Cooke calls me in, and I go into his office. He grilled me for over two hours: 'What are we gonna do? We gotta do something.' I said, 'I tried everything, so we're gonna try some rest.' I sat there, answered all his questions. The phone would ring, and once he was talking to George Allen, coach of the Redskins, so he'd bring him into the conversation.

"Thank goodness when we met the Canadiens in our next game, we got off to a 5–0 lead and hung on for a tie."

That season, the Kings won only 24 games and lost 42, and limped towards the playoffs on a seven-game winless streak. They finished in fourth place in the West Division, 20 points back of first-place St. Louis. Their first-round opponents were the second-place Oakland Seals.

The Kings upset the Seals in seven games. Next were the Blues in the West Final. St. Louis had swept aside Philadelphia four straight. L.A. had taken only 3 of a possible 16 points against the Blues all season.

"We won only five or six games on the road during the regular season, and everyone was calling us homers," Red told the press as his team arrived in St. Louis on the eve of the opening game. "But we took the big games in Oakland to get here."

The Blues swept L.A. aside in four straight, outscoring them 16–5. When the dust of the lost season had settled, Cooke announced that he was looking for a new coach. "At the end of the year, Cooke made it sound like he fired me, but in reality I only had a two-year contract," explained Red.

On June 11, as Red and Andra were packing to leave Los Angeles, the phone rang. It was a reporter from the *Toronto Telegram*, who informed him that he had been selected for induction into the Hockey Hall of Fame.

"You're kidding?" was Red's first reaction.

"What is it, Red?" Andra yelled from the other room.

"They say I've been named to the Hockey Hall of Fame!"

The reporter could hear a distant shriek over the phone.

"She says she's crying too hard to talk," Red said as he came back on the line with the reporter. "You know, we've been so busy packing, I haven't had time to think about hockey. This is, well . . . it's a bolt out of the blue."

Andra composed herself enough to take the receiver. "I'm really not able to talk, I'm so happy," she said, tears of joy streaming down her cheeks. "It's just wonderful for Red. Hockey's his whole life, and this will mean so much more to him than anyone knows."

He had been selected to the Hockey Hall of Fame in a unanimous vote that waived the usual five-year waiting period. The ceremony was slated for later that summer.

But first he needed to get out of California.

"When Andra and I and the kids left Los Angeles for the last time, we were driving for about an hour before we realized we were going in the wrong direction, towards San Francisco," laughed Red. "They had crazy freeways. We were so happy to get out of there!"

Driving north into Canada with no real furniture to bring with them, Red breathed a sigh of relief as they crossed the border. So did Andra.

Casey remembered those last few months in L.A. "Just before we moved from Los Angeles, I was offered a part in a television commercial," she recalled. "Even after we moved, the agent kept phoning to try and have me go back to L.A. for the part. My father said absolutely not — we would stay together as a family, and that was that!"

The Kellys headed to the tranquil peace and quiet of the cottage on Cedar Island.

For the first time in his career, Red didn't have a job.

As he sat on the beach, he was truly content to be away from the frustrations of Hollywood.

• • • • • •

CHAPTER EIGHTEEN

DANCE *with the* PENGUINS

For one summer, Red Kelly had no lineups to worry about, no draft picks to consider, no scouting to do, no travel arrangements to make. It was blissful. He was just a dad with time to play on the beach with his kids.

Then one day in late June, the phone rang at the cottage.

"Donald H. Parsons called me from Detroit," Red recalled. "He was the owner of the Pittsburgh Penguins. He wanted to know if I would be interested in going to Pittsburgh to coach. I said I would have to think about it, but he asked if we could meet. I said sure.

"He sent his chauffeur to pick me up at the cottage and took me over the border to his offices in Detroit, in which there were 45 or so executives. He owned over a dozen American banks. If they found a bank that was floundering, say had minus liquid assets, they would buy it, take it over, put their own manager in there to run it, turn it around and make it profitable. That's how he had made his money at that time.

"I had been on the finance committee in parliament, and in Canada, the banks here had to, by law, have seven to ten per cent cash on hand at all times. But in the States, that wasn't the case. And so Parsons acquired these losing banks. Their shareholders were quite happy because the bank would be turned around, and he did quite well. There had been an article written about him on Wall Street which called him the 'Swinging Banker.' Other bankers were then out to get him. He was highly leveraged, and his operation would usually be on shifting financial ground."

The Penguins, like the Kings, had been admitted in the Great Expansion of 1967, though Parsons was not the original owner. In the spring of 1968, Parsons, originally from Philadelphia, put together a group of 20 investors to buy the team from lawyers Jack McGregor and Peter Block, after which he controlled 80 per cent of the Penguins.

Jack Riley was the general manager, and George Sullivan had been the coach for the first two years, but the Pens hadn't made the playoffs. "You couldn't blame the whole thing on Sullivan," explained Red. "Pittsburgh didn't have a very good lineup and hadn't drafted very well. The ownership was discussing a new coach and looking at four possible candidates when Parsons brought up my name as a fifth. Of course I had played in Detroit, and that's probably why he brought up my name."

"We take over banks and put a manager in there to run that bank," explained Parsons to Red that day. "And we rely on that manager to tell us what that bank needs. So we asked Jack Riley for a coach, gave him five guys to choose from, but he couldn't decide and left it back to us. So we, the board and I, picked you. He didn't. What do you think?"

"I don't know what to say," Red answered. "It's a tough job down there in Pittsburgh. I'll have to think about it." Parsons gave him the spiel about it being a great challenge and Red being just the right

fellow for the job. He understood that Red needed time to think it over and discuss it with his wife.

At the cottage over the next few days, Red discussed the offer, its pros and cons, with Andra. It would mean going back to the States, but he was unemployed. Pittsburgh would be a challenge, and Andra knew Red always relished a challenge. Finally, Red called Parsons and accepted the job. He signed his customary one-year agreement, and on July 2 the Penguins made the announcement that Red Kelly was their new coach.

"We and the Pittsburgh fans are fortunate in having Red Kelly join our organization," Riley said in a statement. "He has always been a big winner. We hope his winning ways will rub off on the players."

"I have one goal in mind," Red said in the same statement. "And that's for the hockey season to start and for the Penguins to wind up in first place in our division. I'm aiming for first place!"

Before leaving for Pittsburgh, Red was inducted into the Hockey Hall of Fame in a ceremony in Toronto on August 21. Joining him in the class of 1969 was the late, diminutive goaltender Roy "Shrimp"

Former Leafs owner Major Conn Smythe presenting Red with his Hockey Hall of Fame plaque on August 21, 1969, in the presence of Jim Vipond. © HOCKEY HALL OF FAME

Worters, Red's former Detroit teammate Sid Abel, 1930s and '40s winger Bryan Hextall, Red Wings owner Bruce Norris and Pacific Coast Hockey League builder Al Leader.

Conn Smythe introduced Red, who had to attend stag. "Women didn't attend the Hockey Hall of Fame induction dinners back then," Andra recalled. "It was a men's-only occasion — ceremony and dinner. I was sorry to have missed it, but what could I do?"

At training camp in Brantford, Ontario, Red surveyed his Penguins and talked to the *Toronto Star*'s Neil McCarl about the difference between playing and coaching. "Basically you can get yourself up when you're a player," Red explained. "Your actions on the ice can lift a team and change the course of a game. Behind the bench, it's a tough thing to do. It's tough to change the course of a game right away. I can talk to the fellows at the end of a period but if I could just call time! But play doesn't stop like that."

Then he talked about his coaching philosophy. "I thought I could do some things with the guys and not treat them the way some coaches do. I don't think I'm a tough coach, but I expect the guys to give me an effort. If you try hard you are going to make mistakes, but I don't mind as long as when I'm working them, they work as hard as they can. We have a lot of fellows on this club who can dig and that can make up for a lot!"

As training camp broke and headed for Pittsburgh, Red and Andra came to a city that seemed down in the dumps. "It was like starting brand new, and the people in Pittsburgh had gotten kinda down on hockey," Red recalled. "Attendance was down. And when we got down there we didn't have great talent, but we had great effort."

The Penguins opened the season with three straight ties, their last one against the powerful Bruins. Reality soon struck, and they won only two games of their first dozen. The attendance woes continued.

Andra Kelly knew why and tried to help the situation, writing a letter to *Pittsburgh Post-Gazette* sports editor Al Abrams, who had always been very critical of the team:

> *Dear Mr. Abrams,*
>
> *The only thing the Penguins need to win is some spirit behind them. When you continually downgrade all of your teams it's a contagious thing. People read you and begin to feel the same way. "Oh what is the use," they say, "they're gonna lose." It certainly doesn't go with the NEW Pittsburgh. I'm puzzled more than upset.*
>
> *My husband and I came here because to him, Pittsburgh represented a challenge. Mr. Abrams, let's get with it with our sports fans. You newspaper people are the ones to influence the people. The Pens are young, exciting, ambitious and proud and believe that Red will try to keep 'em that way but they are not illiterate — they read you too and please don't discourage them.*

Hoping to see you at a hockey game someday — and oh, yes — thanks for the nice things you've written about Red!

— Andra, Mrs. "Red" Kelly.

It was a printed shot across the bow, which the paper ran on the front page. Abrams got the message.

"He invited me to lunch afterwards to try to calm the waters, so to speak," recalled Andra. "I accepted, but I brought all the players' wives with me as well."

In Toronto for a November 12 game against the Leafs, Red spoke to Milt Dunnell about his home-crowd frustrations and played up the Penguins' young, bright star Michel Brière. "By hang, this Michel is an exciting hockey player. I know the people of Pittsburgh would like him — if they'd just come out to see him," raved Red. "Sometimes when I'm watching him, I see the antics of Max Bentley. The boy has good stamina and a great shot. If the other team gives him an opening at all he takes advantage of it. The people of Pittsburgh seem to be hockey conscious. They recognize you and they talk hockey — but they don't come to the games. Still, if we can put some wins together, we can pull them in."

Toronto always had fans, though, and 16,320 spectators packed the Gardens to witness the Penguins, their physical play backed by the stellar goaltending of Les Binkley, win a 3–0 shutout. Red was beside himself with praise for his troops. "This is a better body-checking team than I had in Los Angeles," he boasted to Red Burnett. "They skated and hit for me, checked real well. Les Binkley was in top form and he didn't let me down. If we'd been getting that kind of goaltending all along, we'd have won three of the seven we've lost (thus far)."

The other goaltender in Pittsburgh was veteran Al Smith. Red said he did not have any particular strategy for choosing his starting keeper. "Binkley was my best goaltender, and I would have used Al Smith if Binkley was hurt," he said. "Smith just wasn't as good a goalie as Binkley — he'd let in the odd softie — but if Les was hurt, I'd have to use whatever I had."

The team came to be known as the "Pesky Penguins" in light of their work ethic. "This season is based on a total team effort," Red told the *Toronto Star*'s Frank Orr. "We've received the maximum from every man on the club."

Red knew some of the players from his own playing days. Andy Bathgate was on the Pens that season. He had played the previous two seasons in Vancouver in the Western Hockey League, and was winding down his Hall of Fame career. Red convinced him to return to the Penguins, where he had played in the team's inaugural season. "Andy was not the greatest skater, but he was good around the net. He had a good shot and could really stickhandle," recalled Red. "By this time in his career he had a bit of back trouble. He helped us."

Jean Pronovost was the younger brother of Marcel Pronovost and a key player for the first decade of NHL hockey in Pittsburgh. "Jean was a great player. I couldn't ask for a better player. Did everything I asked of him," recalled Red. "After Jean retired and became a coach, he called to tell me that he used a lot of my drills and techniques."

It was hard to engage the fans in Pittsburgh when the team seemed to be getting bad home press. After a 2–1 victory over the visiting Red Wings on December 3, Red was frustrated to see a great home effort witnessed by a mere 4,116 spectators. Maximum attendance at the Pittsburgh Civic Arena — better known as "the Igloo" — was a dream.

"The first thing we had to do was promote the team and the game," recalled Red. "We ran a hockey school, and we had the son of the morning DJ announcer from WWJ radio station come to the hockey school, and at the end of the two-week session everybody got to play in the game while [the DJ] was there watching.

"He took an interest in the Penguins and was soon talking up the team and the games every morning as you were driving to work. He would make daily comments on the air, in the mornings, about the games — 'Did you see the game last night? A fight broke out,' that kind of thing — talking about the players and that we had a team that was trying. Pittsburgh people understood hard work and the effort, and they slowly started coming out."

Young Conn Kelly had a rough early life in Pittsburgh. "I once fell out of my mother's car while she was driving and came very close to dying," Conn recalled. "Then my sister accidentally hit me in the face with a pitching wedge. I almost lost my eye and missed all of kindergarten. But I remember all of the Penguins coming to visit me in the hospital and bringing me stuffed animals and making me feel pretty special."

The Penguins, led in points by Dean Prentice, Ken Schinkel, Michel Brière and Jean Pronovost, finished second in their division, 26 points ahead of the Kings, but 22 points back of the first-place Blues.

In the team's first ever semifinal appearance, the Pens faced Oakland. Game 1 had 8,051 spectators, and the Pens swept the Seals, setting up a matchup against St. Louis.

The Blues won the first two games on home ice, but the Pens rebounded to a 3–2 win in Game 3, before the largest crowd in franchise history: 12,923 fans. After the Pens defeated the Blues 2–1 in Game 4 — with 39 more spectators than the night before — to even the series, Minnesota coach Wren Blair warned that the Pens were "a hungry bunch." Heading back to St. Louis, Red checked his team in to a different hotel to change things up, but it didn't matter as St. Louis defeated them 5–0 and then 4–3 at the Igloo to eliminate them.

"The capacity crowd in Pittsburgh stood for the last two minutes," Red recalled. "They applauded and applauded, and we couldn't even get our goalie out. I was very proud of this team because they gave me one hundred and twenty-five per cent. The people of Pittsburgh were blue-collar workers, and they appreciated the work ethic. When the game ended, after the players had shaken hands, by the time the last guy got off the ice, the crowd had been standing and applauding for ten minutes. They were as proud of the team as I was. And to think, we lost! It was just fantastic."

Big time hockey had arrived in Pittsburgh and the *Hockey News* selected Red as its coach of the year. In those days, the NHL didn't have a coach's award.

Tragedy would strike the team in the off-season when young Brière, who had led the Penguins with five goals and three assists in the playoffs, including three game-winners, was involved in a single-car accident in Quebec on May 15, and sustained massive head injuries which would leave him in a long-lasting coma.

"The car hit a bump, and Michel was thrown out of it and hit his head on the road. He had so much promise," recalled Red. "He was not a big guy, but he had big hands, was shifty and could really stickhandle. He had real spirit and wasn't afraid of anything. In the playoffs, the Oakland Seals put their big forward on him, but he couldn't touch Brière. He was a true budding star, maybe a superstar.

"Not too long after the accident, I went to see him at the hospital in Montreal. He was still in that coma. I felt so bad, and I wanted to do something to help, so I started talking to him, like it was a game, give him a pep talk. He was unconscious, but I knew he could hear me because he started to react, like a slight grunt now and then, a slight twitch. I knew I was getting a reaction, and I continued talking to him like it was a pre-game. I talked to him for quite a while, telling him to come out of this. That he could do it and come and play hockey again. When I left his room that day, I thought maybe he might get better because I had gotten a bit of a reaction from him." Brière remained in a coma as the 1970–71 season got underway.

Pittsburgh management then added the general manager role to Red's portfolio. "I told the ownership that I didn't really want it, there was too much work just being the coach," Red recalled. "I said that the players needed a lot of attention, and I thought it would be too much. When they continued to insist, I accepted but insisted that Jack Riley stay on as an executive. Don't fire him outright. He could go to the meetings for me; we'd work together. It was my decision to also take on being the GM — and the wrong one. I looked at it afterwards, and I know I made the wrong decision."

There were plenty of tough decisions as GM.

On January 25, Red came home after a long day, headed for the piano and sang. Andra knew something was up.

"When Red plays the piano, it means he's either very happy, very upset or going to make a trade," Andra recalled.

"I traded Glen Sather to New York for Syl Apps Jr.," Red recalled. "Sather had been a fan favourite. At the next game, after the trade, all the signs were up: 'Why Trade Sather?' In the second period, Apps gets a breakaway against Jacques Plante, deked him good and scored. Ha! All the signs came down!

"Sather had been a good team player, a good penalty killer, but had a tough time scoring goals. We needed a centreman, and New York had three centremen plus Syl Apps coming up. Apps wasn't about to break into their lineup with those other three centremen there, and they needed a penalty-killer, so we made the trade."

It would be a tough year in Pittsburgh as the team struggled. Still, Red's coaching talent was appreciated by his players. "I've been playing more years than I care to remember, but I've never played for a better coach," remarked Ken Schinkel at a sports dinner at mid-season. "He is everything a player would want in a coach, and I feel that Pittsburgh should be proud to have him. I guess you'd say he knows how to communicate. Sure, he knows a great deal about the game and how it should be played, but his ability to reach each player and to help them with their problems is what impresses me."

Off the ice, the team's dismal financial situation took a turn for the worse. "Partway through the year Donald Parsons went belly up," Red recalled. "He had once talked about buying the New York Jets, and said he had a fleet of jets. He said, 'Red, you know hockey

— the NHL and the minor leagues? Well, in the banking world, I'm in the minor leagues.'

"Then when tight money came along, banks went to Europe to get financing, but the big banks are in line first to get financing, and Donald Parsons was down the line. Then the other bankers were after him for not having enough liquid assets. Mellon Bank called in his note at 12:01, and at 12:02 the other banks did as well. He lost it all."

The NHL took over the team as of December 1, while Parsons sought a buyer. "Now we're under league ownership for the remainder of the year," recalled Red. "Yet we operated in the black that year because we were getting sellouts, except if it snowed or some dang thing, and the team was playing exciting hockey. Not the greatest hockey, but exciting."

Always looking for an edge, Red had his players wear earmuffs to stifle the loud crowd in St. Louis. "We always seemed to be down when we played there, so I did something different," Red recalled. "The crowd was all above you, and the noise would come right down on you — BOOM, BOOM. I said, 'Well, we'll put earmuffs on.' The players had them all on but soon took them off. By the end of the game, I was the only one left with the earmuffs on.

"It didn't matter. We couldn't win in St. Louis with the Plager brothers there, and Noel Picard. St. Louis wasn't necessarily the best team in the world, but they were rough and tough. And they beat us with their goaltending of Jacques Plante and Glenn Hall. We couldn't match 'em."

The team won only three road games and 18 home games all season, finishing in sixth place and out of the playoffs.

On April 13, nine days after the Penguins season ended, Michel Brière passed away after 11 months in a coma; he was only 21 years old. The Penguins delegation at the funeral included Red, Riley and six players. The following year, another prominent Pittsburgh athlete, baseball icon Roberto Clemente, died in a plane crash;

coincidentally both men wore No. 21 jerseys. No one ever wore No. 21 for the Penguins again, and it was officially retired in 2001.

For the 1971–72 season, Red's third with the Penguins, there was new ownership under a consortium of investors headed by Tad Potter along with Peter Burchfield, Elmore Keener and a returning Peter Block. So impressed were they with their coach that they signed Red to a five-year contract at an annual salary of $50,000. It was a vote of confidence. "I never cared about the salary, even when I played," Red recalled.

GM-coach Kelly was looking around for talent. He first acquired the services of goalie Roy Edwards, a recently retired former Red Wing. "I think Edwards can do a job for us and I think I can sell him on giving it a shot," Red told the press. Other managers thought he was crazy. The move didn't quite work out as Red hoped, as Edwards quit after two wins in 15 games. His departure hurt.

"Roy was a pretty good goaltender, but he just gave up," Red recalled. "He just gave up on hockey, didn't want to play anymore. I tried to convince him to stay, but I couldn't do it. He was playing a lot, too, and we needed him. We sure missed him when he left. It was a very unusual thing. I had never experienced anything like that before."

One cajoling job was successful: Red got his former teammate Tim Horton to come to Pittsburgh. "We flew Tim down with Ron Joyce, his business partner with Tim Horton Donuts. He needed to build warehouses and needed financial backing for those warehouses, so that's what I gave him," recalled Red. "In turn, he agreed to play for me in Pittsburgh. I knew Tim, he was a good team guy, how he would react. I knew what he would do for our team, no question! He agreed to come. His warehouses got his franchises going even more.

"Tim Horton gave me everything I asked for. He played in forty-four games. I remember Alex Delvecchio tripping him in Detroit, taking the feet right out from under him, and he landed on his shoulder. It was right at the end of the period, and then we came off the ice. They took him into the next room, and I went in. His shoulder was up about half a foot out of place! He wanted to go back out and play because he knew I was counting on him. That was the kind of guy he was. I just looked at his shoulder and said, 'Tim, there's no way you're going back out there. Get undressed!'"

The Kellys hosted the team Christmas party at their home. "Attached to the house was a large greenhouse. It was all glass, including the roof, and we had the team Christmas party in there," Red recalled. "Don't you know, it was snowing, and the snow came off the roof of the house, onto the greenhouse. The impact broke through the ceiling, and a pane of glass came flying down right on Les Binkley's head. Wow! He was okay, but it could have been catastrophic. The party moved into the house."

By January 27, the Pens were floundering, having won only 2 of their previous 22 games, and there was talk of resurrecting Red to play. Despite the fact that he had been suiting up for some practices, the 44-year-old Hockey Hall of Famer said he wasn't seriously considering it as an option.

"I suppose there are some people who would like to see me step in and play again," Red told Jim Proudfoot. "Let me answer you this way: I haven't really been practising much. Skating yes, but that's all.

"We just can't put the dang puck in the net and that's the reason for our slump. Listen, we've had the goalie out in the last minute of play 15 times this season! Fifteen times we were within a goal of tying. We really haven't been playing too badly."

With 18 games to go, Red traded unproductive youngster René Robert to the Buffalo Sabres in exchange for his old teammate Eddie Shack. The trade worked to Red's benefit, as Shack picked up 14 points and brought his entertaining style of play to town.

"Shack sure put people in the stands," Red recalled. "Shack was the entertainer. And we needed that in Pittsburgh. We needed a boost, and René Robert was not producing. He had the ability, but he was pouting. We made the deal and Shack would entertain the fans. And

Eddie could still play." (Robert, of course, landed alongside Gilbert Perreault and Rick Martin on the French Connection line in Buffalo.)

Home game attendance shot up by 4,000 fans per game after Shack's arrival, and the Penguins lost only three times in their final 14 games to finish in fourth place. Apps Jr. led the team in scoring with 59 points.

Because Vancouver and Buffalo, new additions to the NHL for the 1970–71 season, had been placed in the East Division, the Chicago Black Hawks had moved to the West Division. It was Chicago against Pittsburgh in the first round of the 1971–72 playoffs — an epic mismatch, as the Hawks had finished with 107 points, 51 more than the Pens. It was a four-game sweep. "They gave us the royal treatment. They had too much power for us," Red remarked.

Red got an unexpected visitor late one summer night. It was the security guard with Eddie Shack and his tiny dog Foo-Foo.

"Mr. Kelly, I've got this guy here who says he wants to talk to you," the guard said.

"It's okay," Red answered with a smile. "I know him."

"Eddie and Foo-Foo come in," Red recalled. "It was clear that he had had a few too many pops. Eddie said he'd had something on his mind for a long time, which had really been bothering him and he wanted to confess to me. I said, 'Ah, well go ahead.'

"He got on his knees in front of a footstool before me, like a confession. He told me that he had taken the credit for one of my goals when we played together in Toronto years earlier, and he was sorry. I had shot the puck but they had given him the goal, but he said he never came a mile of touching it. He said he needed the goal more than I did because he had a bonus for goals. I said, 'It's all in the past now, Ed. Forget about that.'

"He fell asleep on the floor. I went and got a blanket to cover him up. Foo-Foo was lying right beside him on her back with four feet up in the air. I put the blanket over both of them. I didn't put it over

Foo-Foo's head, just his body. Then I thought, *Gosh that's a hard floor, I'd better get a pillow to put under Eddie's head.* I went to move Shackie's head to put the pillow under, and the dog growled: GGGGRRRR! I said, 'Okay, I won't put the pillow under him, Foo-Foo. I'll agree with you.' I left the two of them. Eddie and Foo-Foo were gone by the time I got up in the morning. He was able to walk home, as he didn't live too far from where we lived."

As Red prepared his team for the 1972–73 season, his duties as GM were returned back to Riley. What he didn't know was that the new owners were buddying up to the players. "The ownership group — Peter Block, Elmore Keener, Peter Burchfield — knew beans about hockey," Red recalled. "But they knew how to golf. At training camp, they went golfing with some of my players. I didn't think that was appropriate. If a player had a vendetta against the coach, it can be effected on the golf course."

The Pens started off decently, and at the end of November they had a respectable record of 12 wins against 10 losses.

Rookie defenceman Jack Lynch would later recall his inaugural season and the influence of his new coach for the *Toronto Star* in 2004:

> He and Andra invited the two rookies on the team over for dinner. I couldn't believe that an NHL coach would do that but we were young, just 20, away from home for the first time and he obviously wanted to make sure we were okay.
>
> Red loved to work with us kids and one day after practice I stayed out longer taking extra shots. The other players were long gone but we stayed on the ice working on all kinds of things. I swear he tried to cram his 20–plus years of NHL experience into the next two hours. I loved every minute of the extra attention. The trainers were livid because they wanted to get home.

*I went right home and wrote down on notes every-
thing he had taught me that day. The next day, several of
the older vets brought apples into practice for me to give
to my "teacher." I didn't care about the ribbing. Red was
incredible! I still have my notes.*

Red recalled a situation with Lynch and an old nemesis. "The Penguins had drafted older players and had a poor minor league system. I realized we had to make do with what we've got," Red explained. "So I'm working with Jack Lynch, he was a young player, a good kid who made his fair share of mistakes, so I'm working with him on the ice after practice. The others are gone, and it's just the two of us. All of a sudden, Al Eagleson steps onto the ice and starts talking with Jack Lynch.

"I'm further up the ice, and I see this and the smoke starts coming out of my ears. I thought, *You son of a sea cook!* So I take the puck and I fire it as hard as I could from where I was. It went around the net, around the two corners and just missed Eagleson's shins where he was standing by the boards. It just skinned him. I'm lucky I didn't hit him! Boy, did he get the message and get off the ice in a hurry. There are different ways you can give a message. He got my message."

In January, Red learned the extent to which player dissent can hurt a coach. When a fight broke out in a game, Pens winger Ken Schinkel went for a leisurely skate while the fight was in progress, an infraction that cost him a penalty. The Rangers scored on the ensuing power play en route to a 3–0 win. Red gave Schinkel a public dressing-down after the game. He was livid, as the loss hurt the team in its continuing battle for second place in the West Division. Red didn't know of Schinkel's friendliness with the team's owners. "It was a Saturday morning when they called me in and told me I was fired," Red recalled. "They didn't tell me why, didn't say anything. Just, boom! Just like that! Fired! Guess who they replace me with? Ken Schinkel."

The Penguins team had invited the children of the coaches and players to skate with their parents after the team practice, including the Kellys. "I have bad memories of that Saturday morning," recalled oldest daughter Casey. "My brothers and I were skating, wondering why Dad didn't join us on the ice. After a while he came into the stands and asked us to get off the ice and come to his office. We were puzzled, but did as he requested. Once we arrived at his office, he closed the door and said, 'I've been fired.' We were absolutely shocked by this. Imagine firing someone when his children were right there in the building! And he had made such strides with the team — it didn't make sense to us."

Driving home that morning, kids in the back seat, Red was in shock, angry and disillusioned with hockey. He was out of a job in the middle of the season. The kids were still in school, and Andra was teaching skating to the blind. They had a beautiful house in Pittsburgh, a good life, and had given all of themselves to bettering hockey in Pittsburgh. He had revitalized the Penguins franchise, brought them to the playoffs, built up the fan base. This was how he was rewarded?

As Red got home, shocked and dazed, Andra was just coming in from the nearby Monroeville Mall, which had a skating rink where she gave lessons. In her arms was a full-size tin statue of "Sir George," which she and the kids used to salute as they entered and left the mall; this was such a ritual that she had decided to purchase the statue that morning. As soon as she came into the house, she saw the look on Red's face. "Red?" she asked with concern. "What's wrong?"

He shook his head, hardly knowing what to say.

● ● ● ● ● ●

CHAPTER NINETEEN

COACHING
the LEAFS

After Red's firing, Andra's first reaction was to put the family's Pittsburgh home up for sale.

"I loved Pittsburgh and everything about it," she recalled. "It was just such a great place to live and raise a family. Our house was big; an older home on an old farm, but it was just so warm and cozy. It had a big fireplace, and the neighbourhood was wonderful.

"I had a good job, great skating students and a great group of visually impaired students as well. My figure skating coach had been Edi Scholdan of the Broadmoor Skating Club in Colorado Springs, and I used a lot of his teaching methods. I finished the season with my group but was heartbroken to be leaving them. Suddenly, I got a call out of the blue from Edi Scholdan's daughter, Dixie, who lived in the city, and she agreed to take over my groups when we left Pittsburgh. She used her dad's methods as well, so that was reassuring, but it was still so heartbreaking for me to leave them. I got so attached to my students.

"The kids had to finish school, and Red would be quite occupied trying to get some type of compensation from the Penguins. That took a while. All in all it was a rough few months."

The Penguins sent a letter stating they were going to honour Red's contract, which had four years remaining. "I also had a car that they had supplied me with, but they called that in pretty quickly — no more car," recalled Red. "Next thing I know, Pittsburgh wasn't going to honour the contract either, not a cent, nothing! I couldn't believe it! What was I to do?

"Of course, my next thought was to hire a lawyer and sue the Penguins for breach of contract. Well, try finding a Pittsburgh lawyer to fight the Rockwells in Pittsburgh! Couldn't be done. I didn't know what I would do. I was in a heck of a spot, so I represented myself."

Red met with Penguins ownership and their lawyers on numerous occasions over the next couple of months, but the impasse lasted well into the spring, with no end in sight. The Penguins continued to balk, but Red, knowing he was right, would not let the matter rest.

As he prepared to head north to the cottage, eight NHL and World Hockey Association teams started calling. Three turned out to be serious.

"First I got a call from Coley Hall in Vancouver," recalled Red. "He was associated with the Canucks, had been from their early days. He had a place in Hawaii, so he flew me there to discuss my coaching Vancouver. I was thinking about it."

Then Red got a call from *Globe and Mail* columnist Dick Beddoes. "Red, would you be interested in coming to Toronto to coach?" Beddoes asked. The question caught Red off guard. He had always hoped for a return to Toronto.

"Well maybe," Red answered. "But you're a reporter. How come you're the one asking?"

"I'm actually asking for Harold Ballard," replied Beddoes. He and Ballard were good friends, and Ballard was serving time in

Millhaven Penitentiary on fraud, theft and tax evasion charges. He was soon to be released.

Red said he was interested, and Beddoes said he would pass on the information.

"The next thing I know, I get a call from Harold Ballard from jail, he's still in Millhaven," Red recalled.

"I hear you're interested in coaching my team," Ballard said. "What'll it take moneywise to get you to come to Toronto?"

Red gave him a figure.

"Okay, you're hired!" Ballard answered without hesitation.

Red was dumbstruck.

He collected himself and asked his new boss to hold off on the announcement, since he was still trying to get the Penguins to honour his contract.

Ballard said that he wasn't aware of Red's issues with the Penguins ownership but to keep him informed.

"I found it odd that Ballard didn't know about my situation," Red recalled. "Because all those NHL owners knew what the others were up to. Anyways, the Leafs held off making the announcement for a bit while I was in discussions with Pittsburgh."

At the end of June, the kids were done school, and the Kellys sold their Pittsburgh farmhouse. The next challenge was to secretly shop for a new home in Toronto. Red wanted keep a low profile, as he didn't want word to get out just yet about his new job.

"I had seen this house in Forest Hill before, and it was now for sale," Andra recalled. "Red and I went through it together with a real estate agent, and we introduced ourselves as Mr. and Mrs. Schumaker to the owner, an older lady. This lady just looked at Red, smiled and nodded. After the tour was over and we were leaving, she took me aside and whispered to me with a twinkle in her eye, 'I know who you are. My husband and I are season ticket holders. Red's my husband's favourite player. Your secret is safe with me.'"

They purchased the dark-panelled house on Dunvegan Road just north of downtown and moved in along with the Sir George statue, which got a prominent place in the front hallway.

Other things began to fall into place.

"Finally, the Penguins agreed to honour my contract — but they would only pay me the difference from the time I was let go until somebody else employed me," recalled Red. "They agreed to pay the interim, but that was all. They didn't know I had agreed to coach the Leafs. Nobody knew."

That moment finally came on August 20, 1973, as Red signed a four-year contract to coach the storied Toronto franchise. Jim Gregory was the general manager, but Ballard got all the headlines as the outrageously outspoken owner.

Red spoke to the press about the prospects for his new team. "Outside of the Montreal Canadiens, who are in a class by themselves, there's no reason why we can't be right up there with everybody else," the new coach told the *Toronto Star*'s Jim Proudfoot. "There seems to be good young players at every position." For every veteran on the team, like Dave Keon and Norm Ullman, there were promising youngsters, like Darryl Sittler, Ian Turnbull and Lanny McDonald.

The Leafs started the 1973–74 season decently, and on November 3 his Leafs shut out the visiting Penguins 6–0 to bring their record to six wins against three losses. Returning to Pittsburgh on November 28, Red got the surprise of his life. As he stepped onto the ice to walk to the Leafs bench, the small crowd of 8,425 stood and cheered him. At the end of the first period, again as he walked back across the ice, two banners were lifted high for him to see, stating, "Welcome Red!" and "Love to Andra!"

"I guess they went to a lot of work on those signs," Red remarked after his Leafs had defeated the home team, 4–3. "I imagine they appreciated some of the hockey we showed them in the four years previous." The win put the Leafs in a tie for third place with the Rangers, with 27 points.

As Christmas approached, the Leafs sported a 15–11–6 record. Red was content with the season thus far, as he stated in an article titled, "It's a Merry Christmas for Kelly, He's Happy with His Maple Leafs": "I'm happy with the whole kit and caboodle," he told Red Burnett. "There have been no major disappointments so far. The play of Mike Pelyk has given me great satisfaction. Garry Monahan is in the same category. Norm Ullman is one of our top performers. Ron Ellis is playing sound hockey. The goalies — Ed Johnston, Doug Favell and Dunc Wilson — have been very good. Our young rookies, Ian Turnbull, the Swedes [Inge Hammarstrom and Borje Salming], Lanny McDonald and Bob Neely haven't let us down.

"Sittler is playing strong aggressive hockey. We felt McDonald would be more productive offensively. Neely could be the victim of too much pressure. I look for some big goals from Keon, Rick Kehoe and Tim Ecclestone."

The day after the article, the Leafs paid their first visit of the season to the intimidating Boston Garden, usually a graveyard for visiting teams in its confined space. Though they lost a close one, 4–3, the game set the Leafs on fire, as they won six of their next eight games through January. After a convincing 5–2 victory in Atlanta, Red's boys decided to celebrate at the Marriott Hotel.

"We were staying in two towers. I was in one tower and the players were in another," Red recalled of the January 27 incident. "I got a call a little after midnight from the front desk, a lady saying there were some problems on an upper floor where the players were staying. I got dressed and shot over there, and at the elevator of that other tower I met her, with another manager and the police. Up we go.

"As we got off the elevator, we could hear noise from around the corner. The corridor was littered with glass from plates and a couple of broken gas lights. One of my players was out in the hallway shooting plates, and he didn't have a stitch of clothes on. We had the girl with me, and when this naked shooter's roommate saw me, he was trying to whisper to him from the doorway, to warn him. When he turned around and saw us coming, he was trying to hide behind his hockey stick, which didn't cover much. The team had to pay a couple of thousand dollars in damages so that the police wouldn't arrest him."

On February 21, the hockey world was stunned by the death of Buffalo defenceman Tim Horton in a car crash. He had played at the Gardens the night before, in a 4–2 loss to the Leafs. "I'd sure like to have 18 Tim Hortons on my team," Red commented after hearing the stunning news. "I found him one of the toughest dang guys to beat in the league and when he got you in the corner that was it. He was all man, one of the great competitors in our game."

As the season was drawing to a close and Toronto had secured the fourth and final playoff spot, Red had a few special rookies to look after. "Lanny McDonald was a young guy, a high draft pick, and people were looking for great things from him, but as a rookie he would make some slips here and there, and people would get down on him a little bit," Red recalled. "They were expecting him to be perfect and were getting down on him, and I knew Lanny had the ability but he was just a kid. He's gonna make mistakes. But he had great hands, was a great player, and it would take him time, that's all. I tried to keep the pressure off him."

The season before Red's arrival, Darryl Sittler had finally broken through, with 77 points. The new coach helped as he could. "Sittler worked hard, and I played him a lot. He was big, smart, and he really worked on his stickhandling. He did that himself, and I let him continue practicing that, and I purposely did one-on-one stickhandling drills to help him."

Inge Hammarstrom and Borje Salming were not rookies by age, since both were veterans of Swedish hockey, but they were new to the NHL. With the WHA already making inroads on international talent, Gerry McNamara, the head scout for the Leafs, had signed Hammarstrom and Salming, and they both made the Toronto lineup.

Red was charged with getting the Swedes up to NHL standards. "When they came, I put them in practice, to get them used to the North American game," he recalled. "Salming had a hard go at the beginning and had to learn how to fight back. Salming did, but Hammarstrom never did adapt to the rough stuff. One time in Philly, Inge gets a breakaway on goal, he's all alone, and they're chasing him, can't catch him, but they're hollering at him. They scared him so much he never even got a shot on the net."

As the Leafs entered the playoffs, they had the fourth-best defensive record in the league and the sixth-highest offensive output. But as Red readied his goaltenders for the first series against the powerful Bruins, he had a problem in that he had three of them to keep sharp. During the season he had rotated Dunc Wilson, Doug Favell and Eddie Johnston, going with whoever was winning and changing starters after a loss.

Johnston called the three-goalie system "a little different," but all three got along. Wilson and Favell were jokesters. "I was the experienced guy, the guy that had been there," Johnston said.

"That was not a lot of fun," Doug Favell said. "There was no schedule for playing. It all varied, on injuries, on what guy was playing well and on Red Kelly."

For the playoffs, Red wanted his hottest goalie to keep going. It was an impossible situation.

"We're all established NHL goalies, which made it easier for us to handle the situation, but difficult for Red," Favell told Frank Orr before the playoffs started. "It's satisfying because we made the playoffs and the club came back a long way. But it's been frustrating for all three of us because we haven't played as much as we'd like."

Coach Kelly ended up going with Favell in net for three of the four games, but the goaltending really wouldn't matter, as Boston swept them aside, outscoring the Leafs 16–9. "Boston had a very powerful team, and we weren't able to handle them," Red recalled.

On the eve of the third game against Boston on Good Friday, April 13, Andra's father, Charles McLaughlin, passed away after a seven-month battle with cancer. It was a tough time for Andra, who spent time with him until the end even as her mother continued her own five-year battle with the disease.

"Charles McLaughlin was a pioneer," Red recalled. "He had an aerial survey company in the 1920s and had flown with Charles Lindbergh and Walt Disney, had surveyed the sites for LaGuardia and many large airports in the U.S. We got along great."

As the summer of 1974 unfolded, Red got a good news/bad news letter from defenceman Mike Pelyk, informing him personally that Pelyk was signing with Cincinnati of the WHA and leaving for monetary reasons only. Pelyk thanked Red for playing a major role in his play last season — the best one he said he'd had in six years. Red was pleased for him. "It makes you feel good to get such a letter," Red said to the press. "He had a hang of a year for me. He was a key man — killing penalties, playing defence and the odd shift up front. But there was no way he could pass up that kind of money the WHA offered, over $100,000 a season."

Red wasn't so pleased a few weeks later, when a reporter contacted him for comment on the story that right winger Rick Kehoe, through his agent Alan Eagleson, was demanding to be traded. It was a shock to the coach. "I wish I knew (his reason)," Red answered. "No one around the Gardens has been able to get an explanation. I heard it was because I moved him from Darryl Sittler's line to the Dave Keon line. That doesn't make sense to me. I asked him about it and he said it was fine. His goal output had dropped and I told him not to worry about it. Then he suffered a shoulder injury and missed the last nine games and the playoffs. The next thing I found out was that he doesn't want to play for me."

That summer, Andra's mother succumbed to her cancer. Mrs. McLaughlin had grown very fond of her son-in-law. "Mother just loved Red," Andra recalled. "As she grew too weak to walk, Red would gently pick her up and carry her to and from her bedroom to sit with us. She would say to me softly, 'I just love that man! He is such a good man!'" She passed away just after the start of training camp.

Red was more familiar with his team than he had been at the previous year's training camp. "The difference is like night and day," Red told Red Burnett. "Last year I encountered the coldest, strangest dressing room atmosphere in all my years as a professional player and coach. It was hard to define. It was almost like a room of hostile strangers, and it wasn't all that great when the season ended. Now we have the right kind of atmosphere. Relaxed and friendly."

"That's the kind of camp we had in the Stanley Cup years," Leafs scout Johnny Bower added.

In an exchange of right wingers, Kehoe went to Pittsburgh for Blaine Stoughton. Cowboy Bill Flett came in from the Cup-winning Philadelphia Flyers. He was pleased to be reunited with his old coach.

"Red Kelly was the L.A. coach and he played me a great deal," Cowboy remarked. "He gave me a chance to be a regular in the NHL. I had a good relationship with him and have high regard for his coaching."

On October 23, following a 3–2 loss to the Canadiens at the Gardens, coach Red got angry as his team's record sunk to .500. "We blew the game," said Red, uncharacteristically sounding off to the press. "That third goal should not have beaten Doug Favell. But what about the penalty to Bob Neely when we were winning 2–1? Prior to that they had pulled the feet out from under our guys, hooked and held them with no penalties! Why let so much go and then nab Neely? [John] McCauley deserves all three stars for his effort!"

After the game, referee-in-chief Scotty Morrison paid Red a visit. "I was certainly very perturbed at some of the calls that were being made," Red recalled. "I told that to the referee-in-chief when he came in to see me, and he wasn't very happy about it."

The Leafs had a big roster, with four players having to sit out each game — not conducive to good team chemistry. "The ideal situation of course is to have all players on hand dressing for all the games," Red told Frank Orr. "I know it bruises players' pride to sit out and it doesn't do their conditioning much good either. But it seems a fact of hockey life now to have extra players."

Toronto wasn't the only team doing it; Montreal's GM, Sam Pollock, defended the practice. "It's a sign of the times in hockey to have a big roster," Pollock said. "A team needs extra players to give people a rest occasionally."

In November, the team's defence and goaltending went south as Toronto won only three games. There was unrest in the ranks, and the press gave it good and hard to the two Leafs goalies, Wilson and Favell. "They are allowing more goals than Leafs can score," went one story. "Consequently, Les Leafs are looking like bums. But for the grace of God, and the California Seals, Les Leafs would be dead last in their exclusive little four-team group." Bower came out to practice to work with the struggling goalies.

On November 21, Red was in his office when he received a small cheque from Leafs publicity director and part-time writer Stan Obodiac, who had penned a small biography on him several years earlier. The good news was short-lived, as he was informed that Salming had a shattered heel and would be out for four weeks. Salming had just returned after being out three weeks with a broken finger. "The Leafs had had a slow start that season," Andra recalled. "But when Red came home that day, after hearing that Salming was hurt again, he said to me that he'd never felt so alone."

By the end of November, the Leafs' record was an ugly six wins against 12 losses. The team was beset with injuries to Salming, Turnbull, Sittler, Rod Seiling, Jim McKenny and Keon.

"You have to go with what you've got and do the best you can," Red said. In that light he next took the unusual step of gearing up and participating at full tilt in his practices, which caused speculation among the press that he would put himself into action. "If the man in the blue sweatsuit would only wear a helmet to conceal his bald spot at the Leaf drills these days, he could pass for a shock trooper who has been rushed in to pick up the club," went one story. "He's an excellent skater, this man in the blue fatigues. He handles the puck well, puts the pass on the right stick, and picks the openings inside the posts when he shoots."

When he was asked if he was preparing for a comeback, like his 46-year-old former teammate Gordie Howe in the WHA, Red scoffed. "There's no dang way," Red answered. "I'll say this though, I did have the bounce today and I felt like I had a lot of power. Yeah, I feel pretty dang good. Weight? No problem there. I'm down to 205. But there's no thought of playing again — not for a million dollars. I'll take that back. For a million dollars I'd have to give it some thought." He laughed then added: "I'm just fooling around, trying to get them to move the puck quickly. I can see a lot of improvement. When we get our guys back we'll be okay."

Andra spearheaded a fundraising skate-a-thon to help the family of Bruno and Anna Macri of Salem Avenue, who had lost their house and all their possessions in a November 6 fire. Convincing the Metro Toronto Hockey League to give up six hours of ice time at St. Michael's College Arena, Andra organized and oversaw 3,000 skaters, many of them youngsters in the MTHL, who joined Red, McDonald, Shack and King Clancy on the ice for 50 laps at various times and helped raise over $6,000 for the Macri family.

"I want to say thank you, but just saying it doesn't seem to be enough," an overjoyed Anna Macri told the *Toronto Star*. "There are many people who should be thanked but especially Mrs. Kelly and her husband."

"The coach and all the Kellys are fabulous! They're super!" added 12-year-old Stephen Macri, who, along with his 10-year-old-brother, Joe, had moved in with the Kellys for five days after the fire. Stephen was a minor hockey teammate of Patrick Kelly.

"In Toronto, we weren't ordinary kids with ordinary parents,"

Patrick recalled. "Though I had a *Toronto Star* paper route, and we never missed Sunday mass at Holy Rosary and we would take the subway with Mom to the games at the Gardens, we had other issues.

"People said that my brother and I made hockey teams just because of my father. Our first year in Toronto, I even played as Patrick Shoemaker, to prove myself. Kids at school would want Leafs tickets. We were all redheads, which meant we were called 'carrot tops' at each school. Boys wanted to date my sister because of my dad. People pointed at us at stoplights; we would just slink down below the car window to avoid their stares.

"But we were so proud of my parents, and we were able to experience a lot of great things such as Harold Ballard as Santa Claus, players coming over for dinner like Michel Brière and Denis Herron in Pittsburgh. In Toronto, Inge Hammarstrom, Lanny McDonald, Eddie Shack and Frank Mahovlich often came to dinner."

There was always plenty of criticism and meddling around the Leafs, and not just from Ballard. "Al Eagleson caused me some problems that year," recalled Red. "It was a tough season for us, no question. A lot of injuries, and the wins were sparse for a bit. Some players met with Eagleson after a game, a group that met with him regularly. The players knew what I thought of Eagleson, and that sure didn't help the team and my players' attitude, that's for sure."

As the GM, Jim Gregory had to deal with Eagleson — and Ballard — more than Red did. "Jim wasn't a buffer for Harold, because Harold spoke his mind no matter what," Red recalled. "Gregory had a tough position to be in, not an easy task, and I thought he did a pretty good job. Harold did talk too much, too critical of players. I talked with Gregory more than Ballard. We would have dinner together periodically and talk about the team. I give him a lot of credit for having to deal with Ballard. It would be a tough job that way."

With a cantankerous owner, a meddling player representative and a team beset with injuries, the hockey gods seemed to have issue with the Leafs. But amid the bad spots there was hope. When the

Leafs beat Chicago 6–3 on January 4 to improve their record to 12 wins, 18 losses and seven ties, Cowboy Bill Flett not only defended his coach but also blasted the media who dared to sarcastically remark to him that it had been a great win.

"Great for the man (coach Red Kelly)," Flett told Red Burnett, the sweat dripping from him as he sat at his stall in the dressing room. "He's quite a guy. Instead of using the 'Fire Kelly cry' as a goad, he told us to forget anything we might have heard about Kelly, to concentrate on the game and not Kelly's problems. He gave us a straight from the shoulder talk. He told us what we had to do to beat the Hawks. He stressed that we had to be more physical, play the man as much if not more than the puck. We took his advice and won."

The win sparked a new attitude, and the Leafs went on to win five of their next seven games. A call-up joined the team in mid-January in the guise of a firecracker named Dave "Tiger" Williams, who was promoted from the minors and made his physical presence known in a 4–1 victory in St. Louis.

"Tiger's hitting was a big help," Red told writer Frank Orr. "But we had one of the best overall team efforts of the season with three lines going well both ways, the defence playing soundly and Favell strong in goal. It was a good way to start a six-game road trip. We can be a winning club if we have everyone working hard."

Williams finished his career as the NHL's all-time penalty minute leader. To Red, what Williams really brought to the team was competitiveness. "He was fierce, he was in the game, gave everything of himself in the game and all he had," Red explained. "Can't ask for better than that."

It was not always confined to the ice, either. In Vancouver, Williams and roommate George Ferguson exchanged punches in their hotel room, which resulted in Ferguson sustaining a broken bone in his right hand. Ferguson joined Salming, Brian Glennie, Bob Neely, McDonald and Turnbull on the injury list.

The Toronto press didn't help matters. "The Maple Leafs touring sad-sack carnival limped home today, following a week of horror shows on the West Coast," started the story by Frank Orr. "More hockey skill has been played in house league peewee games."

"I have never seen anything like it," Red told Orr, in trying to explain the team's bad luck. "How can one team get so many injuries to defencemen?"

Orr laid out what he thought was wrong with the Leafs. "Kelly might not have to shoulder the load of trying to motivate a team totally lacking internal leadership, and suffering from a dearth of professionalism which its high payroll would seem to demand," he wrote. "Although Leafs owner Harold Ballard has said he plans no immediate changes ... he won't wait much longer. Leafs do have some players who care and try but not enough to carry the team's unmotivated, unaggressive passengers and out-of-condition high-livers."

When they lost 8–3 to the Penguins on home ice on February 15, things were pretty quiet in the Leafs dressing room. "Too many injuries and too many guys not carrying their weight," Red said quietly afterwards.

Red kept the faith and tried to keep the team positive until some of his injured players returned. When they did, one after the other, Red's faith in his team was rewarded as his boys caught fire, embarking on a 13-game undefeated streak. Finally, the Toronto press had to write positively about the team as the wins stacked up.

Toronto ended the season hot, losing only five times in their final 23, ending up in third place in the newly created Adams Division consisting of Buffalo, Boston, Toronto and, oddly, the California Golden Seals. The NHL had added teams in Kansas City and Washington, creating an 18-team league divided into four divisions.

In a very unorthodox 1975 playoff setup, the 12th-place Leafs had to face the fourth-seeded Los Angeles Kings in a best-out-of-three preliminary-round series. The Kings were heavily favoured, as they had 27 more points than the Leafs, and would host the first and third game. It helped that the Leafs started the series at complete full strength, something that hadn't happened all year.

Gord McRae, who had been the primary goalie for Toronto's farm team, the Oklahoma City Blazers of the Central Hockey League, got the starting assignment for Game 1. He was hot and kept the score close until the Leafs tied it up late in the game to force overtime. The Kings had their hands full with an aggressive Leafs checking game but pulled out the win, 3–2. The Leafs returned to the Gardens full of confidence for Game 2, and returned the favour with an identical 3–2 OT win.

The rubber match had everything in it: great goaltending between McRae and L.A.'s Rogie Vachon, nifty passing and tight checking. Williams continued to bring emotion to the team and became embroiled in a second-period brawl, for which he was ejected along with his foe, Dave Hutchison. The Leafs fed off Tiger's effort and upset the Kings 2–1, moving on to face the defending Stanley Cup champion, Philadelphia Flyers.

"We're a different team now," Red told the press after the win. "We have some young players in the lineup. We've come together as a unit. Turnbull is back on defence and playing well and we're getting excellent goaltending from Gord McRae."

"It was nip and tuck," Red recalled of the series. "Bob Pulford was coaching L.A. He used Dan Maloney like Gordie Howe, rushing in there to knock us off the puck. Their game was built around him. We used the same method we used to use playing Detroit and Howe — move the puck quickly before getting checked. We didn't monkey with the puck, we moved the puck quickly. Boom! That's how we beat 'em. It threw L.A. off, and we were effective."

Red savoured the moment before preparing for the Flyers.

Game 1 in Philly was close as the Leafs entered the third period with a 3–2 lead. The Flyers roared back with a four-goal outburst for a 6–3 win. The score was not indicative of the close game, as Flyers coach Fred Shero observed. "If Leafs had got that game, they'd be in the driver's seat, sky high and full of confidence," Shero said. "They came too close for comfort. We had to win to be in command."

"In the third period, we were trying to do too much as individuals and it cost us," Red said after the game. "But we'll be here tomorrow. Don't forget, we lost the first game to Los Angeles."

Leafs owner Harold Ballard didn't help the cause when he went public with his criticism of Inge Hammarstrom's lack of physical play. "Hammarstrom could skate into the corner with six eggs in his pocket," Ballard bellowed, "and not crack one of them."

"Harold sure had a penchant for making headlines," Red recalled of this particular incident. "He sometimes said things that weren't helpful to the team. Inge certainly had trouble playing against the Flyers, no question. Their goon squad certainly went after him, but Harold didn't help either. It was not right. That tells the other teams that that's the kind of player he is."

The next day, the *Globe and Mail* published a poetic piece by noted Toronto writer June Callwood on Red that demonstrated the personal side of a coach who had experienced a tough season:

> He's a pale, exhausted, silent man, holding himself together these days by means of his touchstones: family, God and the renewable earth. He has in him a poetic, wild-Irish feel for universal mystery and a farmer's stubborn patience, bone-deep after generations of watching weather playfully destroy a crop and then planting again under the same bland sky.
>
> It has been a hard year for Leonard Patrick Kelly, called Red. His line of work is hockey. A player for 20 years . . . a coach these past seven seasons, of which this last one has been the worst. In private when he is feeling fine, Red Kelly will walk in the rain singing Irish songs, or gather people around a piano for a sing-song or will dance all

night — he loves to dance — but his public behaviour is stiff and reserved. He is uncomfortable in cities. He is always conscious that they are built on arable land — that's why people clustered there in the first place — and he mourns for the good growing soil under the pavement.

Farming is a religious experience for him. "You're closer to God out there," he says with conviction. "Much closer to God." He hasn't had that sense of peacefulness in a while. "Sometimes," he says bleakly, "I think that I don't know how to relax now."

The Toronto team he is coaching now has not been wonderful. He absorbs criticism and taunts with inflexible mild politeness . . . His family is closing ranks around him. "We all stick together," he says. He has a warm wife, the former professional skater Andra McLaughlin, and children with names out of a song about shamrocks: Casey, Patrick, Conn and Kitty.

And he rests himself in church. "It's like being near God, eh? It's like being in that field." Red Kelly has the best support system in town.

The next game was a mismatch, as the Flyers outshot the Leafs 29–13 en route to a 3–0 win that was kept close due to the great play of McRae.

Shero did not believe that the move to Maple Leaf Gardens would matter. "Their home crowd won't motivate them," said the Flyers coach. "Most of the people in Toronto think it is unsophisticated to cheer a home team goal. They come to see a good hockey game, not to see the home team win."

The Leafs came out flying in Game 3, forcing Flyers goalie Bernie Parent to make many great saves. Then Philadelphia took over, and the Toronto fans wouldn't have a goal to cheer about, as the Flyers won 2–0.

When reporters implied to the Flyers that the Leafs were push-overs, the Flyers were gracious in victory. "Don't underestimate the Leafs," said Philadelphia captain Bobby Clarke. "They gave it their best tonight. We were just a little too good. We have that necessary experience and we do things while they're thinking about it. Their young players will be better next season."

Next season came quickly, as the Flyers won a hard-fought 4–3 battle in which Toronto led twice and came back to tie it in the third to send it into overtime, where Moose Dupont sent the Flyers to the next round — and eventual second straight Cup.

"We improved step by step," Red observed in post-game analysis. "Six of our fellows were new to Stanley Cup play. We made little mistakes which hurt us. Experience is the only thing which corrects such mistakes."

Ballard wasn't so apologetic:

> We thought we had a contender this season, and we were wrong," boomed Ballard. "I don't want to make the same mistakes again! King and I will make the final decisions when we meet with our staff. We're going to scout all future playoff games, in all leagues. Then we'll plan our moves.
>
> When we saw how young players dominated the NHL All-Star Game in mid-season, we realized we had a lot of work to do. It is a young player's game. We owe a lot to the fans for their loyalty and everything possible will be done to give them a winner. I'm not ready to discuss numbers . . . or discuss the coaching.

As Red left the Gardens that night of April 19 and drove to his Forest Hill home with Andra and the kids, he hadn't heard Ballard's rant but would hear about it in the days to follow. He had come to expect it. While the Toronto press liked to beat down Leafs players and their coaches, Red was defended by a veteran writer who had written positive pieces about him before: Margaret Scott in *Weekend Magazine.*

The downgrading of Red Kelly as coach of the Toronto Maple Leafs has been slickly accomplished by a combination of oblique inferences and skillful innuendos. While the snipers ground out their material, much of it inaccurate, some of it unfounded, Kelly remained verbally handcuffed. He had to walk carefully to make certain he trod in Punch Imlach's old footprints. He was not a meaty bone to be gnawed upon by the press at regular intervals. Kelly appears to have inherited Imlach's ghost.

He is not totally responsible for Toronto's problems. The fact that Kelly rejects profanity and measures his liquor apparently wounds some of his detractors. Odd, how we insist that sport project high standards for the young to follow, then gripe when a coach complies. Does anyone actually believe that today's players would be more receptive to the fire and brimstone approach of Eddie Shore at his volatile best?

The player of today is vastly different from the player of five or ten years ago. Be it good or bad, the difference is termed evolution. Obviously no-cut contracts, salaries that out-strip the incomes of coaches, and lawyers willing to dash to the rescue of maligned athletes, change the concept of manipulating players. They are no longer willing to be cowed.

Kelly has been accused of lacking inventiveness and shunning innovations. Untrue! He studied Russian skating films and incorporated them into his own. Some of the techniques currently deployed by Bob Pulford were used by Kelly when he coached Los Angeles. He even conducted practices to the strains of music. Has any coach ever pleased all of his players all of the time?

The Kellys live in a large comfortable home in Forest Hill. As a couple they have never been able nor willing to install an invisible barrier between themselves and their teams. Red has never publicly berated his men and it cuts him when other people do so.

Andra has always described her husband's heart as a hockey puck. Not black and definitely not hard, but totally part of the game. Whatever affects him disturbs her.

Someday, a marketing genius will make a fortune packaging an old game, known as "What's Wrong with the Maple Leafs?" It will be a top seller regardless of the team's league standing.

Like all human beings Red Kelly is imperfect. He has never walked on water but he has had considerable experience skating on thin ice.

• • • • • •

CHAPTER TWENTY

KATE SMITH *vs.*
PYRAMID POWER

Meeting with Harold Ballard and King Clancy after the 1975 play-offs to discuss the past season must have been tense for Red Kelly. There had been talk of him being out of job, so he went in not knowing what to think. Still, the late-season surge by the Leafs and the elimination of the Kings had to mean something.

"You can't jump overboard unless you have a good life preserver," Ballard cryptically told the press. Though it wasn't exactly a strong vote of confidence, it meant Red still had his job for the time being.

Red attended the annual NHL draft in Montreal with GM Jim Gregory and was ecstatic when they picked up goalie Wayne Thomas from Montreal in exchange for a draft pick. "I'm tickled pink," Red exclaimed. "Inconsistent goaltending was a problem last year until Gordie McRae joined the team. He gave a boost to the club's confidence. There are many reasons why I'm enthusiastic about next season — Thomas and McRae in goal, two really excellent young defencemen like Borje Salming and Ian Turnbull, and being set on two lines which I'm not afraid of using against anybody." Those lines were George Ferguson between Lanny McDonald and Errol Thompson, and Darryl Sittler centering Tiger Williams and Ron Ellis. "We'll take a long look at Jack Valiquette as a centre, too, and maybe give Pat Boutette a shot at left wing," Red added.

When Flyers coach Fred Shero was asked at the meetings about coaching in Toronto, he pointed a finger at Ballard. "The only way a coach has a chance is if he's in charge and there aren't other people connected with the team who are quoted all the time with assessments of players," said Shero.

As training camp began in mid-September, Harold was sounding off again about his team, to which coach Kelly answered, "By hang, Harold knocked the Bobby Orr contract stories off the sports pages — for one day anyhow." Orr and his agent, Alan Eagleson, had made headlines when Orr signed a 10-year deal with Boston worth $4 million.

And Ballard wasn't done. The Leafs owner said Dave Keon and Norm Ullman were washed up and didn't have a place on the team. He gave them permission to look for new teams, but his NHL asking price for their release was so high that it forced both men to play in the WHA. When Sittler was appointed captain on September 10, he took exception at the way Ballard had treated the two Leafs icons.

"I thought the Keon and Ullman situation was handled very badly," Sittler said within minutes of accepting the C. "I know Mr. Ballard is noted for being outspoken, but in this case I thought it was dead wrong. These are guys who had done a lot for the Toronto club and I thought they deserved more consideration. You don't see that sort of thing happening in Montreal."

Red couldn't comment on the Sittler appointment — he was home with a bout of pneumonia.

When Inge Hammarstrom sat out a pre-season game against the Flyers with a supposed pinched nerve in his neck, Ballard was on the hunt again, stating how odd it was that Hammarstrom seemed

*Red in a pensive mood behind the bench of the
Toronto Maple Leafs. Coaching the Leafs was never easy,
especially with the meddlesome Harold Ballard around.*

ill whenever they faced the Flyers. "Hammarstrom was injured. He couldn't turn his head," Red said, defending his player. "He received treatment from the club doctor, and it's still bothering him a little. Inge never has ducked a game against Philadelphia or any other club."

The Swedish winger weighed in. "In Europe, my game was skating, moving the puck and scoring goals," Hammarstrom said. "Those were the things I did well enough for the Leafs to offer me a contract. Surely they didn't think that I was going to become a tough guy just by flying across the Atlantic Ocean."

Even Bobby Hull, starring with the WHA's Winnipeg Jets, got in on the conversation. "Hammarstrom has as much pure skill as anyone around," Hull commented. "I'd love to have him on my team. Tell Mr. Ballard that if he doesn't like Swedish players any more, the Jets will be happy to [take Hammarstrom], and take that Salming off his hands too."

In the pre-season games, Red felt the team was jelling — and getting tougher. "Every time they pushed, we pushed back," Red told reporters after a tie with Philadelphia. "When they found out that we weren't going to run and hide, they soon stopped the nonsense. We've been playing well as a team. There is a great feeling of that team idea among the players. Sometimes young players need a couple of years to get the hang of how things are done in the NHL. Some players make it quickly, others need time."

Ballard wasn't buying it and did not agree with his coach's assessment. "We're talking to anyone who will talk to us about deals," he boomed. "We'd like to get more muscle. The winning teams these days are those like Philadelphia Flyers and New York Islanders who have big, strong, young players who knock people down and aren't afraid to scrap."

A few days later, in a question-and-answer session with writer Frank Orr, Red tried to downplay his concerns with Ballard's rants, and his job security, and talked instead about his team. "I couldn't care less about that," Red said in reference to Ballard and his job threats.

> *It's the least of my worries. I knew it would be rough. I knew we'd have to struggle for a couple of years but I also figured that by the end of four years we could turn the team around to be right up there at the Stanley Cup door.*
>
> *We're young because the majority of our experienced players are gone. Our key nucleus is good, young, solid players with two or three years' experience and some with four or five. We'll be a club that works hard, we'll make mistakes but we'll improve. Our goaltending is stronger, we have the nucleus of a good hockey team but it might be necessary for one or two additions to make it a real Stanley Cup contender.*

"How much control of the team should a coach have?" Orr asked.

"The players must feel that the coach is the one man running the team, the one who decides which players are used and instructs them how to play on the ice," replied Red. "The players must have the confidence that the coach has the authority. If there's doubt about it, then the player often is unable to give his full playing ability for the coach to use."

Red worked with some of his younger players, especially Turnbull. "I used to get on him for going up the ice and taking his sweet time coming back," Red recalled. "I had no problem with him going up the ice. You get the chance, you go! Keep everything in front of you. But don't come back next week! You're a defenceman first and foremost. You come back, and fast. He could be a bit stubborn at times, which is not always a bad thing. But he was a great player."

When Andra was interviewed at length in mid-October by the *Toronto Star*'s Jane O'Hara, she talked about her own frustrations of being the coach's wife in Toronto.

> *(Hockey) is what he loves and I don't resent it. There's nothing he'd rather be doing although secretly I think he'd love to put on the skates and get back into action again. My biggest gripe is with the fans at the Gardens. They just aren't giving the team enough support and I really can't understand it. In every other city in the NHL the fans lie down and die for their team, win or lose. But not Leaf fans. Last year when Buffalo would come to town, I'd say "Well, here come the Toronto Sabres." The Gardens would go crazy when Buffalo scored, the organist would start playing that Sabres dance song and I'd get so shaking angry that I'd have to leave the building.*
>
> *Last (season) was the hardest Red's ever had to face. He has never been one to bring hockey home, but last season was an exception. With all the injuries the Leafs had, he*

just couldn't relax. When the team's winning, it's good, but when they're losing, it's awful. The publicity is upsetting to both Red and myself but especially to the children. The kids don't say much but when they hear the kids at school talking, or listen to the radio or read the newspapers, I know they feel it.

Last winter for example we were sitting eating dinner and a sports broadcast came on saying Red was going to be fired. The kids started crying right there even though there was no basis for the story. You can't stop reading the papers to avoid the publicity and besides I wouldn't want to. I'm not anti-press in the least. I try to keep my mind off it by doing my community work and keeping myself busy.

This year I'm just not going to listen to any foolish talk until I hear it in person from Mr. Ballard's lips. All along he's been very fair to us and I'll always remember him as the man who brought us back home.

If it was tough to be in Toronto as a coach, it could also be tough on the players, as exemplified when Ron Ellis announced his retirement before the season began, despite having come off the most productive season in his career. "That surprised me. I was blind-sided, you could say," recalled Red. "I tried to talk him into staying, but he had decided for his own personal reasons. He was still playing good hockey as far as I was concerned. I needed him, and his leaving left a hole to fill."

Ellis said that he was mentally burned out. "I realized I wasn't going to do any good playing and I couldn't be an asset to the team," Ellis recalled. "I took the game home with me too much. It was just part of my personality. I had just finished 11 full seasons, so I retired for the good of my family."

But as always, there was the ever-present sniping of Ballard, who let it be known that he was tired of waiting for youngsters Bob

Neely and Lanny McDonald to fulfill their promise; they were now expendable. Rumour had McDonald going to Atlanta. It didn't help his confidence.

"At this point Lanny had trouble shooting," Red recalled. "He would miscue on his shots, but I had no doubt in my mind, he had great tools, good hands, good shot and was a good team player. There was never any doubt about him in my mind about his talent."

As October flipped into November, McDonald had two goals. When Red made him a healthy scratch for one game, McDonald was seething. "I wanted to sock Red," he later told Frank Orr. "At the time I couldn't understand what he was trying to do and we would butt heads a little bit. It really hurt. Red wanted me to take a long range view of a game and maybe see what I wasn't doing. I never felt Red was down on me. He kept telling me to work away and things would straighten up."

At this time, Andra was teaching skating classes for the visually impaired. One of her helpers was Lanny's new bride, Ardell. Knowing her husband was really down on himself, feeling the pressure of hockey in Toronto and the trade talk, Ardell suggested Lanny come out to the classes, as a change of atmosphere.

"I'd been feeling sorry for myself because things with the Leafs were going badly," McDonald told Orr. "I needed a wakening up and those kids, some with very little eyesight, supplied it. After a half hour with them, I knew any problems I had were nothing."

Not long after, in a game in Kansas City on November 7, Red placed McDonald on a line with centre Stan Weir and winger Errol Thompson. They got scored against. "When we came back to the bench, Red growled at us, and I figured I'd be on the bench again," McDonald recalled. "But the next shift, he sent us back out and we scored the tying goal. That gave me a lift."

The next night in St. Louis, McDonald notched a pair in a 3–3 tie, got another in Vancouver and then another in California. Lanny McDonald had arrived, and it gave the Leafs a lift.

Andra was constantly excited in her role of teaching skating to the blind, as discovered by *Toronto Star* reporter Warren Gerrard, who visited her at the North York Victoria Village Arena. Skates and helmets for the skaters were provided by the Maple Leafs. Andra had 15 students ranging from 5 to 49 years of age from all parts of the Toronto region. Arranged through the North York Recreation Department, the Canadian Institute for the Blind and skating instructor Barb Russell, Andra's program was a great success. "Just because a person is blind isn't an excuse not to skate," Andra said.

A month later, the *Globe and Mail* sent reporter Nora McCabe out to witness Andra's program. "Aren't they marvellous?" Andra said as she watched her students, each helped by one of her core of volunteers. "When you think most of them are totally blind, that some are partially paralyzed . . . it takes some kind of courage to come out here and learn to skate. Boy do you know any regular athlete with courage to top this?"

An early December losing streak culminating in a 5–3 loss to the Islanders sunk the Leafs record to nine wins against 11 losses.

Ballard's rants created headlines. "Some reporters were great, like Red Burnett, George Gross or Milt Dunnell," Red recalled. "You could talk to them and trust that they wouldn't slant a quote or a story differently other than the way you meant it. But there were others that you knew were just trying to sell papers and create headlines, and you had to be careful what you said to them."

In early November, it was an on-ice incident that created headlines: Detroit's Dan Maloney attacked Brian Glennie from behind and, after Glennie went down, repeatedly picked him up by the neck and dropped his head back to the ice. Maloney was charged with assault causing bodily harm.

Leafs doctor John Evans testified in a preliminary hearing that Glennie had suffered a mild concussion and a 45-second bout of amnesia. Red told the judge that punches had indeed been thrown, but that Maloney had not been regarded as a dirty player. Maloney would be acquitted the following summer, but the attorney general of Ontario, Roy McMurtry, vowed to clean up hockey violence.

Eagleson was also trouble in that third year. "He was a disruptive force with the players and was always undermining me," said Kelly. "I knew what he thought of me, and he knew what I thought of him. We weren't best of buddies! It certainly stemmed back to my defeating him in politics. He definitely had some of my players in his corner, and was poisoning and influencing their opinion of me and the team."

One day, Johnny Bower, who still liked to don the pads at Leafs practices, came to Red after facing a couple of McDonald blasts. "That kid has one of the toughest shots I've ever faced," Bower said.

"Go and tell Lanny," Red suggested. "Also tell him the angles from which he'd be most effective. It's better that he should get the information from a goalie than from me."

Bower did, and towards the end of December, McDonald started to really hit his stride as a goal scorer, which silenced the boo-birds and his owner. The Leafs started winning, improving their record to 14 wins against 13 losses. Some of the media began calling Red "Doctor Kelly" in tribute to his patience, encouragement and handling of McDonald, and his belief that the kid from a farm in Craigmyle, Alberta, would click.

On the ice, Red put Sittler as the pivot on a line with Lanny McDonald and Errol Thompson. Ballard did not see Sittler as the "super centre" that he wanted. "We'd set off a time bomb if we had a heck of a centre in there," Ballard said.

The explosion happened on February 7 against Boston and goalie Dave Reece; Sittler rewrote the NHL record books, notching an unbelievable six goals and four assists in an 11–4 rout at the Gardens. "It was a night when every time I had the puck, something seemed to happen," Sittler said. "Undoubtedly, Mr. Ballard will think his little blast inspired me to set the record but it just isn't that way."

Red was asked if he felt at all sorry for the Bruins as the score mounted. "Hang, no," he answered. "It isn't often I get a chance to feel that comfortable. Anyway, I played for the Leafs the night the Bruins beat us 11–0 here at the Gardens."

"It was Reece's last NHL game," Red recalled. "Once Sittler's points started, I just kept throwing him out there. Things were going well for him, so I gave him the opportunity, and he scored the goals. It was unbelievable, really. Never saw anything like it."

Ballard never uttered another word about needing a "super centre." In fact, he declared the feat "was a greater thing than what Henderson did in Moscow," alluding to Paul Henderson's heroics for Team Canada at the 1972 Summit Series against the Soviet Union. The next night, in a 4–1 win against Minnesota, Sittler got one assist and didn't get a single shot on goal. "That gets you back to Earth," he said.

The Leafs finished the season with 34 wins, 31 losses and 15 ties, to finish in third place in the four-team Adams Division. Super Centre Sittler became the first Leaf to ever hit 100 points, and the winger Ballard wanted to trade, McDonald, finished second in team scoring with 93 points.

The Leafs defeated the Penguins in three games in the first playoff series to move on against the defending Stanley Cup Champions from Philadelphia — again.

When the Flyers emerged from the NHL pack with a physical and aggressive style of play in the early 1970s, they were nicknamed the "Broad Street Bullies." Their rough ways had won them two consecutive Stanley Cups. Red knew he had to have an answer to the bullying tactics that Fred Shero's boys employed, as his team had lost to them all year.

"The goon squad was in Philadelphia," recalled Red. "That was the type of hockey they played. But I made some changes and brought up Kurt Walker. He was a good, rugged, physical guy who could both play hockey and get physical as the situation warranted. And he was left-handed and he swung from the left side."

The Flyers won the first two games on home ice, 4–1 and 3–1, but Walker made his presence known in the second game, when he and Dave "the Hammer" Schultz went at each other at the very end of the third period. "Dave Schultz, of all guys, yelled to me on the bench in Philadelphia, 'Red, where did you get that goon?'" Red recalled. "It was the first time Schultz had ever spoken to me, so I knew that Kurt Walker was getting to him."

The Leafs hadn't backed down. They were ready as the series shifted back to Toronto. Red knew he needed a strategy against the Flyers, maybe even a little magic.

It came to him via Andra, in the shape of a pyramid. "Casey had bad headaches, so we tried whatever we could to get the headaches to go away," recalled Red. "Andra had read about the power of pyramids, so we tried a small one under her pillow, and her headaches disappeared. Andra suggested it for the team. I was ready to try anything."

Prior to Game 3 at the Gardens, Red placed small pyramids under the Leafs bench. Whether it was the presence of the secret pyramids or not, there was definitely some electricity in the air.

Three minutes in, Walker went after Schultz, and the two squared off in a dandy that saw Walker ejected from the game. It set the tone: 30 seconds later, the captains, Sittler and Bobby Clarke, went at it and were sent off. Ten minutes later, Sittler and Gary Dornhoefer fought. Later, Jim Watson, Pat Boutette, Orest Kindrachuk and Tiger Williams squared off and were sent off together.

The Leafs didn't back down and emerged with a 2–1 lead in the first period. The brawl-filled second was worse, but the Leafs stood their ground. At 17:29, all hell broke loose as the Flyers went after Salming and Turnbull, but the defence pair fought back, each receiving fighting penalties. It was the first fight of Salming's career. The Flyers spent most of the period short-handed, and the Leafs outshot them 27–5, but the great goaltending of Bernie Parent in the Philadelphia net kept the game close at 5–3. It was brawl after brawl as referee Dave Newell called 12 minor penalties, seven major fighting penalties and three game misconducts in that second period alone.

The game calmed down somewhat in the third, with only four minor penalties and one game misconduct issued as the Leafs outshot the Flyers by a total of 52–28 and won 5–4.

"It's been a long time since we got carried away like that," commented Schultz. "Usually we have discipline but in that game we didn't and it cost us."

"Our team has much courage," commented Shero. "Leafs are a young team that's improving and trying to develop that courage. When teams like that meet, there's certain to be hard-hitting and aggressive play and yes, even fights."

"They really attacked Borje, who was paired with Ian Turnbull," Red recalled. "They wouldn't attack Turnbull, but they really went after Borje. Turnbull was a pretty good defenceman, a typical Canadian. He could handle the rough going and didn't hesitate to get into it."

The fourth affair, two days later, was much calmer. With the pyramids still a secret under the bench, Toronto played determined hockey and evened the series with a 4–3 win. Red's strategies, one psychic and one strategic, had worked.

"Shero would have four guys in the corner, all on one side, with one defenceman back. He'd run his goons in there like that and how did we compete with that? They used to always come out with the puck, they'd get in there quick," recalled Red. "To counter that, I pulled my off-winger to the front of the net, just in front of the defenceman, and I had my centreman stay up just inside the blue line. When the defenceman got the puck, boom, he passed right to that centreman. Then the off-winger in front of the net broke out quick and the puck was to him, boom. Now we have a two-on-one. And that's how we played against them and won."

Now it was back to Philadelphia and the crazy atmosphere of the Spectrum, with its raucous fans and their secret weapon. Kate

Smith, a contralto singer who had been a radio and TV star from the 1930s through the '50s, would walk onto the ice and belt out "God Bless America." The fans and the Flyers both fed off her performance, and many attributed the back-to-back Stanley Cup wins as evidence of her power and inspiration. Used only when a win was necessary — at a price of $5,000 per appearance — her presence was like an extra player on the ice.

Fired up, Philadelphia whipped the Leafs 7–1 as the series shifted back to Toronto.

Finally, Red went public with his Pyramid Power theory. He revealed the pyramids' presence around the Gardens and under the Leafs bench during the two wins on home ice.

"I didn't have the right stuff with me in Philadelphia. I just had part of a pyramid," he commented with a sparkle in his eye. "So we lost."

He explained his theory of the pyramids to his players. "It's a plastic model of a pyramid," detailed Sittler after the game. "Red brought it into our dressing room and hung it up. This was a do-or-die game for us. I took the six sticks I was going to use and put them under the pyramid. Then I stood under the pyramid for four minutes — not any more, not any less — to get its vibration. A lot of guys saw what I was doing, and soon each guy was standing under the pyramid. I still get vibrations from this stick."

Sittler scored a playoff-record-tying five goals and added an assist to lead the Leafs past the Flyers 8–5. Defenceman Claire Alexander stood under the pyramid for an extended length, as Sittler had, and played a standout game, with a goal and an assist. The Flyers' undisciplined no-holds-barred hockey proved a tonic for Red and his team. The second and third periods were full of fights and penalties again, but the Leafs were up to the task. Tiger Williams outpunched Schultz in one fight, while Leaf Dave Dunn outboxed Bob "Hound Dog" Kelly in another.

"It's working, isn't it?" Red mused to the press afterwards when asked about the pyramid theory. "People don't know why the pyramids in Egypt were built or even how. But there always has seemed to be some strange waves given off by them. It has been proven that things shaped like pyramids can do strange and wonderful things.

"They can make plants grow, sharpen razor blades. They can make miracles happen. And that's what we need against Philadelphia. To hear people talk, we're not supposed to have a chance so we really need that extra help. I think they can influence events. They must, because without a miracle, there's no way we can beat Philadelphia. That's what I keep hearing anyway."

Shero called it "one of the worst games this club has ever played. Leafs are just too good a team to play that way against and expect to win."

The series was headed back to the Spectrum for the deciding game, where the Leafs hadn't won in five years. They certainly needed an advantage to fight off the Flyers. Perhaps it would be Pyramid Power. The players believed in it, as did many Torontonians, who sent Red a barrage of pyramids in all shapes and sizes before the game. It made headlines.

But Red Kelly also had an ulterior motive for introducing Pyramid Power.

"I was trying to do some stuff to distract things away from Harold Ballard saying things about the club," Red remembered. "I was trying to get the guys thinking hockey and positively, and never mind this other stuff and Kate Smith. Pyramid Power caught everyone's attention, especially after Sittler put his sticks under there and he got all those points. Suddenly, everyone bought into it and it grew bigger and bigger from there."

Prior to Game 7, the press had a field day with the mystic battle of "Kate versus the Pyramids."

"For Game 7, I had a twelve-foot-tall pyramid placed right in the dressing room at the Spectrum," Red recalled. "I had gotten it made, and three players at a time sat under it for four minutes. The last guy to sit under it was Tiger Williams, and when he came out he said, 'Thank God I don't play for Philadelphia! I'd hate to have to sit under Kate Smith for four minutes!'"

Though Smith was not in the house this night, her recorded version of the anthem still whipped the crowd into a frenzy, and the mystical battle was on. The Leafs entered the game with only four defencemen, with Glennie and McKenny out.

Leafs forward Jack Valiquette silenced the building by scoring the game's first goal just after the initial minute. Though the Flyers tied it, Toronto went ahead on a subsequent power play. The mystical effects of Pyramid Power imploded when Claire Alexander stepped on Ross Lonsberry's stick and crashed into the boards early in the second period. He left on a stretcher with a broken heel, and the Leafs were down another defenceman. His loss deflated the team.

"Claire Alexander was very quick, had a good shot and could respond quickly," Red recalled. "That changed the game right there. We had no replacements, I mean nobody as good as Alexander. He had been playing really well for us."

From then on it was downhill. In the next four minutes the Flyers pushed the play into the Toronto end and poured four quick goals behind Wayne Thomas to go ahead 5–2. It ended 7–3.

After the handshakes were over, the Leafs packed up their equipment — and pyramids — to head home. Even though they had won, the Flyers were uncharacteristically subdued in their dressing room, cognizant of the fact that they had just barely survived a war.

"I'm just relieved to get that series over with," said Flyers defenceman Joe Watson. "You've got to hand it to the Leafs. They gave us all we could handle. I think they're on the verge of becoming a great team. Leafs are like we were (a few years ago) — young and tough, with a super goalie. You could see we were the team of the future then. This Toronto club is exactly the same. Playing against them, you can sense it. In fact it's hard to say what would have happened right here tonight if they hadn't run into injuries. That's what finally tipped the scales our way."

Pyramids or no pyramids, Red Kelly certainly agreed. His team had pushed the Stanley Cup champions to the brink, but their injuries had disabled them and they came up just a touch short. Still, it had been a great team effort. As Red and his disappointed troops flew northward out of the City of Brotherly Love, he wondered if his restless city, its restless press and its restless owner would agree.

CHAPTER TWENTY-ONE

· · · · · ·

NEGATIVE IONS

Coach Kelly wondered about the future as he headed off for the summer of 1976. He was entering the fourth year of a four-year contract with Toronto, his 33rd year in hockey. He visited the farm near Simcoe, spending time with his parents and family, and enjoyed quiet time at his cottage.

When Red attended the Windsor Kinsmen Sports Celebrity Dinner in mid-June along with Montreal star goalie Ken Dryden, Red was asked why the Leafs seemed to always be behind the Canadiens in terms of success — the Habs had just beaten Philadelphia for the Stanley Cup.

"It's a matter of policy," Red carefully told *Windsor Star* writer Jack Dulmage, explaining that in the past the Leafs had sold farm teams based in Rochester and Vancouver, and peddled players to expansion teams, leaving themselves with an inadequate supply of farmhands. "A lot of money was made in those transactions."

By comparison, Sam Pollock, the general manager in Montreal, collected draft picks for expendable talent and money. "The only way to prevent Montreal from stockpiling draft choices is for other teams to stop trading them to Montreal," he said. "We have a young, growing team and we'll carefully guard our draft choices. This wasn't a good draft year. Not a bumper crop. That's because underage players were drafted the year before, spoiling it. But next year should be good."

Red also talked about the trial of Dan Maloney, the seeming increase in hockey violence, the Province of Ontario's attempt to curb it, and the NHL's response with new penalties for instigating and fighting. The NHL had acted quickly because there was such an outcry, Red said.

> *I agree they had to do something. The referees are in for a hard time. It's easy to see retaliation, but often they don't see what caused it. There could be injustices.*
>
> *Pat Boutette and Tiger Williams showed a little moxie this past winter. They helped us to turn it around. Our players gave all they had against the Flyers and for the first time, were able to come out of the playoffs with their heads held high. I just hope we can pick up where we left off when the next season rolls around.*

The Leafs season began with a loss in Colorado, followed by a grand home-opener on October 9, as Toronto celebrated 60 years of having a team in the NHL and 50 years as the Maple Leafs. They topped the Boston Bruins 7–5, but it would prove to be the only win in their first nine games. Then Errol Thompson broke his wrist in the second week of the schedule; he had been an integral part of the line with Sittler and McDonald.

Things got better in their next 18 games, and by December 7, Toronto was in second place in their division, only two points out of fourth place overall.

Red was trying to keep his hopes realistic. "I'd like to be first in our division, if we could," Red told the *Toronto Star*.

But our aims, right from the beginning, have been, to be sure of making the playoffs, and to go into those playoffs in the best condition possible.

This year if we can move further up, we might get home ice advantage in the second series as well. That might be the most important thing we can do. Sittler and McDonald have been coming through in a big way. I'm looking forward to what they'll do when Thompson rejoins them sometime next month. Brian Glennie is having a superb season. That's made up for a lot.

Rookie goaltender Mike Palmateer had won Toronto hearts when he backstopped the Toronto Marlies to a Memorial Cup victory two years before. Now the acrobatic left-handed goalie was gradually replacing Wayne Thomas in the number one spot. "He was a good little goalie, small, great effort every night, great reflexes, quick," recalled Red. "I was quite happy with him. He often won games for us."

A three-game home stand started off badly on February 5, when Toronto lost to the Flyers 7–5. They had tied the game after being down 5–2, but defensive giveaways by Claire Alexander and Jim McKenny directly resulted in the Flyers go-ahead goals, which had Red fuming.

"There's really no excuse for blowing the game after tying it the way we did," Red told the *Toronto Star*. "We didn't quit when we were down. It's simply a case of being short in a certain area (defence) and that is hurting us."

A major U.S. television network contacted Red to see if he would talk about his experiences with Pyramid Power. The call coincided with a visit from a group of university students from California who also wanted to discuss pyramids. "They were supposed to be making a picture," Red recalled. "They sent a crew in from San Francisco to film us, and we talked pyramids. It had turned the team around in those previous playoffs, without question — the players had bought into it."

By late February, the Leafs offence was firing on all cylinders but was in tough. In two games, a 6–6 tie with Pittsburgh and a 10–8 win over Chicago, the Leafs lost defenceman Claire Alexander to a broken leg, Kurt Walker to strained knee ligaments and Borje Salming to a bruised hip. They had already been without defenceman Brian Glennie and forward Stan Weir. The 30-goal weekend had Red shaking his head. "In my thirty years in the National Hockey League as a player and coach, I can't remember anything like these games," he told reporters. "We should rename the league the National Basketball Association," added Ballard.

Reflecting back, Red explained that hockey is an odd game. "Some days you're going to have a shutout, and some days you're going to get bombed. That's hockey. The biggest thing is to score that first goal. Once you break that shutout, then goals come more easily. You've changed the outcome of the game by getting that first goal. The longer you go in a game without scoring, the tougher it gets to score."

With a lack of defensive depth in the Toronto lineup, Red had to pull back winger Bob Neely to defence to pair with Mike Pelyk; McKenny and Turnbull made a solid pair.

As February ended and the Leafs lost three close games in a row, Ballard was at it again, stating he was not happy with the results and that Kelly's job would be on trial for the remaining 16 regular season games. To Red, it was just background noise.

"When you're after big game, you're not side-tracked by bunny tracks," Red told the *Toronto Star*. "Mr. Ballard hired me and he can fire me. If he's dissatisfied, it's his prerogative to make a decision. We've been moving up, improving each year. At the moment I'm interested only in the hockey club. When you lose five guys to injuries, it's hard to fill the gap."

On March 17, a nice little distraction occurred in Leafland when Lanny McDonald's wife, Ardell, delivered a healthy eight-pound, nine-ounce girl, whom they named Andra — Ardell and Andra

Kelly had grown very close as they continued working with blind skating students.

Red liked being home with the family, and his children certainly knew when Dad was home. "Game day meals when Dad was playing, and then when coaching, never changed," Patrick Kelly recalled. "It was always steak, baked potato, canned peas and fruit salad made from frozen strawberries, canned pineapple, canned mandarins and bananas. It's a combination I still love to this day."

In late March, an accident during practice would change the mechanics of the season for Red. "The puck came around the boards where I was standing during scrimmage, and Lanny McDonald was barrelling over to get it," recalled Red. "Lanny had a habit of keeping his head down. I thought he was going to run right smack into me if I stayed there, so I pushed myself away from the boards, about four or five feet out. Lanny had seen me along the boards and veered to go around me where I had been, and he hit me. He went down. I didn't go down, but it shook me up pretty bad. I had to go to St. Michael's Hospital. I couldn't stand up straight, it was so painful."

After a battery of tests, the diagnosis was two slipped discs and pinched nerves. The treatment lasted well past the end of the season. "They would hang me from my neck, to ease the pain," Red recalled. "Not just once but every week, and sometimes every day. I didn't blame Lanny. Accidents happen, but it was a painful year."

Despite the pain, Red carried on, though sometimes he would have to forgo lacing up the skates for practice. It wasn't easy, and his team didn't help matters. In a 7–5 loss to Boston, his power play iced the puck three times during one opposing penalty. When his power play unit came to the bench afterwards, Red asked them if they realized that they were the ones with the man advantage.

"Things like that can't be excused," Red explained after the game. "What most people don't understand though is that we have a play that exploits a long pass down the middle. We've scored some important goals on this play this season. When it goes wrong though, the puck goes the length of the ice (for an icing)."

Their play seemed inconsistent, but the Leafs could still manage great efforts, such as a 3–3 tie at the Forum against the hot Canadiens on March 30 — Montreal's 60-win season, with eight losses and 12 ties, gave them the best winning percentage (.825) ever during an NHL season, a record that still stands.

The Leafs went winless in their final seven games to finish with a 33–32–15 record, good enough for seventh place in their division. They would face Pittsburgh again, but this time the Pens had home ice advantage in the best-of-three preliminary-round series.

"Pittsburgh has an offence which can be very explosive," Red commented. "What we have to produce is a solid, two-way game with good back-checking so our defence isn't isolated against their quick guys. Last year we were bumping the Penguins off the puck and that is what we have to do again."

The Leafs summoned Pelyk and Alain "Bam-Bam" Bélanger from their Dallas farm club to sub in for the injured. The injuries and call-ups were getting to Ballard. "We're running our own private airline between here and Dallas," the grumpy Leafs boss declared. "If we play as poorly as we did in Boston (a 7–4 season ending loss), we're fortunate to have even one home (playoff) game. I've been sounding off about this team being better than last season's club. We're two points lower in the standings."

What Ballard didn't directly mention was the fact that each Leafs home playoff game meant an extra $160,000 in the owner's pockets, not counting revenues from concessions and the Hot Stove Lounge, a restaurant and bar in the Gardens.

Having had success with Pyramid Power, Red tried something new. "Kelly Sprays Leafs with 'IONS' – Eureka They Win!" was the headline in the *Toronto Star* after the Leafs emerged with an opening 4–2 triumph. "Pox on Pyramid Power. Blah to bio-rhythms. Ions are in!" the story continued.

Coach Kelly turned physicist and explained negative ions. "Upgrading the number of negative ions in our dressing room before the game helped us deliver a strong game on the ice," Red explained after the game.

> *It was an Ion victory! It's been established scientifically that the nature of the ions in the atmosphere govern people's outlook. When there are too many positive ions people are listless and not interested in what they are doing. When the ion field around them is negative, they operate at a much higher level.*
>
> *Yesterday morning I noticed that the air in our dressing room and the arena was stale and stagnant, the atmosphere where positive ions flourish. So I sprayed some negative ions in the room and we played a really strong game. I even sprayed some on Johnny Bower and he was so full of pep last night that he probably could have won the Olympic high jump.*

His players thought they contributed to the win as much as the ions. "I don't know anything about ions," observed Thompson. "Actually I thought our good checking and Wayne Thomas' goaltending had a lot to do with it."

Prior to Game 2 in Toronto, Sittler talked about what the Leafs needed to do. "It's a matter of discipline," he said. "It's a mental thing. If we put our minds to it, we could play the style that wins for us all the time."

The press were having fun with Red, calling him "The Ionic Man." He played along. "I can't tell you where I get my supply of ions," Red said. "I may reveal how I do it at a later date. It's real. It's scientific. An imbalance of positive ions could be compared to a stagnant pond, compared to fresh, running water. You notice after it rains when the air is charged with negative ions, you actually feel uplifted. I intend to spray our room again tonight."

It didn't quite work, as the Penguins upset the Leafs 6–4. The jinx of the home team continued as Toronto went into Pittsburgh and eliminated the Pens with a 5–2 win.

Now it was on to meet the Flyers again.

In the opener at the Spectrum on April 11, the Leafs jumped out to an early 3–0 lead just nine minutes into the game. "Flyers started slowly, and we were able to get on top of them, force mistakes and produce goals," Red said after the 3–2 Toronto victory. "By the middle of the second period Flyers were rolling but we were able to hold them off with a big team effort. It's an extremely big win for us."

Flyers captain Bobby Clarke agreed. "They're a smart team now with a great deal of pride. A few people figured we'd have no trouble blowing them out of the rink but we knew differently."

With confidence — and a ton of negative ions in their dressing room — Toronto beat the Flyers handily 4–1 in Game 2. Tiger Williams told gleeful Toronto fans on *Hockey Night in Canada* that he thought the Flyers were "done like dinner."

In Game 3, the Flyers started out badly, spotting the Leafs a 2–0 lead, but tied it up going into the third. Things seemed tense until Thompson scored on a backhander to put the Leafs ahead 3–2 with 4:09 left in the game.

In the final minute, the Flyers pulled goalie Wayne Stephenson for an extra attacker. Buzzing around the Toronto net, the Flyers pressed. With 38 seconds left, Rick MacLeish tied it for Philadelphia and then scored again a few minutes into overtime to steal the game for the Flyers.

The Leafs regrouped from that heartbreaking loss and played strong hockey in Game 4; with only six minutes left in the game, they had the Flyers down 5–2.

It is a loss that is still clear in Coach Kelly's mind.

"Then Philadelphia scores to make it 5–3," Red recalled. "There was a faceoff in our end. Philadelphia won the draw and got the puck to their blue line. My winger didn't go out to the blue line when we lost the draw, like he was supposed to. Their defenceman shoots and they score. Now it's 5–4. That was the first mistake.

"Then the Flyers pulled their goaltender and forced a faceoff in our end with seconds remaining. I put out my best line and we win the draw. Great! The puck goes back to my best defenceman. The Flyers had a big defenceman as their sixth attacker, and when the puck came back to my defenceman, that big guy was right on him. He lifted his stick, and the puck went to my other defenceman.

"Now there is nobody within a country mile of him. All he had to do was put the puck out over the blue line and the game is over and we'd win the game. Instead, he winds up and slaps it! Slaps it! They stopped the puck and, boom, it's in our net! The game was tied, and then they win it in the overtime. Two mistakes we made. So, what are you going to do? I can't change anything from behind the bench. I put the men out there that I thought were capable in that situation, and they made two crucial mistakes. The series is now tied, and it flipped the momentum back to them. But the Flyers never quit in both those games. They came back."

Back in the City of Brotherly Love, the Flyers and Bernie Parent shut out the Leafs 2–0 to go up three games to two.

For Red, still in constant pain from the collision with McDonald, the return home enabled him to return to hospital for treatments. "I continued to hang from my neck at the hospital," Red recalled. "To ease the pain." What didn't help his pain was that the Leafs had seven players out with injuries for Game 6.

In a penalty-laden first period, Turnbull's power play goal put Toronto in front 1–0. The Leafs were granted seven minutes of power play time when Paul Holmgren cross-checked Leafs rookie Bruce Boudreau into the boards and punched him to the ice, and then the Flyers were assessed a bench minor. It was the opportunity Toronto needed, but when they could only muster one shot on net during that entire power play stretch, the writing was on the wall. "When you kill seven straight short-handed minutes in the other guy's building, it gives the team a good feeling and a lift," Shero said.

Early in the second period, Clarke intercepted Ferguson's cross-ice pass in front of the Toronto net and beat Thomas to tie the game. McDonald put the Leafs ahead, but the Flyers tied it back up before the second period ended. In the third period, Lanny notched his 10th playoff goal to put the Buds in front again, but the Flyers fought back. With memories of past Leafs-Flyers brawls fresh in the officials' minds, the tide turned against the Leafs when a third-period minor staring match between Williams and Kelly resulted in 10-minute misconducts assessed to both men by referee Dave Newell.

"That was a bad penalty by the referee," Red would say after the game. "Bob Kelly had no points in the series and Tiger Williams had quite a few. The Flyers sent their guy off the bench to start something."

"The referee was just a gutless (so and so)," Williams said. "Neither of us was doing anything and he hands out 10-minute misconducts. For what? Standing around?"

With Williams, an effective firecracker, watching from the sidelines, MacLeish tied the score minutes later, and Philadelphia scored the go-ahead goal with two and half minutes remaining. The Flyers held on, and Toronto was out. It was heartbreaking.

"What really hurts about losing this series is just how close we came to winning it," Red said afterwards. "I'm proud of my guys because we had seven players injured and we extended a team which finished 34 points ahead of us during the season to six games, lost two in overtime and one by one goal. Take seven players away from the Flyers and see how well they do. We battled right to the end with everything we had."

The Flyers agreed.

"The Leafs are better this year than last year," said Shero. "They couldn't have won the series last year but this year they came too close even with their injuries. That shows how they've improved. They also had more experience this year and really gave it a shot."

"They sure deserved to win the first two games and were in every game," added Clarke. "We also had a little luck. We've played one hundred games this year, but right now it feels like two hundred."

Red blamed his team's loss on Bobby Clarke. The Flyers "were ready to quit, you know. He simply would not let them. One thing I recall about the Philadelphia bench is that whenever he wasn't on the ice, Clarke was standing up at the bench cheering his mates on. He must have been dead-tired but that's the kind of competitor Clarke is. There's no doubt about it — we'd have won but for Clarke."

With disappointment reigning in Leafland again, the inevitable speculation about Red's coaching future started immediately. "Red Kelly's job is as secure as mine and I'm not gonna get fired," declared Ballard that night. "There'll be some changes, you can bet on that. We never should have blown two good chances the way we did."

When asked about his status, Red wouldn't bite. "My future?" he answered. "I have a contract that runs out in September. I'm a Celt. We don't ask or give any favours. They bury us straight up so we're ready for the fight in the next world."

Nobody was more disappointed than Red as he left the Gardens that night. For the next week, the Toronto sports pundits weighed in on the Toronto coaching debate, using unnamed sources to criticize Red. He ignored it all. He had enough trouble just dealing with his neck and spine pain.

The Kellys went on a holiday south, but Red ended up spending most of it in bed; he had difficulty lifting his head. Back home, he went to hospital every day, placed in traction and hanging from his neck. He also had a hanging device on a door at home. He was unable to attend the NHL draft in early June.

"I fully intended to be there for the first couple of rounds at least, but I just didn't feel up to it," he told Jim Proudfoot from his bed.

"I don't feel a hang of a lot better but at least I'm taller. I'm hoping some good things happen in the next little while."

On June 16, Red was summoned to see Ballard in his office at the Gardens. Red knew his contract was up, and after ten years he had had enough with coaching.

Ballard "told me he had decided on a change," Red calmly told the press.

> *I said fine and congratulated him on getting into the Hall of Fame. He didn't offer me another chance at the job. My understanding was that I'm through.*
>
> *Actually I'd been considering the situation for quite a while and I'd pretty well made up my mind to get out. Because of that I wasn't too upset when I met Mr. Ballard yesterday. It didn't really fizz on me. I was in that frame of mind when I went in.*
>
> *Things have changed in hockey. The game I've known all my life has undergone a big change and not necessarily in the right direction. It might be on the way back but it's got a long way to go.*
>
> *Overall I've had a pretty good four years here. I feel we played some pretty good hockey in that time. The best part was seeing some good young players develop . . . Now with four of the first 30 junior draft choices this year, the club should be ready for big things.*

Four decades later, Red is comfortable with his coaching legacy. "Harold offered me to stay on in another capacity there, but I told him I wasn't interested. But looking back, a coach is just like a player. You make mistakes, like a rookie, but you learned and tried not to make the same mistake twice. As a player, you went out on the ice and changed the game directly. What you did on the ice changed that game. A coach can tell a player certain things to do or not to do, but when the player is out on that ice, they're on their own. If a pothole suddenly pops up in the road, the driver has to react themselves. Hockey players are like that. They themselves have to react to what's happening on that ice. They don't have time to ask the coach, 'What do I do now?'"

For the first time in his life, Red was completely out of hockey.

There was no question he would miss it.

The real question was, "Well, what do I do now?"

• • • • • •

CHAPTER TWENTY-TWO

AIRPLANES, ACCOLADES
and the ANSWER
to WHY

"Legend," according to the *Oxford Dictionary*, is a Middle English word taken from the Old French word *legende*. It can mean "A traditional story sometimes regarded as historical" or "an extremely famous or notorious (or good) person, in a particular field."

A "living legend" describes "someone who is extremely famous during the time that they are alive." The adjective of this is "legendary."

Leonard "Red" Kelly qualified on all fronts. He could not walk anywhere without being recognized, greeted and sought out.

No longer involved in hockey through the rest of 1977, Red still felt the effects of the Lanny McDonald collision, and he continued with the daily visits to St. Michael's Hospital, hanging in traction from his neck to help relieve the spinal pain. By September he was starting to feel a little better.

As the kids' school year started, Red became immersed in the daily life of Andra's world: getting the four kids to various figure skating lessons, hockey games, school sports and activities throughout the Toronto region. Patrick was now 15 and played hockey for the

St. Michael's midgets. Conn was 14 and played for the bantam Toronto Toros. Seventeen-year-old Casey and nine-year-old Kitty were both deeply involved in figure and speed skating. "I'm taking a lot of driving off Andra's shoulders now," he told the *Toronto Star*. "I realize what a tremendous job she did in the last few years. You know, we had a little rink in the backyard and the kids wanted me to play with them." He was making up for lost time.

As much as he enjoyed being home, Red was restless to find something else to do. Even though he had a strong connection to the family farm near Simcoe, it was well managed by his brother, Joe. Red's new interest would come through his in-laws, the McLaughlins.

The year before, Red had become a director on the board of McLaughlin Research Corporation, founded by Andra's late father, Charles. Based in Long Island, New York, the company was family-run, with Andra and her brothers on the board. "The company was into a lot of technical research," Red explained. "In the 1960s, my father-in-law, Charles, backed the development of a maintenance system to be installed on submarines. Then they took it a step further and developed a maintenance system to be installed on executive jets. It was called Computer Aircraft Maintenance Programs, or CAMP for short.

"CAMP Systems was a built-in maintenance schedule system. It would tell the owner what to do, when to do it, how to do it and the tools needed to do it on their aircrafts. It also informed them that while they were going into the bowels of an aircraft to change something, nearby parts or mechanisms were coming due, perhaps in another couple of flying-time hours, so it was beneficial and economical to do both at the same time and not have to go back in repeatedly. It made it easy, safer and, in the end, economical. There was nothing like this in Canada, so it was my job to try and get contracts up in Canada with Canadian companies."

His office was at Pearson International Airport, in a hangar. "I saw right out on the runway. I had a girl who worked three days a week with me," recalled Red. "The general aviation pilots would come in and have breakfast or lunch right in the hangar, so I got to know a lot of the pilots, the maintenance staff. Of course, they knew me through hockey, but they soon knew about CAMP, that I was in that business, that I wasn't a fly-by-night thing."

And his oldest daughter became a big help. "Casey later came to work for me at CAMP Systems. She was my chief cook and bottle washer there. Casey basically ran my office and everything."

They worked together for 17 years. "I saw first-hand how my father dealt with employees and customers," explained Casey. "My father always likened business to the sports world. We were always a team — his philosophy was that every employee had a different role to play on the team, equally important, always contributing towards the same goal of keeping the customer happy."

Since his branch was a subsidiary of an American company, Red had to present a Canadian business case to the government for approval. The Foreign Investment Review Agency gave him its seal of approval on December 23. "It took me a year to make the first sale," he said, adding that governments, mining and oil companies were targeted. "We installed the system on TransCanada Pipeline helicopters, on Falcons, Sabreliners, even old aircraft. Our biggest goal was to get on board the new Challenger jet that Bombardier was rolling out, and we did. CAMP Systems was up and running in Canada, and we eventually grew to an office staff of about fifteen or so."

"I thought it was a great product to bring here," Red told the *Toronto Sun*. "Apart from Toronto, we have clients in Calgary, Edmonton, Vancouver and Montreal. If you had asked me what a Westwind was a few months ago, I would have said it was a wind blowing out of the west. Anyway, I know a lot more now."

Even though he became immersed in the business world, the sports world continued to recognize and honour the redhead from Simcoe. He had been inducted into the Detroit Red Wings Hall of Fame in 1969 and the Canadian Sports Hall of Fame in 1975.

Celebrated Detroit sports writer Joe Falls listed Red as number nine in his list of greatest Detroit sports stars of all time and number five on his greatest Red Wings list of all time. In 1980, Red was the given the "Achievement in Life Award" from the *Encyclopaedia Britannica* for "Achievement in Sports."

Red was never far from the public eye, as the Toronto press often sought him out for comment about what was wrong with the Maple Leafs. It was a Toronto pastime.

In 1978, Roger Neilson coached the Leafs to the semifinals, beating the Kings and then the ascendant Islanders before losing to the eventual champion Canadiens. "I was happy they won. Why would I be disappointed?" reflected Red. "They played the Islanders, and their big centreman Trottier had the broken jaw. That's one of the reasons why they beat them. Then they lost four straight to Montreal."

In early July 1981, Pete and Frances Kelly celebrated their 60th wedding anniversary. There was a special mass at St. Cecilia's Church in Port Dover, and a gathering of 1,500 at the Port Dover Lions Community Centre. Nanticoke Mayor John Pow acted as master of ceremonies. "The faith of the Kellys was solid as the native rock," Pow told the crowd. "Their home was their castle; their children, their pride and joy; their friends were their rubies; the door of their home always open to their friends." Greetings were brought by all levels of government and members of the family. Guests danced to the sounds of the Swaying Brass Orchestra. Both Pete and Frances would live into their 90s and were extremely proud of their community roots and their family.

In the late 1980s, Red and many former players got together occasionally to socialize and reminisce. Often, discussion came around to the fact that some players' monthly pension benefits weren't nearly adequate, especially compared to other sports. Many older players had minuscule monthly payments despite their long years of NHL service. When former Leaf Carl Brewer, Susan Foster and others got serious and started looking into the NHL pension funds, they were shocked to find them completely mismanaged. They knew that Ted Lindsay and Doug Harvey had tried without success to form a players' union so many years before and had wanted to investigate the pension funds. The new group felt it was time to revisit the situation.

"There were meetings that we started attending up at Eddie and Norma Shack's house," Red recalled. "Keith McCreary was in on that. A lot of people were there. I recommended to Keith that they get Leo Reise involved on the committee because he had been there from day one and he was good with numbers, so they did get him. Then we got onto Eagleson and his slippery trail. That was another kettle of fish."

The NHL claimed it had $31.9 million dollars in total in the pension plan for old and new players. Contrast that with the baseball pension plan that was also started in 1947, the same year as the NHL: it had well over $500 million in pension fund assets built up. Though there were obviously fewer hockey players involved than baseball players, something was clearly wrong. "We were very upset," said Red. "There was a lot of money involved that we felt belonged to us. Some older guys were having trouble making ends meet. We had trouble getting to the bottom of things, so we had to go to court."

In 1991, 1,300 former players filed a joint lawsuit against the NHL in a Toronto court. Justice George Adams spent the next 18 months talking to both sides and reviewing hundreds of NHL and pension society documents dating back to 1947. In October 1992, Justice Adams ruled in favour of the former NHL players and awarded them $43 million in accumulated funds and interest. The NHL appealed, to no avail, and the award stood. Red himself had a steady income, but he had given his dues like the others, and he was especially happy for his colleagues. "It was money owed to us, and it sure helped some other guys out."

Brewer was one of the keys behind the lawsuit. Red will admit that during their playing days, he and Carl did not exactly know what to make of each other. "I sometimes wondered if he liked me or not, and he wondered, too, and he said so when he saw me in the hospital one time," chuckled Red. When Brewer died in August 2001, Andra and Red arranged for his funeral at their church.

In April 1989, St. Michael's held its second annual Celebrity Dinner, and Red was the guest of honour. Funds from the dinner were used to establish a scholarship at the school in Red's name. St. Michael's alumni Frank Mahovlich, Ted Lindsay and Dick Duff were on hand. A few months later, Red was the recipient of the Hockey Achievement Award given at a gala dinner at New York's Waldorf Astoria Hotel, organized by the Canadian Society of New York and particularly its ardent president, Paul Levesque. Guests were welcomed by former Canadian ambassador to Iran Ken Taylor.

When Harold Ballard passed away at the age of 86 in April 1990, Red commented to the press that, "Harold was Harold. There weren't many like him. He said what he wanted to say. Nothing he did surprised me."

Despite Ballard's legendary crustiness, Andra Kelly had a different take on the grumpy curmudgeon of Maple Leaf Gardens. "We used to have an annual carnival for and with the blind skaters, and 1981 was the Year of the Disabled Child," she recalled. "I had gone to see Harold Ballard, and I took a couple of the blind children with me, and Harold had the blind children sitting on his knees. I asked him about donating the Gardens so we could put on this show. He readily agreed. In April of 1981, we put on The VICKIE show. It stood for 'Visually Impaired Children's Ice Extravaganza.' We had 14,000 people there!

"The California Drill Precision team from Los Angeles came, as did Stash Serafin, a blind skater from Philadelphia, arranged by Toller Cranston. And Toller, Brian Orser, Tracey Wainman — all the top skaters in Canada donated their time. They were terrific. It was very successful, and Mr. Ballard donating the Gardens enabled us to accommodate the larger crowd, and it helped us to raise a lot of money for the visually impaired."

In the late 1990s, Red headed to Colorado Springs to participate in an annual old-timers game. Then he got an invitation to attend the 1991 All-Star Game in Chicago and laced up the skates in a "Heroes of Hockey" match. A few months later, Red agreed to don the skates again in a charity event to help establish a Toronto Maple Leafs Alumni Association. With the Leafs struggling during those years, the alumni thought it would be a way to raise money for a good cause while helping to improve the image of a tarnished organization. New Leafs president Donald Giffin said it was a priority to reconcile with former Leafs greats. "We're not here to tell today's players what to do," Red said at the promotional press conference. "But I think there'll just be a better feeling around the place."

Before a packed house, the old Leafs defeated the old Habs 5–1, and Red got the bug to play. He participated in a few more old-timers games — and at one of them, his competitiveness got the better of him. "This one tournament in Lake Placid, Gordie Howe was playing on one of the other teams," recalled Red. "At this stage,

I hadn't played much hockey and was in terrible shape. The game was tied and Howe's right behind me and I've got the puck. I said to myself, 'There's no dang way he's going to catch me,' so I turn it on. Of course, he can't catch me, but he reaches in between my legs with his stick and says, 'Guess who, Red?' I said, 'I don't need to guess, I know who.' We beat them and later won the whole thing.

"After that old-timers tournament, I drove back across the border, and I pulled in to this restaurant. I turned the motor off, opened the door to get out, but my legs wouldn't move! I thought, *Holy mackerel, what's this?* That showed how much I had used those legs all of a sudden without being in shape. I eventually moved my legs with my hands and got one leg out and then the other one and eventually got them going again, but that was quite a scare. An old lesson learned."

Then, in 1998, Red was named number 22 on the *Hockey News* list of the top 50 players of all time. "Just another list," Red told the *Times-Reformer.*

> *I don't think you can compare unless you put them on the ice together. It is publicity. It is great for* The Hockey News *and great hype for the game. How are you going to make a list? Who has seen all the players? When you double the number of players, you have to say the league is not as strong. Then another six (teams) come in. I don't think the players from the '50s got enough credit.*
>
> *When I broke in I played against some really tough guys. When I retired (1967) and went to L.A. and coached I used to practice with the guys all the time. I would have had no problem playing with them. Don't take anything away from Gretzky (No. 1). He has been at the top of the game for a long time. He plays away at the periphery but he always did shy away from the hitting. It doesn't mean he wouldn't have played well back then but . . . he would have been tested.*

In 1997, after 20 years in the aircraft CAMP Systems business, Red sold his Canadian company to the Blackstone Group of New York; McLaughlin sold the American version as well. For the first time in his life, Red was totally free to do as he pleased.

Red was acknowledged back home when he was elected to the Norfolk County Sports Hall of Recognition. On May 20, 1998, he was inducted into the Michigan Sports Hall of Fame; three years later, he was inducted into the Ontario Sport Legends Hall of Fame.

In 2001, No. 4 was the honorary chairman of an event called "An Evening of Leaf Legends," a fundraiser for Campbell House. The recent deaths of Brewer and Billy Harris were on the attendees' minds, said Ron Ellis, but so was Red. "Number one, we're getting together because we're happy to support a good cause in the city," said Ellis. "And number two, we're happy to support Red Kelly, that's the kind of respect we have for him."

"The deaths of old teammates can really hit you," said Red. "Because you were so close and together day in and day out, and you go through the tough times and you go through the good times, you know things about each other that really, nobody else knows. That makes you bond as a group."

After eight Stanley Cups, Red got another chance to hang out with the storied trophy in August 2001. Rob Blake of the champion Colorado Avalanche brought the Cup to Port Dover, and his former neighbour and distant relative (third cousin once removed) Red Kelly was with him on the float that wheeled through an excited town. A year later, on June 30, Port Dover held a day in his honour, and the road in front of the old homestead was renamed "Red Kelly Line."

In January 2002, Red was named a member of the Order of Canada. As his children wanted to be present when he received the medal, governor general Adrienne Clarkson presented it to him in Vancouver later that year. Also in January, Canada Post issued a set of six stamps commemorating NHL stars; Red was chosen along with Glenn Hall, Tim Horton, Howie Morenz, Guy Lafleur and Phil Esposito.

There is still one honour that has eluded Red, decidedly out of his control. Jerry Green of the *Detroit News* campaigned for years to have Red's No. 4 sweater retired by the Red Wings at the Joe Louis Arena. Green surmised that the reason it hadn't happened was Red's having balked at his trade to New York in 1960.

When Green spoke about the subject to Jimmy Devellano, senior vice-president of the Red Wings, Devellano shrugged him off saying: "There's no way we want twenty sweaters retired and have them get lost. This is for very, very elite players. Those who have played twenty years for us or won some Stanley Cups for us." Green was flabbergasted by the response and pointed out Kelly's 13 seasons with the Red Wings, four Detroit Stanley Cups, three Lady Byngs, a Norris, six First Team All-Star selections and two Second Team All-Star selections.

Gordie Howe agreed with Green, saying that Red's number "should have been there before the others. We never won a thing after he left us!"

So did Ted Lindsay when Green campaigned again a couple of years later. "It's like politics," Lindsay said. "I think he belongs there for what he did for the Red Wings. It was not his fault that he won four Stanley Cups in Toronto. That was Adams's stupidity. He could play hockey with his feet better than most could play it with sticks."

In their 2014 hockey book, *100 Things Red Wing Fans Should Know & Do Before They Die*, writers Bob Duff and Kevin Allen listed the oversight, appropriately, at number four. "There's a sense of foreboding when some look up at the retired numbers hung at the Joe Louis Arena rafters. Or should that be four-boding?" wrote the duo. "Many veteran watchers of the team are convinced that there's been a huge oversight in terms of which sweaters have earned a place of honor in the Wings franchise. They are convinced that

Red Kelly's No. 4 should also be up top, and they have a valid point ... Hockey people viewed Kelly as Detroit's true catalyst, the one player they couldn't do without, even more so than Gordie Howe ... Isn't it time that the Wings embraced all that Kelly brought to the team and gave his number the recognition it deserves?"

No. 4 is not sure what's up. "I don't know why. It's their opinion, their decision, not mine. I have no say in it," said Red diplomatically. "Maybe because old No. 4 came back to haunt them a little bit. I played extra hard against them, you bet your boots. I don't think it's the present owners. Mrs. Ilitch [wife of Wings owner Mike] has come up and kissed me on the cheek, and that wouldn't have happened if I had still been in the doghouse. She used to watch us play as a fan. Devellano is dead set against me, I can tell you that. When we met at the Hockey Hall of Fame, we had a little talk there. I was nice, but he gave me the double talk, I guess he didn't care for my play or something. The whole number retiring thing is in their hands. Two or three writers have tried to promote it but have been shut out."

In 2003, Red, who had already overcome two heart attacks and heart surgery, had an 18-month battle with colon cancer and won after a long struggle, but it wasn't easy. In a touching and well-written story about Red's struggles — and his faith in God, the doctors, Andra and his family and friends — Red relayed to the *Toronto Star*'s Paul Hunter that "I was that close to being gone. It was touch and go for a while there. I wouldn't recommend it to anyone."

"While the priests at his church, Holy Rosary, provided support," wrote Hunter, "Kelly's hockey mentality, a stoic resilience built up through 1,480 regular season and playoff games, also helped him cope with his illness and obscured his uncertainty."

"You're hurt. You get hurt in hockey and you take care of it and you get better," Red told Hunter. "I'm hurt. There's no use fighting it. Accept it. Get better and get back. That was my attitude."

"We did a lot of rosaries. Lots," added Andra.

Best wishes came to Red from a who's who of the hockey world, and from strangers who showed up at the house with holy water from Lourdes, France. He was home recuperating, but not able to have visitors yet, when Eddie Shack showed up at the house. Andra told him about the doctor's order. So Shack backed up a few steps on the front lawn, cupped his hands to his mouth and yelled up to the second-floor window in a voice the whole neighbourhood must have heard: "Hey, Leonard! I hope you're feeling better!"

By October, Red had recovered well enough to attend his induction into the Etobicoke Sports Hall of Fame. The next month, he and Andra drove to Newport, Rhode Island, to attend Conn's wedding. At one point during the reception, which was held in an old mansion, Andra noticed the orchestra setting up in an adjoining room. She whispered to Red, "Let's just sneak in there and have a little dance." The orchestra played them a waltz. As they slowly glided about, guests drifted in to watch, including Red's sister Laureen. "That was the most wonderful thing," Laureen said through tears. "To see Leonard dancing again,"

It was a busy time. Upon his return to Ontario, Red was inducted into St. Michael's College's Order of St. Michael in a ceremony near and dear to his heart. It's the highest honour the school can bestow, recognizing a member of the college's community "whose life is exemplary and a model for students; who has made a significant contribution to the spiritual, academic or material welfare of the school."

When the NHL strike ensured that there would be no Stanley Cup winners to parade the coveted trophy around their communities in the summer of 2005, the league generated some much-needed positive publicity by choosing 25 past Cup winners to be given the trophy for a day. It was called the "Silver and Grey Tour." Red was the first to have it. He and Dick Duff brought the Cup back to their shared alma mater, St. Michael's.

On October 4, 2006, the Toronto Maple Leafs beat the Detroit Red Wings after raising a banner marked "No. 4 Kelly" to the rafters of the Air Canada Centre, where a No. 4 for Hap Day also hangs. The

Leafs, however, only have two numbers officially retired: Bill Barilko's No. 5 and Ace Bailey's No. 6. The rest are "honoured numbers."

"I'm proud to have won four Stanley Cups with the Leafs," Red told the crowd. "I was fortunate to have those things happen. But I never, ever dreamed that I'd be hung from the top of the building."

In March 2007, the surviving members of the 1967 Cup–winning Leafs were feted with a 40th Anniversary Dinner at the Metro Toronto Convention Centre, where they autographed a sweater for Canadian prime minister Stephen Harper. Harper wrote to Red after the event, thanking him and the others for the sweater: "Your team's legendary performance continues to inspire Toronto Maple Leaf hockey fans to this day."

In 2009, a new Port Dover billboard stating "Home of Champions" was unveiled, with Red's picture alongside those of goalie Rick Wamsley and defenceman Jassen Cullimore.

In February 2013, Red and Laureen returned to help brother Joe celebrate his 90th birthday at the Port Dover Legion. The *Simcoe Reformer* covered the event. "Joe Kelly was the man of the hour at the celebration," wrote Monte Sonnenberg. "A fitter senior would be hard to imagine. He looked natty in a black suit and red tie and spent much of the party on his feet visiting with his many well-wishers. He walks and talks like a man closer to 60 than 100."

In the fall of 2014, Canada Post issued a new set of stamps depicting the NHL's greatest Original Six defencemen. Red Kelly was present at the Hockey Hall of Fame to represent the Red Wings, along with fellow honourees Pierre Pilote of Chicago, Harry Howell of New York and Bobby Orr of Boston. Toronto's Tim Horton and Montreal's Doug Harvey were represented by their families.

NHL coach Mike Babcock is a great believer in hockey history, tradition and heroes. In Detroit, to act as an inspiration to his Red Wings, he set aside three empty dressing room lockers, inscribed and dedicated to three greats of Detroit's past: Gordie Howe, Alex Delvecchio and Ted Lindsay. Hired in the summer of 2015 to kickstart a lost franchise, Babcock brought his locker room tradition to the Toronto Maple Leafs, setting aside lockers for Leafs greats George Armstrong, Johnny Bower and Red Kelly.

• • • • • •

In his 90th year, Red doesn't get back home to Simcoe–Port Dover as much as he'd like to, but he often talks of life on the farm. He and Andra still live in the same Forest Hill home they've shared for the past 40 years. He continues to get requests for card signings and memorabilia shows. He attends when he can, and he is always very popular. He still gets an amazing amount of fan mail just about every day, and there's not a week that goes by that he doesn't take the time to answer every request personally. Hockey is all about the fans, he says, and anybody associated with the game should never forget that.

Yet, despite all of the awards and all the accolades he's received over the years, there is no question that Red regards his marriage to Andra and the births of their children and grandchildren to be the greatest accomplishments of all. When he speaks about any of them, his proud Irish eyes light up. "I am proud of my faith and I am so proud of my family; Andra too," he said. "Sports have always been a big part of our lives and their lives; it's in their blood, our children and grandchildren."

Casey, their eldest, was a figure skater and international skating judge, as well as a champion speed skater in her division. Like her mother, Casey taught figure skating on a volunteer basis for many years. There are not many in the Canadian figure skating circles that don't know Casey, from the late, legendary coach Sheldon Galbraith to champion Toller Cranston to present-day champions. "I was seven when my father stopped playing hockey, so I remember the coaching years more than the playing years," Casey recalled. "My dad gave my children their first skates when they were two years old. Surprisingly to some, these were figure skates, not hockey skates. He said they should learn to skate the right way first, before they could try hockey.

"My father always encouraged us with our various lessons: piano, singing, bagpipes, drums, drama, skating and hockey. For a big anniversary about ten years ago or so, my parents gave each other a grand piano — my dad still likes to sit and play and sing. He has a lovely voice and sounds a lot like Bing Crosby.

"My mother and father go to church every Sunday, unless they are very ill. We often attend with them. They always go together, and even if they are travelling, they look for the local Catholic church. I look at my dad as a spiritual, religious, loyal, devoted, family-oriented, respectful, honest man. He has constantly fought against the odds all his life, and has overcome many obstacles and physical ailments because of his strong determination. He and my mother are so devoted to each other and their family."

Casey is married to James Waddell. Their children, George, Charles and Bruce, play minor hockey, figure skate, play musical instruments and sing — a definite Kelly trait. Casey lives nearby in Toronto and is always checking in on her parents.

Like his father, grandfather and great-grandfather before him, first-born son, Patrick, attended, played hockey at and graduated from St. Michael's College in 1981. Tough and determined, he took up speed skating at the advanced age of 22 while working as a draftsman in California. One day, during a practice at the Paramount rink, his foot hit the ice at the wrong angle and he flew into the boards and shattered his leg in seven places. "They took me to the hospital and operated on me," he told the *Toronto Sun*'s George Gross. "They told me that I would probably not be able to walk with the same gait, let alone skate."

Using that Kelly self-drive and stubbornness, Patrick worked at his rehabilitation, determined to participate in the Olympic Games. Eighteen months after his horrific accident, Patrick became a two-time Canadian speed skating champion. With Red, Andra and the family cheering him on, he participated in the 1992 Albertville Olympics, where he fell twice. He regrouped and was on the Canadian team at the 1994 Lillehammer Olympics. It was there he met his future wife, Karen Courtland, a pairs skater on the U.S. Olympic figure skating team.

Patrick earned an MBA from the University of Calgary and graduated with an engineering degree from McGill University, where he played on the varsity hockey team along with Mike Babcock. Patrick and Karen married in 2004.

"We run two skating related companies, Peak Edge Performance and IRUM Ice," Patrick added. "We work with both professional and developing athletes, from beginner through to the NHL or Disney On Ice and consult in design, engineering and building of ice rinks."

He can quickly list off many memories: "at every school we attended, we were redheads, the carrot-tops; summers at Cedar Island, and me and Conn performing 'We are Working on the Railroad' in concert; working on the farm with Grampa; hot chocolate after Dad's games, at the kitchen table, discussing hockey situations; playing ball hockey and catch with Dad; making 'dang sure' that we didn't slow anyone down when golfing — even if we rushed our shots tremendously; at the kitchen table, enduring hours of figure skating politics, especially after Dad started working in the non-NHL world. But most of all, I can remember not wanting to ever disappoint Dad."

Like his father and brother, Conn played hockey. "I didn't have a chance to really see Conn play much hockey or to help him, so this one time I rented an hour of ice time," recalled Red. "I went out with him to show him a few things. He was getting older, and it's sometimes harder to teach an older player than a young one. Conn was a true Irishman too — we can be stubborn, and like to argue. That's sometimes a good thing.

"So I said to him, 'Now, Conn, I only have one hour of ice time, one hour to give you a few pointers, so I don't want you to argue with me, just listen and do what I say.' I showed him a few things, and we started to argue a little bit, and I stopped him and said, 'Stop, don't argue, just do what I say.' And so he did, and I was able to show him how to shoot, to use the stick, how to turn, to check, a bunch of little things that I thought would help him. He listened, and he used those tips later, and I thought afterwards, *If only I had been able to show him when he was younger.*"

Conn played at St. Michael's and then with the Henry Carr Crusaders, who won the Junior B championship. He went out to the Maritimes for a year but had to come home when he developed mononucleosis. Conn attended and graduated from University of Western Michigan. "My father used to put in his own foursome every year in the Pro-Am Golf Tournament at the Canadian Open," Conn recalled. "In 1991, our team won the lottery and honour of playing with Jack Nicklaus. I was twenty-seven at the time, and it was a lot of fun. The foursome was myself, Dad, Frank Mahovlich and my uncle Douglas McLaughlin. We showed up in the morning at the first tee, and, because of Jack, there was a great crowd of people to watch him play. But just as Jack and his caddie (his son) got ready to start, they noticed that Frank and Dad had a huge crowd around them and were busy signing autographs. I was standing by Jack, and he asked me, 'Who are those guys?' No one had mentioned who he was playing with. I said they were former NHL stars and they had 14 Stanley Cups between them. Jack got all excited and said he wanted their autographs as well."

Conn launched into another story of celebrity from Christmas 2006. The phone rang and Conn answered. "The gentleman asked if my father was home, but I said he wasn't. The man said he was Evel Knievel. I was thinking the guy was crazy, but he went on to tell me how my father had been a big influence on him when he was a young man. Evel had been a pretty good hockey player and was at a hockey school out in Grand Forks, North Dakota, where Dad had instructed him. I didn't know at the time that Evel was dying, but he didn't sound very good. He said he wanted to talk with my dad.

When Dad got home, I asked him if it was true, and he said it was, that he had been talking with Evel for several weeks now."

Their children are in awe of the dance skills of Red and Andra. "My parents were good dancers," Conn said. "It was their partnership on the floor that had all who watched them impressed. My mother could go with whatever Dad could throw at her. She was an amazing dancer, and my father likened his dancing to skating at the rink, smoothly weaving in and out of the corners. Right when you thought they would knock into someone else on the crowded floor, they would swiftly and with elegance dart away and around. You could really see his skating in his dance movements. But, like their marriage, it was the team effort. It wasn't so much that my father led but that my mother trusted him, that he would never put her in harm's way. Their marriage seemed to me to be like that."

His sister, Kitty, concurred. "My favourite times with my father are when we dance together or when I see him dancing with Mom. He and Mom are like Fred Astaire and Ginger Rogers. They could dance any dance. And when I dance with my father, he can lead me in any form of dance."

Conn lives in Rhode Island and is married to Molly Ann McShane. They have one daughter, Maeve, who loves Irish dancing and plays ice hockey with her grandfather's gusto.

In late 2014, Conn and Patrick got a surprise from their father. The Toronto Maple Leafs had presented former Leafs who had won Stanley Cups in the 1960s with Stanley Cup rings. Red suddenly had four new rings. "I wanted to surprise Conn and Patrick with the Stanley Cup rings from the year they were born, so they got them as Christmas presents," Red said. "Patrick got the 1962 Stanley Cup ring, and Conn the '64 ring. Conn was unusually speechless and put it on right away. Patrick was equally touched."

"When Dad gave me that ring . . . wow; 1964 was the year I was born and the one in which I'm pictured sitting in the Cup doing a load," Conn recalled. "It's pretty special. I love wearing it, especially at

Boston Bruins games, and I love to show it to the visiting Leafs fans when they're playing in Boston. Leafs fans love to see it. I think it kind of gives them hope that great things may be just around the corner."

The résumé for one Kitty Kelly, Red and Andra's youngest, clearly demonstrates that she inherited her mother's figure skating and artistic flair, while from her father she received introspection and athleticism. Determination she got from both in spades. It's a Kelly-McLaughlin trait.

As an amateur, Kitty competed nationally and internationally for Canada. She was a double gold medallist in figures and freestyle in both Canada and the United States. Turning pro, she performed as a principal in Ice Capades for seven years, appeared in two TV specials and skated with Ice Theatre of New York and Ice-Semblé in Chicago. While in Chicago, she got her theatre degree at Northwestern University, and she also studied drama at Yale.

For over 15 years now, she has coached skaters who have competed at every level. She founded the Redwood City Ice Theatre as director and choreographer. In 2014, she founded Ashburn Theatre On Ice, whose junior team was ranked 11th in the U.S. Happily married to Kevin McGorry, with four red-headed children, Shawn, Andra, Molly and Katey, Kitty lives in Ashburn, Virginia.

As the youngest, Kitty has a unique and eloquent perspective on a life lived. "I never played hockey, I couldn't stand hockey," she admitted. "When I went to the Leafs games I would always fall asleep, and then later when I had to attend my brothers' games, I couldn't wait to get home. It wasn't until I was married and teaching in Redwood City that I finally put on a pair of hockey skates and found out what I had been missing. I didn't know my father as a great hockey player. I was born after he had finished playing. I only knew him as a great dad, soft and reflective. He taught me to be quiet and faithful. We went to church every Sunday, either to eleven o'clock or twelve thirty mass. There was never a time when we did not attend. It was here that I really felt I knew my dad best. Just sitting in mass, listening and praying, and what I observed within him. My dad is simple in that way. He likes the quiet moments. He taught me to listen and trust in God, to have faith."

Andra would often rent the ice at the local Forest Hill arena for her daughter to practise. "On several occasions, Dad, with his old skates and old blue hockey bag, would come out and skate with me," recalled Kitty. "He would bring a stick and hockey puck and shoot while I was skating. There was never a moment that I was afraid while he was out there. He was so adept at what he was doing. There was fluidity with his stick handling and precision with his slapshots. When he skated, I saw the rhythm to his movement. It was like he was skating to the music I was playing. This was the first time I saw the great hockey player in my father."

Music is another key to the family. "If you step into the house on Dunvegan, there are days when all you hear is music," said Kitty. "We all had to learn to play the piano. Even now you may chance to hear my dad playing the piano and singing along. He has a great voice. When I was singing in a play at Northwestern University, Dad told me that he once wanted to be a singer and dancer, and I believe he could have done both. His lullabies put my kids to sleep, and to this day, my girls love to hear their grandfather sing."

At one point, Kitty was helping hockey players with conditioning in Los Angeles. "I thought I'd better be wearing hockey skates if I was going to attempt such a feat, so I got some," recalled Kitty. "My husband, Kevin, wanted to join, and the next thing I knew we were playing in a beginner's hockey league. I loved it. Not long after, Dad had been asked to attend the All-Star Game in Los Angeles, so he and Mom flew to see us in San Francisco afterwards.

"Now, Dad had seen me skate in the Ice Capades, and I'd performed at Madison Square Garden, Joe Louis Arena, Maple Leaf Gardens, Ice Theatre of New York, but when Dad saw me playing hockey, well, his eyes just glowed with excitement. I'd never seen him happier about anything I had done before. Next, he started giving Kevin and me pointers on plays, stickhandling, and body cues from other players."

There were many lessons through the years. "What I've learned from [Red and Andra] is that not everything comes easy. You have to be patient and persistent, work for it, and somewhere along the way you'll find joy and passion in what you are meant to do," said Kitty. "Things may not always go your way, but if you respect what you do with the right intentions, then the rest doesn't really matter. The prize isn't always the Stanley Cup at the end of a game, a medal after a performance or an award you get; it's the route you take to get there and the lessons learned along the way. That's what my parents taught me."

Patrick sees his parents as role models. "My mother and father, through their love for each other and us, not only have been an inspiration for me and the rest of my family, they are the pinnacle for which I believe all parents should strive," concluded Patrick.

· · · · · ·

Red Kelly, the "Lady Bynger," has led quite a life: a life of faith, inspiration, hope; working for God, his family, his team, his country, his sport; leading, teaching and inspiring by a quiet, determined example.

Yet Red cannot help but harken back to the day so long ago when he was four years old, saved from drowning in the Lynn River by Stanton Berton, who himself would lose his life just a few short months later.

Why him and not me? Red always wondered.

The answer today is simple . . .

So he could grow to become Red Kelly.

SELECTED BIBLIOGRAPHY

Of course, research is paramount to the accuracy and completion of any biography. With a hockey career spanning over 30 years, and a life approaching 90 years, Red Kelly's amazing story had more written and video material than you could shake a hockey stick at. Priceless periodicals such as the *Thurible* (the St. Michael's yearbook), *Star Weekly* and *Canadian Weekly Magazine*, *Weekend Magazine*, *Hockey Pictorial*, *Hockey Illustrated*, *Liberty Magazine*, *Sports Illustrated* and the *Hockey News* proved timeless and instrumental.

The following books were invaluable references in telling *The Red Kelly Story*.

Batten, Jack. *Hockey Dynasty*. Pagurian Press. 1969.
Batten, Jack. *The Leafs*. Key Porter. 1994.
Baun, Bob, and Anne Logan. *Lowering The Boom*. Stoddart. 2000.
Beddoes, Dick. *Pal Hal*. Macmillan. 1989.
Brewitt, Ross. *Clear The Track*. Stoddart. 1997.

Cole, Stephen. *The Last Hurrah*. Viking. 1996.

Coleman, Charles. *Trail of the Stanley Cup – Vol. 3*. NHL. 1976.

Cox, Damien, and Gord Stellick. *'67*. Wiley. 2004.

Cruise, David, and Alison Griffiths. *Net Worth*. Viking. 1991.

Duff, Bob. *The China Wall*. Immortal Investments. 2006.

Duff, Bob. *Detroit Red Wings*. Biblioasis. 2013

Duff, Bob. *Marcel Pronovost*. Biblioasis. 2012.

Dupuis, David M. *Sawchuk*. Stoddart. 1998.

Dupuis, David M., L. Waxy Gregoire and Pierre Pilote. *Heart of the Blackhawks*. ECW. 2013.

Ellis, Ron, with Kevin Shea. *Over the Boards*. FENN. 2002.

Foster, Susan. *The Power of Two*. Fenn. 2006.

Harris, Billy. *The Glory Years*. Prentice Hall. 1989.

Howe, Gordie. *Mr. Hockey*. Viking. 2014.

Hunter, Douglas. *Open Ice*. Viking. 1994.

Imlach, Punch, and Scott Young. *Heaven and Hell in the NHL*. McClelland & Stewart. 1982.

Imlach, Punch, and Scott Young. *Hockey Is A Battle*. Macmillan. 1969.

Jenish, D'Arcy. *The Stanley Cup*. McClelland & Stewart. 1992.

Kincaide, Richard. *Legends of the Detroit Red Wings*. Sports Publishing. 2013.

Lawton, James. *Tiger*. Douglas & McIntyre. 1984.

MacSkimming, Roy. *Gordie*. Greystone. 1994.

Mahovlich, Ted. *The Big M*. Sports Masters. 1999.

McDonald, Lanny, and Steve Simmons. *Lanny*. McGraw-Hill. 1987.

McDougall, Bruce. *The Last Hockey Game*. Goose Lane. 2014.

McFarlane, Brian. *Legendary Stanley Cup Stories*. Key Porter. 2008.

McFarlane, Brian. *One Hundred Years of Hockey*. Deneau. 1989.

Miller, Bob. *Tales from the Los Angeles Kings Locker Room*. Sports Publishing. 2013.

Obodiac, Stan. *Red Kelly*. Clarke, Irwin. 1971.

Podnieks, Andrew, Pavel Barta, Dmitri Ryzkov and others. *Kings of the Ice*. NDE Publishing. 2002.

Shea, Kevin, with Larry Colle and Paul Patskou. *St. Michael's College*. FENN. 2008.

Shea, Kevin, with Paul Patskou, Roly Harris and Paul Bruno. *Toronto Maple Leafs*. Firefly. 2010.

Sittler, Darryl, with Allan Turowetz and Chrys Goyens. *Sittler*. Macmillan. 1991.

Thurible, The. St. Michael's College. 1944–47.

ACKNOWLEDGEMENTS

It is amazing to think that Red Kelly had never had a true biography or autobiography written about him until now. True, Stan Obodiac did publish a short young-adult book in the 1970s that touched on Red's amazing story, but it really just skimmed the surface. Yet, knowing Red's sincere humility and modesty, it is not surprising. Despite his "Okay, let's do it," it took more than the three of us to tell his story.

We would like to thank Jack David, Michael Holmes and David Caron from ECW Press for believing in this legend's story. Thanks as well to the team: Crissy Calhoun, Erin Creasey, Rachel Ironstone, editors Greg Oliver, Peter Norman and Richard Kamchen for their contributions. Thanks as well to Craig Campbell at the Hockey Hall of Fame and Bob Duff of the *Windsor Star* for helping tie up loose ends. Thanks to former MPP Garfield Dunlop for his continued support.

Thanks as well to former teammates, players and staff whose observations and comments from past projects were useful in the telling of this story: Marcel Pronovost, Ted Lindsay, Alex Delvecchio, Glenn Hall, Johnny Wilson, Leo Reise, Budd Lynch, Jiggs McDonald, Pierre Pilote, Wayne Rutledge, Ron Ellis, Jimmy Peters, Jimmy Skinner, Lefty Wilson and Danny Wood.

We thank the men and women who covered, reported and wrote about the game during Red's career and life. Their observations, reports, stories, columns and pieces make every biographer's work so much easier and more complete. These great journalists of Red's time set the writing bar high, and we owe the following a great debt for their amazing work and contributions: Paul Chandler, Bill Brennan, Lewis H. Walter, John Walter, Marshall Dann, Pete Waldmeir, J.E. O'Brien, M.F Drunkenbrod, *Detroit News;* Dana Mozley, John Gillooly, Jack Parr, Harry Stapler, *Detroit Free Press;* Frank Orr, George Gross, Jim Proudfoot, Milt Dunnell, Red Burnett, Joe Perlove, Fred Cederberg, Neil MacCarl, Jim Kernaghan, Gordon Campbell, Paul Rimstead, W.R. Wheatley, Jim Hunt, Ken McKee, Joe Taylor, *Toronto Star;* Louis Cauz, Scott Young, Jim Vipond, Rex MacLeod, Neil Davidson, *Globe and Mail;* Hal Walker, Bob Hesketh, *Toronto Telegram;* Jack Dulmage, *Windsor Star;* Trent Frayne, *Toronto Star Weekly* magazine; Jack Parks, *London Free Press;* Jean Sonmor, *Toronto Sun;* Red Fisher, *Montreal Star;* Ken Kal, *Inside Hockeytown;* Dave Warner, *Canadian Register;* Herb Ralby, *Boston Globe;* Baz O'Meara, *Winnipeg Herald;* Dink Carroll, *Montreal Gazette;* Vince Lunny, *Montreal Herald;* Pete Kehoe, *Simcoe Reformer;* Jack Wells, *Winnipeg Tribune;* Sterling Taylor, *Ottawa Journal.*

Other writers whose work helped our research immeasurably included: Joe Perlove, Jack Laing, Zena Cherry, Margaret Scott, Andy O'Brien, Bill Furlong, Allan Wegemer, Ken McKenzie, Walter Gray, Greg Allen, E.A. Batchelor Jr., John Gomez, R.W. Hewitson, Frank Kenesson, Annis Stukus, Len Bramson, Jack Wells, Elmer Ferguson, Eugene Gallmeier, Al Nickleson, Arnold Bruner, Tom Alderman, Thelma Dickman, Gord Walker, Gil Smith and Pete Axthelm, to name but a few.

Thanks to Red's children: Casey, Patrick, Conn and Kitty. Your memories and insights into your parents' lives helped make the book complete. We know they are as proud of you as you are of them.

Last but not least, our greatest debt is to the incomparable duo, Red and Andra Kelly. It is impossible to thank one without the other. You were both so accommodating to our many questions, visits and intrusions! Andra was forever finding pictures and articles "upstairs." Thank goodness. You are a true team. We feel so humbled and blessed that you chose us to tell your story after all this time. It has been such a joy and privilege to work with you both. Thank you for your trust, insight, patience and friendship. We hope you are as proud of the final product as we are. Thank you both for saying yes!

David M. Dupuis and Waxy L. Gregoire